ROUTLEDGE LIBRARY EDITIONS: POLITICAL THOUGHT AND POLITICAL PHILOSOPHY

Volume 45

MARXISM AND PHENOMENOLOGY

MARXISM AND PHENOMENOLOGY
Theories of Crisis and their Synthesis

SHIRLEY R. PIKE

LONDON AND NEW YORK

First published in 1986 by Croom Helm Ltd

This edition first published in 2020
by Routledge
2 Park Square, Milton Park, Abingdon, Oxon OX14 4RN

and by Routledge
52 Vanderbilt Avenue, New York, NY 10017

Routledge is an imprint of the Taylor & Francis Group, an informa business

© 1986 Shirley R. Pike

All rights reserved. No part of this book may be reprinted or reproduced or utilised in any form or by any electronic, mechanical, or other means, now known or hereafter invented, including photocopying and recording, or in any information storage or retrieval system, without permission in writing from the publishers.

Trademark notice: Product or corporate names may be trademarks or registered trademarks, and are used only for identification and explanation without intent to infringe.

British Library Cataloguing in Publication Data
A catalogue record for this book is available from the British Library

ISBN: 978-0-367-21961-1 (Set)
ISBN: 978-0-429-35434-2 (Set) (ebk)
ISBN: 978-0-367-24787-4 (Volume 45) (hbk)
ISBN: 978-0-367-24790-4 (Volume 45) (pbk)
ISBN: 978-0-429-28441-0 (Volume 45) (ebk)

Publisher's Note
The publisher has gone to great lengths to ensure the quality of this reprint but points out that some imperfections in the original copies may be apparent.

Disclaimer
The publisher has made every effort to trace copyright holders and would welcome correspondence from those they have been unable to trace.

CONTENTS

Preface

Introduction   1

PART I   MARXISM AND PHENOMENOLOGY   7

1. The Possibility of a Synthesis   9

   Defining the Synthesis   9
   Basic Traditions in Marx and Husserl   14
   Idealism, Materialism and the Natural
      Attitude   17
   Dialectical Materialism and Subjective
      Idealism   19
   The Kantian Legacy   24
   Duality and Dialectic   29

2. Hegel, Marx and Husserl   35

   The Idealist Tradition   36
   Phenomenology in Hegel and Husserl   38
   The Concept of Totality   42
   Hegelian Marxism in Lukács   46
   Hegelian Themes in Sartre and Kojève   50
   The Structure of Consciousness   52

PART II   THE CRISIS OF SCIENCE AND THE ANALYSIS
OF CAPITALISM   59

3. Structure and Scientificity   61

   The Structuralist Synthesis   62
   Science and Ideology in Althusser and
      Foucault   66
   Structure, System and Totality   71
   Scientific Realism and Phenomenology   74
   Structure, Consciousness and Causality   79

Contents

4. The Crisis of Science	91
The Concept of Crisis	92
Scientificity in Marx and Husserl	96
Theorising the Life-world	101
Alienation and the Ontological Question	108
Teleology and Causality	113
PART III THE SYNTHESIS OF MARXISM AND PHENOMENOLOGY	123
5. The Question of History	125
Historicity in Husserl	126
Historicism and Hermeneutics	129
Historico-genetic Analysis in Marx and Husserl	135
Time, Sedimentation and Language	141
Consciousness and History in Existentialist Marxism	147
6. Conclusion: Phenomenological Marxism	159
The Nature of the Synthesis	160
Phenomenological Marxism - The Contribution of Enzo Paci	171
Towards Husserlian Marxism	178
Glossary	187
Bibliography	193
Index	197

For Don

PREFACE

This book has two main themes - the nature of theoretical synthesis in the social sciences, and the possibilities for a synthesis of Marxism and phenomenology. Integral to the study of these issues is an understanding of the theory of crisis and of the development of Marxist theory. I hope that all these themes finally converge to leave the reader, not with answers, but with the same kinds of questions which started me thinking and writing. The Introduction provides a summary from which the reader can gauge the scope of the work. As it states, the book has three parts, in each of which the two chapters have an affinity. However, Chapter One sets out the framework for what follows, and needs to be read before approaching any other part out of sequence.

A number of people have contributed generously of their time, energy and ideas to the writing of this book. I am grateful to staff and fellow students of sociology at the University of Essex for helping me to think through the issues and priorities of the subject. In particular, I am indebted to Ian Craib for his unstinted help at every stage of the work. Any coherence or lucidity that this book may have is due mainly to him. I should also like to thank Ted Benton for his interest and encouragement. My thanks must go to Linda George for her skill, efficiency and attention to detail in the production of the book. I should also like to thank my editor, Peter Sowden, for guiding me through the complexities of the process.

I wish to thank my family and friends for their tolerant support of my determination to complete the research. David Ryles and David Mansfield have helped considerably by reading and commenting on parts of the draft. Finally, I wish to thank my

Preface

husband, Donald Pike, for his comments on the final draft and in the preparation of the index. His critical gifts and incisive understanding have sustained my efforts with characteristic generosity throughout.

INTRODUCTION

Characteristic of twentieth century thought is a fragmentation of disciplines, a challenging of dogmatisms, and a loss of cohesion. This is generally interpreted as a crisis of philosophy and the social sciences. For Marxists, the concept of crisis has always been central, but the attenuation of the crisis at the political level appears to threaten the impetus for revolutionary action. The crisis in Marxist theory is reflected among radicals in retrenchment and internecine conflict. One response from radical theoreticians has been the development of phenomenological Marxism. Because many theoretical difficulties are unresolved, the efforts of the phenomenological Marxists to give new directions to Marxist theory have not been consolidated. Not only has the potential of phenomenological Marxism as a tool of analysis been unfulfilled, but its programmatic implications are as yet unrealised. This is owing, in part, to problems with the interpretation of Husserl's work. Also, there is a tendency for neo-orthodox Marxists to dismiss phenomenological Marxism as a simplistic humanism, revisionist and incompatible with Marxist science. It is my intention to enquire into these theoretical difficulties which are impeding advances in phenomenological Marxism. This enquiry raises the further problem of relating two apparently disparate philosophical perspectives. The book is organised to allow both theoretical and meta-theoretical discussion of these questions to run parallel. In this way I hope to combine a critique of current Marxist theory with an exploration of problems germane to other aspects of the philosophy of the social sciences.

The first part of the book examines the philosophical backgrounds of Marxism and phenomen-

Introduction

ology through a critical exposition of the traditions from which they arose. I look at what is involved in relating two systems of ideas, that process which has characterised the development of Marxist thought in this century. Chapter One begins by asking in what sense two frameworks of thought can be analysed as a basis for claiming a theoretical synthesis. Is it enough to show that they relate on traditional conceptual levels or should they articulate in other ways? Formalised levels of analysis - logic, epistemology, ontology and methodology - are used as a focus as they become appropriate, and the question of their relative significance as organising criteria is raised.

Chapter One continues by examining the problem of relating Husserl and Marx, given the differences in their philosophical backgrounds. At first sight the possibility of a liaison between dialectical materialism and subjective idealism appears remote, but these orthodox representations of Marxism and Husserlian phenomenology deserve to come under scrutiny. Points of contact are sought first in the empiricist and rationalist traditions exemplified by Descartes, Kant and Hegel. These traditions are the sources of the antagonism between idealism and materialism, philosophy and science, ideology and science, and theory and practice. Such antimonies are problematic for synthesising the two systems of thought. The first chapter therefore serves as an analytical introduction, and attempts to lay down some parameters for examining a synthesis. It asks what constitutes a system of thought and, subsequently, what constraints operate as one system yields to another in the making of a synthesis. How may the consequent gains and losses be evaluated? What degree of theoretical coherence may be forfeited? The need for such lines of enquiry to be traced to their limits is characteristic of phenomenology and is also in accordance with Marxism's claim to be a radical analysis. It is in this context that the work of the leading phenomenological Marxist, Enzo Paci, is introduced.

Chapter Two begins with a comparison of Husserl's phenomenology with that of Hegel. Since Marx emerges from Hegel historically this is an important pivot from which to consider the theories of consciousness in Husserl and Marx. There would appear to be fundamental differences between them which hinge on the question of the dialectic. In order for phenomenology to achieve a synthesis with Marxism it would have to be interpreted as

Introduction

dialectical in essence. The possibility of this is considered through a discussion of a central concept in Hegel and Marx - the totality. This leads to an examination of Hegelian Marxism as exemplified by the work of Lukács. The claims of Paci to transcend this theoretical position by offering a truly phenomenological Marxism are assessed.

Hegel's concept of totality and its relevance to Marxist analysis is a key issue. Can it be related in any sense to Husserl's concept of the premundane world, the Lebenswelt, and thus supply a basic element of liaison between Husserl and Marx? The point is made that this concept originates within the idealist tradition and may not be altogether compatible with either Marx or Husserl. Husserl's rejection of metaphysics would preclude a liaison unless Marx's analysis of the concrete world is free from metaphysical materialism. The treatment of science and philosophy by both Hegel and Husserl is discussed in this context. The study of Hegel indicates the problem of historicism which is dealt with fully in a later discussion of history and consciousness. The chapter closes with a consideration of the recent revival in Hegelian studies and what this implies for the present state of Marxist philosophy.

The second part of the book develops the theme of the relationship of science to philosophy. In reaction to the dominant positivism of his time, Husserl regarded this relationship as a crisis. For Marx, the crisis was generated by the contradictions of capitalism, and its resolution required a revolutionary science. In Chapter Three, questions of philosophy and science are given a particular focus by considering another branch of contemporary Marxist analysis. The scientific Marxism of Althusser is examined by looking first at its basis in structuralist theory - a discussion of Foucault's work provides illumination here. The Hegelian concepts which are transformed into central elements of Althusser's theory are then considered. His attempt to fuse a version of structuralism with Marxist science demonstrates the problems in the reconciliation of two philosophical perspectives. The claim that structuralist Marxism is free from the ideological contamination which characterises other Marxisms, and is thus truly scientific, brings us to the question of scientificity itself. In what sense does phenomenology challenge these conceptions of science? Can phenomenology provide a more satisfactory foundation on which to establish Marxism as a

Introduction

scientific theory? Questions of science and ideology, totality and intersubjectivity, and teleology and causality are important for this analysis. The chapter concludes with an assessment of the scientific realist position in contemporary Marxist theory and develops a critique based on the phenomenological view of the real and the concrete.

Chapter Four focuses on the crisis of science as perceived by Marx and Husserl. Phenomenological Marxism claims to relate their perceptions by means of a radical reinterpretation of scientificity. The chapter continues to examine the corpus of work by both philosophers but gives more attention to their mature writings. Husserl's overriding concern was to establish phenomenology as a rigorous science. His last major work viewed the crisis of the sciences in terms of its meaning for mankind's future. However, the theorising of the intersubjective world is not fully developed and is not, in its embryonic stage, compatible with the Marxist analysis of the social structure. Paci and Piccone claim that the crisis of the sciences and the crisis of capitalism are aspects of the same crisis but their proposed synthesis presents considerable difficulties. One approach towards resolving these difficulties is to consider what may be termed the epistemology of crisis. Theorists from various traditions have used the concept of crisis as a metaphor to explore the growth of scientific knowledge, the contradictions of the social structure, and the predicament of Western culture. Marxist theorists are concerned to explain the attenuation of crisis in the structure of late capitalism. The search for a rational solution to the crisis through a liberating praxis raises questions of ontology. In discussing the ontology of labour I consider Marx's concept of alienation in relation to Husserl's concept of occlusion. The theory of the life-world is important in this context. Finally, the tension between teleological and causal explanation in the natural and human sciences is examined. This raises basic questions concerning the scientificity of the two frameworks. Are the teleological explanations of phenomenology compatible with a Marxist science? Would Marxism vitiate its claims to be scientific by a phenomenological interpretation? Such enquiries are fundamental for any possible synthesis.

The theme of the third part of the book is the structure of consciousness within the experience of capitalism. The approach is through ontological and epistemological enquiries aimed at explicating the

Introduction

basis of phenomenological Marxism, its systematisation and development and its explanatory power. It is necessary to consider Husserl's historico-genetic analysis as an answer to the problem of history in phenomenology. The question of whether phenomenology can account for the historical is given prominence in the work of Carr and Ricoeur. If the earlier version of phenomenology as a science of the description of essence has been superseded by phenomenology as an account of a historical intersubjective world, then a case can be made for a synthesis with Marxism.

Chapter Five begins by reviewing the claim that Husserl developed a theory of the historical a priori. This is followed by a discussion of historicism in Marxist theory in which the concept of historicity is analysed. It is important to understand the development of these concepts in the hermeneutic tradition and in aspects of existentialist theory. The relationships between history, knowledge, language and ontology are considered with reference to Dilthey, Husserl, Heidegger, Sartre and Merleau-Ponty. Husserl's theory of language as the horizon of all possibilities provokes the question of the prepredicative determinants of those possibilities. The answer appears to lie in our concept of experience. It is in the organising of experience that intentionality, as the basis of consciousness, precedes both language and logic. The concept of intentionality as a central element in Husserl is examined. The proposal that phenomenological Marxism should be developed as a philologico-genetic critique is questioned. The problem here is that the analysis of language alone is not adequate to the understanding of either the structure of consciousness or of society. How would a synthesis with Marxism contribute a more concrete structural analysis, and how should this be theorised?

The final chapter weighs the arguments concerning the possibility of a synthesis. It analyses the claims of the phenomenological Marxists and attempts to identify those areas of conceptualisation which need development. It takes up the question of the programmatic aspects of Marxism and asks what, in concrete terms, a synthesis with phenomenology could hope to achieve. To bring the enquiry back to the metatheoretical level I look at the alternative forms of the liaison expressed either as a phenomenological Marxism or as a Marxist phenomenology. What do these formulations imply and how do these terms constrain the analysis? Would the synthesis of Marxism and

Introduction

phenomenology be better represented as a Husserlian Marxism? In conclusion, the chapter sets out these questions and findings schematically and reviews the work as a whole. It suggests areas where further research is necessary, given the implications of a synthesis of Marxism and phenomenology for the philosophy of the social sciences.

PART I

MARXISM AND PHENOMENOLOGY

Chapter One

THE POSSIBILITY OF A SYNTHESIS

Defining the Synthesis

The notion of a theoretical synthesis is fundamental to this enquiry. It therefore needs clarification at the outset. For a term in such general philosophical use we would expect to find criteria by which to isolate, inspect and evaluate a synthesis. But is the synthesis as a theoretical construct such a distinctive entity? What is its epistemological and linguistic status? To answer such questions I do not intend to examine exhaustively the usage of the term in the history of philosophical discourse, though some aspects of its origin as philosophical currency are illuminating. My main intention is to analyse the concept and its theoretical implications. A preliminary question is whether we can distinguish a synthesis from a theory or theoretical framework. If we make a distinction between a theory and a synthesis, then a synthesis of separate theories cannot become a new theory; it will retain a distinctive character by definition. What, then, is a synthesis and why is it important as an object of study?

The synthesis is a particular mode of theorising. It is the outcome of relating two frameworks of ideas in such a way that they each inform and regulate the other, producing new questions, insights and problems. This process of bringing theories into conjunction can be deconstructive on many levels, provoking new uses of old concepts, suggesting new problems and giving rise to new combinations of thought. Without this kind of stimulus, philosophical endeavours are stultified. In its broadest sense, synthesis can be defined as the process by which philosophy has developed, a process of adaptation in conceptual structures to changing modes of argument, conjecture and assertion.(1) Inherent in this type

The Possibility of a Synthesis

of definition is the basic concept of an origin, tangential to which alternative ideas arise and against which new constructs are evaluated. These may then become assimilated to the degree where a qualitative change can be identified.(2)

The term 'synthesis' could also be used to describe the mode of development of the traditional areas of philosophical investigation, from their origins in Greek thought to their institutionalisation in modern academic philosophy. It is, however, doubtful that such a broad application of the term is useful in describing the growth of philosophical discourse. The term becomes inevitably restricted by its association with certain specific theories. It was in early use to define an integral aspect of the dialectical process. Dialectic, denoting the process of dialogical reasoning, appears before Plato and Aristotle in the paradoxes of Zeno.(3) Its earliest usage did not include the notion of synthesis as later developed by Kant,(4) Fichte,(5) and Hegel.(6) In Fichte and Hegel the synthesis is not the mere outcome of a process of dialectical opposition of antithesis to thesis which it resolves – the synthesis elevated thought to a higher logical status.

The concept of a synthesis as an element of dialectic is worth considering in more detail here. In the dialectics of Hegel and Fichte it signifies the closure of the dialectical procedure and becomes transformed into the thesis for the next stage of the process. The synthesis designates a resolution which, when we turn to examine it, has become a different theoretical entity, the new thesis. By contrast, Aristotle's scheme of dialectics as set out in *Topica*(7) does not develop the concept of synthesis as a closure. According to Aristotle, the dialectic as an on-going interaction between two sets of premises was not sufficient to yield new knowledge or scientific knowledge. For this, inductive reasoning could be the only basis. Aristotle's account of the dialectical process itself is consonant with my claim that synthesis is a distinct type of theoretical framework. Aristotle regarded dialectic as a process of interplay; reasoning was held to be dialectical if the epistemological status of the premises was that of the true and the self-evident. The value of dialectic was three-fold: it was useful in training the intellect; useful in challenging the premises of an antagonist in general discussion; and useful in examining first principles of the sciences (a priori and unprovable): 'Dialectic is a process of criticism wherein lies the path to the principles of

The Possibility of a Synthesis

all inquiries.'(8) With this emphasis on its critical force, Aristotle's account of dialectic as an unresolved interplay is particularly instructive for, and consonant with, my view of synthesis as:

a) a liaison which provokes the questioning of fundamental principles;
b) a relationship of theories which continually stimulates critical evaluation of concepts;
c) a theoretical construct which, in its dialectic nature, demonstrates the processes of consciousness to be themselves reflexive and dialectical.

If we take the process of dynamic interplay to be its fundamental character, then what emerges as a synthesis is distinct from a theory. It is primarily a mode of theorising. However, the synthesis should not be regarded as a methodology only; such a notion would be limiting and inaccurate.(9) A synthesis will display more than its dynamics. It will have a distinctive epistemology and ontology. The process of synthesising is obviously a methodology but the synthesis itself, I would argue, can achieve a discrete theoretical status.

The term 'synthesis' retains connotations which provide us with a context for its examination. My intention is, however, to give the concept of synthesis a more specific reference. I propose to examine attempts to relate distinct and disparate frameworks of thought. The merger of certain theoretical traditions is common to the history of philosophy. Marxist thought in the twentieth century has been under constant revision and therefore allows us to exmaine closely the process of theoretical synthesis. The attempts to synthesise the work of Marx with other perspectives have been made in response to conditions of crisis and conceptual impasse. Where, at a particular historical juncture, the current theory has failed in either explanatory power or effectiveness as a spur to revolutionary action, the consequent disillusionment has impelled Marxism in new directions.(10) It is my intention to explore the origins of those frameworks from which four branches of Marxist thought - Hegelian, structuralist, existentialist and phenomenological - derive.

Before attempting an analysis of these theoretical systems it is essential to define the construct which stands as the basis of the enquiry - the theory itself. This preliminary should enable us to isolate criteria for analysing and assessing a synthesis. Perhaps the most simple and cogent way of

The Possibility of a Synthesis

characterising a theory is in terms of the types of enquiry it opens up. These can be codified within a schema of four levels of analysis - logical, epistemological, ontological and methodological.(11) It is accepted practice in philosophy to employ these categories to develop lines of enquiry as follows:

- i) logical enquiry - into the internal coherence, structure and consistency of a theory.
- ii) epistemological enquiry - into what counts as knowledge; how new knowledge is created; how concepts are formed, their truth status and meaning.
- iii) ontological enquiry - into the nature and meaning of existence, into theoretical entities and their 'real' existence and appearance.
- iv) methodological enquiry - into the methods of investigation; the validation of forthcoming data; the principles by which resulting material is organised.

These traditional modes of enquiry(12) are the guidelines for my analysis but will not be employed systematically throughout. Such a procedure would impose unnecessary constraints. However, for the initial task of formulating the criteria of a synthesis of two frameworks of thought I have retained these categories. The criteria relate to the format above as follows:

- i) logic - the task here would be to discover to what extent logical coherence is possible; also, to identify related aspects of structure;
- ii) epistemology - the conceptual structure of elements which form the synthesis must be shown as capable of producing new knowledge; the status of concepts must be clarified together with their relationships; the possibility of equating or substituting concepts must be examined;
- iii) ontology - basic assumptions concerning the nature of a priori principles and 'givens' must be demonstrated as compatible;
- iv) methodology - the enquiry must look for compatibility in methods of gaining data, analysing propositions and establishing truths.

These necessary elements of analysis are pre-

The Possibility of a Synthesis

sented in a formalised way in this schema. I am not, however, proposing to follow such a systematic analysis but to operate with these criteria in a flexible manner, the intention being to discover how the various aspects of a synthesis inform and illuminate one another. It should be possible to identify the constraints which become operational when one framework of thought yields to another. The gains and losses need evaluating in terms of the criteria stated. Can we claim, for instance, that a particular theoretical liaison is a forced synthesis, unacceptable in that the ideas of its originators have been distorted and misrepresented? We have already defined the synthesis as distinct from the theory. The point to be stressed in formulating criteria for its evaluation is that, although the levels of analysis parallel those used to examine theories, at each level emphasis is on the degree of compatibility. We should expect the synthesis to display inconsistencies at certain levels. Where the greatest compatibility overall can be demonstrated we would take this as the measure of success of one synthesis against another.

The question is raised in the preamble as to whether phenomenology is able to render an interpretation of Marx which would overcome classic problems within Marxism. Alternatively, can phenomenology be given a Marxist interpretation? Though questions in a similar form may be posed throughout this analysis, it is important to emphasise that a theoretical synthesis can and must be distinguished from a theoretical interpretation of one theory from the standpoint of another. The synthesis, as I have defined it, must be susceptible of logical, ontological and epistemological evaluations, according to certain established criteria which I hope to demonstrate. By contrast, the procedure of interpretation remains in a hermeneutic relationship to the theory under scrutiny and the outcome, the interpretation itself, is bound to retain a peripheral character in relation to the original theory.

The synthesis is a distinct type of theoretical construct. It is subject to the same kinds of epistemological enquiry as other modes of theorising but it retains a distinctive character as an interplay of ideas. Although, as a duologue, it carries the potential for unity, it is always susceptible of deconstruction and recombination. This account has so far not intended to explain modes of theory construction but to suggest that a theoretical

The Possibility of a Synthesis

synthesis can be more productive of new ideas because of its hybrid nature, its origins in disparate traditions. We should expect it to retain the dynamic tension of the dialectic.

We may not extend the scope of our enquiry by tracing the sources of certain theoretical standpoints. In this we attempt to follow the injunctions of both Marx and Husserl to go back to foundational ideas. To Marx this meant drawing back the veil on the processes at work in society. Similarly, Husserl intended phenomenology to be a first philosophy by which to examine the presuppositions of philosophy itself.

Basic Traditions in Marx and Husserl

The investigation of the possibilities for a liaison between Marx and Husserl must begin with an account of the traditions evident in their work. This is essential to an understanding of their basic assumptions, their use of concepts and their original contributions to philosophy. At the outset we are compelled to recognise the disparate nature of two traditions, dialectical materialism and subjective idealism. These at first seem irreconcilable, representing as they do a polarity of thought which continues to dominate Western philosophy. The dualities inherent in these traditions will be considered later in this chapter, and in subsequent chapters I will be tracing a more specific aetiology. At this initial stage it is more useful to outline Husserl's development and to contrast this with the development of Marx's work. Husserl's philosophy has been variously interpreted as phenomenalism, transcendentalism and subjective idealism. We need to examine these evaluations. Likewise, interpreters of Marx present a confusing diversity of readings. Epistemological difficulties appear to centre around opposed postulates, and grappling with such antimonies as subject/object, appearance/reality, concrete/abstract seems to be the perennial task for Marxist commentators. I begin this enquiry into basic propositions by asking whether we can establish any epistemological affinity between Marx and Husserl.

For Husserl, the abiding task was to establish a pure theory, beyond all the dilemmas of empiricism, as the basis of truth. His phenomenology developed from the point where he began to undercut the established conventions of philosophy and to seek the founding activities of consciousness itself.

The Possibility of a Synthesis

When Marx writes: 'To be radical is to grasp things at the root. But for man the root is man himself',(13) he gives us a true expression of Husserl's guiding principle also. Husserl's radical return to subjectivity was intended to establish the essence of human thought. From this point of agreement, therefore, it might be argued that a humanist version of Marxism is compatible with phenomenology. This would be an erroneous conclusion based on the interpretation of both theories as merely anthropocentric. The questions with which both Husserl and Marx are concerned are basically epistemological. At the early stage of his thought, Marx was developing a critique of Hegel which was to lead to a fundamental rejection of idealism. Husserl also was to take a direction away from an idealist standpoint. This movement away from idealism can be claimed as another point of contact between Husserl and Marx.

We have seen that the radical attitude, in the metaphorical sense of stripping away all surface material to disclose the foundations of thought, does epitomise the basic philosophical attitude of both theorists. We may associate the radical attitude in Husserl with the basic principle of phenomenology - that it should establish 'philosophy as a rigorous science'. From the essay of 1913, which bears this title, to his last work on the theme of crisis, this remained Husserl's overall project. It was a goal pursued in the spirit of rationalism.(14) On the following points, therefore, we find a measure of agreement between Marx and Husserl - the radical attitude, the rejection of idealism and the desire for scientific rigour.

The early work of Husserl derived from his concern to demonstrate the futility of the 'psychologism'(15) whch had begun to dominate certain branches of nineteenth century thinking. In Brentano's(16) elevation of psychology to a supreme position in the sciences, and in Mill's(17) claim that psychology was foundational to logic, Husserl detected what he believed to be the basic error of empirical thought - the claim that inductive generalisations had the status of natural laws. By opposing this, Husserl reaffirmed the Kantian distinction between contingent and necessary truths. His pursuit of a pure theory led Husserl to examine formal logic. But the demonstrable purity of its internal consistencies failed to satisfy Husserl's criterion for a pure theory since it employed concepts, the grounds of which were never examined. It was to this task of examining the underlying

The Possibility of a Synthesis

assumptions of logical categories and concepts that Husserl next addressed himself.

The project of discovering a synthetic a priori which had ultimately eluded Kant, was successfully resolved, in Husserl's view, within the terms of his own eidetic enquiry. He rejected the empiricist 'presumption' that we can be aware of nothing but the particulars of experience. By the intuitive apprehension of 'essences' we gain a synthetic knowledge of universals. These abstract entities are, in the early stages of Husserl's thought, 'given' to intuition.(18) This givenness was emphasised by Husserl's choice of the term 'descriptive psychology' for phenomenology. At this stage Husserl was not concerned with the causation of 'acts' of thought. Later he was to explore these by the processes of 'egological' and 'transcendental' reduction which he evolved. After <u>Logical Investigations</u> Husserl ceased to rely on the 'givenness' of essences to experience as the basis for phenomenology. His search for certainty led him to Descartes. The methodology of the <u>epoché</u>, first employed in <u>Ideas</u>,(19) followed the Cartesian method of doubt. Husserl believed that such a procedure could be sufficiently rigorous to remove all cognitive redundancies, eventually yielding the pure form of consciousness.

<u>The Cartesian Meditations</u>(20) marked the beginning of a phase in which the return to subjectivity is pushed to its limits. The idea that a methodology of reduction could be developed to enable the immanence of individual experience to be transcended led Husserl, in some respects, on a path parallel to Hegel. But the whole basic organicist postulate of the Hegelian system of Absolute Idealism was anathema to Husserl. While both Hegel and Husserl examined the structure of consciousness, for Hegel, the reality of the world and our experience of it is an expression of the Absolute revealing itself in the socio-historical sphere. For Husserl, however, the central question in this phase is how we are made aware of the reality of the world. Descartes's method of doubt reduced all certitude to the <u>cogito</u>.(21) But the paradox of the Cartesian reduction was that it led initially to a solipsist position. Husserl's idea was that the bracketing out of the self would yield transcendentally reduced data as a basic level of truth from which the reality of the world could be reconstructed, or constituted. This process of transcending the monadic ego brought Husserl to the point of positing the intersubjective world at a

The Possibility of a Synthesis

preconceptual primordial level. But, he asks, what are the elements in the process by which this is accomplished? The answer appears in the fifth <u>Meditation</u> that cognition takes the form of intentionality. Our consciousness is always aware of something, directed towards something; therefore, we can be aware of others. But are they the mere 'appresentation' of others' egos which we construct in the solipsistic sense? Husserl saw the primordial world as peopled not merely by others' consciousnesses, but as a sphere existent in nature. The corporeality of others is the essentially constituted first object. But the individual must be thought of as a psychophysical entity. Therefore, to perceive another person corporeally is to perceive another ego, not as a separated-out analogue but as a psychophysical reality.(22)

From <u>Cartesian Meditations</u> we get the first statements of Husserl's intersubjective phenomenology. The chief concern at this point in his work would appear to be:

a) to establish a pure presuppositionless logic - in fact, a basic structure, an a priori of being;
b) to resist charges that his philosophy led to solipsism by theorising the intersubjective world;
c) to acknowledge that his position was a form of subjective idealism and yet to insist upon the concrete nature of man.

The ambiguity of the last point suggests that a link can be forged between Husserl's work and Marx's, since the postulate of concreteness can be taken as a departure from idealism. But before we can begin to examine attempts to synthesise the two frameworks it is important to outline the rejection by both philosophers of any naive notions concerning the concreteness or materiality of the world.

Idealism, Materialism and the Natural Attitude

Husserl and Marx shared the concern that cognition should be closely examined to reveal the sources of intellectual deception - categories of thought which distort the understanding by falsely abstracting from the concreteness of experience. Paradoxically, these abstract categories are those unquestioned assumptions by means of which the consciousness experiences the world naturalistically (in Husserl's terms, the 'natural attitude'). Therefore, what appears as concrete 'reality' is, for Marx, an ideological misrepresentation. Marx's intention was to reveal the errors in the analysis of society offered by contemporary economic theory, but also in his philosophical critique Marx resisted the natural attitude. He strongly rejected the naive assertion of 'materiality' as a direct emanation from matter; the Hegelian legacy made this untenable.

We find in Husserl a similar rejection of simplistically derived categories of thought. Phenomenology must challenge the natural attitude, the perception of the world as a taken-for-granted construct. It is evident from <u>Cartesian Meditations</u>(24) and <u>Ideas</u>(25) that Husserl saw phenomenology as the method by which the natural attitude could be suspended or 'bracketed'. The world could then be apprehended transcendentally. At this stage of his thought Husserl was preoccupied with what he considered to be a fundamentally new form of 'transcendental idealism', distinct from both psychological idealism, 'a senseful world from senseless sensuous data', and from Kantian idealism, 'a systematic egological science'. Husserl conceives this idealism to be the essence of phenomenology. He makes a vigorous defence of this position in the name of 'concreteness':

> This idealism is not a product of sportive argumentations, a prize to be won in the dialectical contest with 'realisms'. It is <u>sense-explication</u> achieved <u>by actual work</u>, an explication carried out as regards every type of existent ever conceivable by me, the ego, and specifically as regards the transcendency actually given to me beforehand through experience: Nature, culture, the world as a whole. But that signifies: systematic uncovering of the constituting intentionality itself. <u>The proof of this idealism is therefore phenomenology itself</u>. Only some-one who misunderstands either the deepest sense of intentional method, or that of transcendental reduction, or perhaps both, can attempt to separate phenomenology from transcendental idealism. (26)

However, it is from this point that the combination of concreteness and intersubjectivity carries Husserl in the direction of the life-world to a position more compatible with Marx's materialism.

Both Marx and Husserl were highly critical of the philosophy of their day; Marx regarded academic

The Possibility of a Synthesis

philosophy with hostility,(27) while Husserl castigated its failure to fulfil its primary tasks. Traditional practices of critical analysis and reflection fail by remaining within the natural attitude; only by developing a correct critique can the world be grasped in its true meaning. The overcoming of the natural attitude is, therefore, a common theme in addressing the crisis of philosophy.

Dialectical Materialism and Subjective Idealism

The philosophical distance between dialectical materialism and subjective idealism seems to be an insurmountable barrier separating Husserl and Marx. How can two theorists from distinctly opposed traditions be related, let alone reconciled, in a synthesis? The apparent incompatibility could be overcome only if it were demonstrated that both Marx and Husserl had moved from their original positions. This would require a reappraisal of their work and a challenge to orthodox assessments. One of the most incisive reappraisals of phenomenology and Marxism is to be found in the work of the Italian theorist, Enzo Paci, who persuasively argues that a synthesis can be achieved.

Paci's major work, <u>The Function of the Sciences and the Meaning of Man</u>,(28) is a rigorous attempt to establish a phenomenological Marxist perspective. As the leader of a left-wing Husserlian group, Paci came to prominence in the 1960s and 70s. The crisis in Marxist theory of the period engendered a reappraisal of the possibilities for a phenomenological Marxism to supersede earlier abortive attempts by Marcuse(29) and Tran Duc Thao.(30) Paci's work finds the affinity of Marx and Husserl in their critical responses to the predicament of reified and alienated human experience. These insights challenge doctrinaire positions within both dialectical materialism and subjective idealism. This innovative approach was paralleled by other developments in radical thinking but has not yet received the wide critical attention given to the Althusserians and the Hegelian Marxists. To explore the possibility that Marx and Husserl moved towards a common ground, we need to examine the concepts they came to reject. We have already noted that both theorists were critical of a naive idealist position. What radical critique did they make of the materialist epistemology? Materialism in its naive form holds that all thought emanates directly from matter. In 1847 Vogt wrote that 'the brain secretes thought just as the liver secretes bile'.(31) In a radical reaction against the 'respectability' of idealism, the materialists had turned to science as the source of truths empirically derived. The discoveries of physiology, physics and the other natural sciences appeared to confirm their theories of knowledge. In reaction, Marx turned to Feuerbach for illumination. Feuerbach had inverted the Hegelian system by placing man at the centre of the world. Concerning the theory of knowledge he wrote: 'I do not generate the object from the thought, but the thought from the object: and I hold that alone to be an object which has an existence beyond one's own brain.'(32) It was the process of the generation of thought which engaged Marx's attention. Knowledge could not be explained by a naive theory of reflection. It was the world that existed beyond the brain, inaccessible except via perception and cognition, that Marx discerned as a world in constant flux.(33) He rejected 'the abstract materialism of natural science, a materialism that excludes history and its process'.(34) Marx's materialism was able to grasp both the dialectical nature of the historical process and the reflexive nature of consciousness within the one theory. The link was thus forged between a dialectical materialism as Marxist philosophy and a historical materialism as Marxist science.

If we are to take Marxian materialism to be a theory of representation we must also accept the view that materiality is causal and that material conditions are fundamentally the determination of social life and thought. Can such a view be in any way compatible with Husserl's claim that the ideation of the subject, his consciousness, is the source of all knowledge about the world? It is on the question of causality that there appears at first to be an unbridgeable gap between Marx and Husserl. Marx totally rejected the idealism of Hegel, an Absolute Idealism in which causality derives from the progress of the Absolute. Marx ascribed causal power to the economic structure of society. This materialist view is diametrically opposed to Husserl's initial idealist standpoint on precategorical causality. However, certain interpreters of Husserl see in his later work a retreat from transcendentalism to a position more compatible with Marx. As Paci puts it, in the <u>Lebenswelt</u>:

> ... 'lived' causality is precategorical ... the category of cause ... can be grasped intuitivel and allows for a categorical intuition ... This

The Possibility of a Synthesis

> means that we must discover the precategorical origin of the category of cause in order to become aware that causality is a way in which nature is given to me as material nature. (35)

Paci is hopeful that the problems raised by the dichotomy of materialism and idealism can be overcome by rejecting the traditional oppositon between them. He sees in Husserl's later work the possibility of a synthesis which would overcome traditional difficulties. The implications of this will be considered in a later section.

Related to the traditional opposition of materialism and idealism are the problematical dichotomies of abstract and concrete, subject and object. Marx deals extensively with the dialectic of the abstract and the concrete in the works preceding <u>Capital</u>. This is essential for establishing what he believes to be the correct analytical method for a critique of bourgeois economic theory. It is also necessary for clarifying his position regarding his use of Hegelian terminology and method.(36) As we have seen, Husserl is also claiming to reveal concrete reality by phenomenological analysis. The dichotomy of categories of thought and modalities of experience presents perennial epistemological difficulties in Marx's theory. In addition to difficulties with the abstract and the concrete, the positing of subject and object in the dialectic causes many problems. Can we say that phenomenology is able to offer any resolution of these? Before we consider attempts by phenomenological Marxists to solve some of these basic dilemmas, we need to look at Husserl's idea of the concrete and his mode of constituting the object. In the broad field of phenomenology since Husserl we are unlikely to find any consistent opinion on these matters. As Spiegelberg remarks, on the question of whether phenomenology explores only subjective phenomena: 'Husserl's conception of phenomenology as the attempt to find objective essences in the very heart of subjectivity is by no means common ground for all phenomenologists.'(37) Spiegelberg attempts to cut through some of the 'nearly hopeless confusion' by criticising characterisations of phenomenology as either reflective introspection, private intuitionism or phenomenalism. He concludes that it is an empiricism no more and no less objective than any approach based on 'pure' uncensored experience. All experience is basically 'subjective' in the sense that it is our own experience. No empirical knowledge how ever purged and 'objectified', can elude the subjective matrix of all experience.(38)

Basic to Husserl's phenomenology is the return to subjectivity. In its early phase, his work is often referred to as a subjective idealism. Piccone is doubtful that this is a correct reading. His doubts seem well founded, since Husserl resisted any naive characterisation of his work. His theory of intersubjectivity enabled Husserl to escape the limitations of a naive realist or idealist position. Neither of these can give an adequate analysis of knowledge. Idealism presents 'the given' entirely as projected forms and categories, whereas realism is the belief that the structures of perception and conceptualisation are informative about a world of actual existents and the relations between them. Piccone sees these positions as being unable to thematise the relation between concept and object, or to furnish any criteria of truth or knowledge:

> Idealism fails because any criterion it offers must be strictly system-generated and thus incapable of applying to the system as a whole. Realism fails because any concept derived from such a system is limited by the conditions of derivation, ie. any criterion of knowledge or truth can only apply circularly ... The only way to escape such a static system of constructs is to develop a philosophy which has a basis and a goal that cannot be grasped in necessarily limited systems of categories. For Husserl, the basis is the life-world. (39)

That Husserl finally rests his philosophy on the concept of the precategorical life-world is the basic premiss of Paci's attempt to relate Husserl and Marx. Piccone endorses his claim that the life-world can be equated with the world of material needs. I shall be discussing this claim when I consider questions of ontology and historicity in a later section. For the moment, I intend to follow lines of thought in Husserl concerning the pre-categorical nature of the life-world and the category of the object.

In Kantian philosophy the basic elements of truth were yielded up by 'things in themselves'. Phenomenology goes beyond the phenomena, as mere appearances, to the essence of things. Knowledge of essences is made available by subjective insight via the process of _epochê_. But we are still bound to conceptualise our experience, to constitute objects of thought. In the first section of _Crisis_(40)

The Possibility of a Synthesis

Husserl considers the precategorical world as the world of the possibility of its categorisation or formal constitution. This is made clear in his account of the Galilean mathematisation of nature. With the development of pure geometry and arithmetic an ideal praxis of 'pure thinking' evolved. The abstraction from nature meant that objects were constituted in a rational coherent system. Within this we shift from a priori theory to empirical enquiry 'so familiarly' that the separation of the forms of thought from experiential activity is rare.(41) In other words, a grid of categories is superimposed on our apperception of the world by inductive and deductive logic. The methodology of pure geometry and mathematics appeared to overcome the relativity of subjective interpretations, but for Husserl it represents 'the sort of naivete of a priori self-evidence'. Husserl's view is that subjectivity is not relativistic. The pre-categorical world has a 'causal style', or invariance, which makes its formalisation via hypotheses, induction and prediction possible. Thus intuition can lead to knowledge of the true a priori, 'a universal causal regulation'. And what of objects? For Husserl what is available empirically as sense data is: '... the concreteness of sensibly intuited bodies of their being in actual and possible experience.'(42)

Phenomenology claims to dissect what we take to be irrefutable assertions concerning objects in space and time, and to reveal the underlying concrete world as the source of categorisation. Thus the precategorical world is the foundation of knowledge wherein we find the essence of all phenomena. Husserl's account of the mathematisation of the natural world illuminates the theme of <u>Crisis</u> - the revelation of how science has obscured the meaning and purpose of humanity. The historical treatment of this theme opens up possibilities of relating it to historical materialism. Phenomenological Marxists claim that the subjective awareness of the precategorical world enables us to be wary of categorisations which reify human thought. It also enables us to 'periodically reconstitute those very categories and their institutional otherness that human praxis constantly render obsolete'.(43)

We must now ask whether Husserl's method of constituting the object can in any way be related to Marx's object of knowledge, 'the concrete in thought'. Husserl's early programme investigated the things themselves by phenomenological analysis. This 'turn to the object' was surpassed by a more radical

The Possibility of a Synthesis

enterprise, that of investigating the conscious processes of the knowing subject. This project pervades the whole of Husserl's work. Lying dormant even in the earlier phase was the insight that in the structures of consciousness there was a parallel between the subjective act of knowing and the objective referent:(44) It is worth noting here that the relationship between subject and object is thought of as asymptotic by Husserl and not in any sense as a dialectic of subject and object. The attempts of such theorists as Merleau-Ponty to discern a dialectic in Husserl's phenomenological method will be under consideration later.

In discovering how objects are formulated by the subject's consciousness, the central notion for Husserl is the concept of intentionality. This concept was first formulated by Brentano as the notion that consciousness is always directed toward an object's immanence in the mental 'act'. Thus intentionality was characteristic of all psychical phenomena, including feelings. Husserl modified this conception so that acts of consciousness directed toward the object itself became 'intentions' and the objects, as targets, 'intentional objects'.(45) Husserl's theory goes beyond the empiricist notion of selective attention towards objects available as sense data. Phenomenology intuits the essences of objects (their universal and invariant underlying structures) and by the process of intentionality 'constitutes' them from perceptual experience of particulars. Thus the 'objectivity' of objects is traced to the conscious intentions of the subject. An important distinction to be made here is that the object is not constructed or created by consciousness, but is assumed to be an object 'given' to consciousness and made available in the intentional act. This distinction demarcates phenomenology from subjective idealism. Husserl clarifies this as follows: '... the recurring expression that in an act "objects are constituted" always designates the act's character of <u>rendering the object present</u> ... not "constituting" in the actual sense.'(46)

The Kantian Legacy

We now must consider a further aspect of the distinction between phenomenology and subjective idealism. As a prelude to this, necessary to the understanding of a possible link with Marxism, we trace a common influence, Kant. His ideas pervaded nineteenth century thought and the growth of natural

The Possibility of a Synthesis

science. Kant's influence, profound as it is in many branches of philosophy, has as its most distinctive attribute its critical character. Thus at points of crisis the injunction 'Back to Kant!' has been a call to re-examine fundamental principles. Both Marx and Husserl responded to this demand for radical reappraisal in philosophy. Marx's reaction to Kant is demonstrated through his rejection of Hegel.(47) There is little evidence to suggest that Marx approached Kant direct. Kant's ideas came to Marx through the filter of neo-Kantian radicalism. Husserl also came to Kant indirectly through the work of Brentano,(48) who influenced The Philosophy of Arithmetic, Husserl's earliest major work. Later, however, he made a close study of Kant. During the period of Logical Investigations and Ideas the main influences were Descartes, the Pre-Kantian empiricists, Locke, Berkeley, Hume, Mill and Leibniz, Bolzano and Lotze. Kant's direct influence was felt in the post-1917 period of First Philosophy, Formal and Transcendental Logic and Crisis. It is particularly in Crisis that Husserl makes a positive evaluation of Kant's ideas.(49)

The epistemological level is the most basic for the possibility of linking phenomenology and Marxism via the Kantian legacy. It is, however, difficult to forgo a consideration of Kant's ethical influence. His search for the underlying principles of all knowledge extended to the sphere of ethics. Influenced as he was by Rousseau, the critical thrust of his philosophy was made in defence of the new science which appeared endangered by scepticism. It is the critical spirit in Kant which reverberates in both Husserl and Marx. Teleologically, therefore, there are common resonances. However, in the epistemologies we find profound differences.

Marx came to Kant through Hegel.(50) Though he commented directly on Kant's political writings, Marx had no knowledge of The Critique of Pure Reason or The Critique of Practical Reason except through Hegel's work. We need to understand the response of Hegel to Kant in those areas of epistemology which Marx set himself to overturn. The crucial questions concern the phenomena/noumena distinction, teleology and the category of experience.

Kant's desire to save science through the distinction of synthetic from analytic knowledge required the further concession to empiricism of making certain a priori knowledge accessible to consciousness. The solution for Kant was to assert a priori the forms in which the contents of

The Possibility of a Synthesis

experience are perceived. Science thus enquires into nature via the perceived phenomena, unlocking this knowledge in given forms and categories. Hegel's rejection of this constraint upon the scientific accessibility of realities stemmed from his conception of the teleological nature of human knowledge and expereince. Following Fichte and Schelling's neo-Kantian conception of the historical self, Hegel developed his system of 'dialectical self-realisation'. The progress of the Absolute Spirit via the dialectical processes of history is the unifying element in his system, and the principle of unity is paramount in all its aspects. The accessibility of the thing-in-itself to the self-conscious ego is held by Hegel to be an active historical unfolding, not the static enquiry of Kant's transcendental apperception.(51) This historical element is what Marx has transformed in his dialectic of history into conceptions of the materiality and mutability of human experience. The sensory apprehensible manifold which overlies reality for Kant and obscures the thing-in-itself is, for Marx, the source of mystification; it is given its ideological interpretation by those who command both material resources and the means of expression.

Kant's attempt to rescue science and religion, and Hegel's task of rendering metaphysics as history are both rejected by Marx as bourgeois philosophies. However, his early attempts(52) to overturn Hegel are still made, I submit, within the problematic of the stultifying dualism of realism and idealism. We are obviously left within metaphysics when we address the question of the real, the concept and the system as Marx defines them in his early works. I shall be examining later those works which demonstrate the change of direction in Marx's thought and which may yield the greatest possibilities for a synthesis with phenomenology.

It is possible to give a more detailed account of Kant's influence on Husserl since he made extensive critical comment. Husserl regards the Kantian system as: '... the first attempt, and one carried out with impressive scientific seriousness, at a truly universal transcendental philosophy meant to be a <u>rigorous science</u> ...'(53) According to Husserl, Kant fails to achieve the radical investigation to be found in Cartesian philosophy. Kant, by going back to 'knowing subjectivity as the primal locus of all objective formations of sense and ontic validities, is on the way towards fulfilling the true task of philosophy'. Husserl uses the term

The Possibility of a Synthesis

'transcendental philosophy' in the broadest sense,(54) giving it teleological significance. The reflexive mode of enquiry into knowledge will yield a direction out of the crisis 'striving forward from vague <u>dynamis</u> towards its <u>energeia</u>'.(55) Thus, the pursuit of the rational and the ethical are common concerns for Husserl.

Husserl takes issue with Kant over numerous points. These are usefully outlined by Kockelmans who takes up the distinctions in their work concerning the pure ego.(56) Two points of difference seem to me of particular importance. First, Kant's concept of the a priori is inadequate for Husserl. Husserl applauds Kant's reproach to rationalism(57) for its neglect of the foundations of knowledge. Kant asks how an exact science of nature is possible. But Kant's enquiry rests on unquestioned presuppositions which co-determine the meanings of his questions. Kant takes the a priori character of space and time as invariant particulars. These pure 'forms' make it possible to develop the judgements of mathematics, geometry and arithmetic, ie. those synthetic a priori judgements in the natural sciences which are descriptive of space and time. But Kant's conceptions of what is a priori rests on his acceptance of the world as it is with the sciences as cultural facts, their truths and methods taken as valid. Husserl insistently questions such assumptions. He asserts that this taken-for-granted world is a naive conception. Kant's method of investigating the nature of science is wholly inadequate, 'a theoretical-logical substruction ... of something that is in principle not perceivable ... not experiencable in its own proper being'.(58) Secondly, Kant's conception of the subject is misconceived. In Kant's subjectivism the intuiting self operates at a level which creates its own difficulties. Kant fails to achieve a truly subjective enquiry through using what is, in Husserl's view, a spurious methodology - constructive inference of the formal a priori. Husserl describes this as 'mythical concept-formation'.(59) His own theory demands an essentially different regressive method, a thoroughly intuitive disclosing method of enquiry into things taken-for-granted by philosophers and scientists, the '... unspoken grounding of (their) cognitive accomplishments, hidden in respect to its deeper mediating function. Further, there must be a systematic disclosure of the intentionality which vitally holds sway and is sedimented in this ground ...'(60) The ground is the life-world which,

The Possibility of a Synthesis

unlike Kant's noumenal sphere, is accessible and experiencable. Thus Husserl introduces the concept of a non-formal material a priori exhibited by eidetic enquiry.

The objection may be made that Husserl's methodology renders the a priori accessible only in a theoretical sense and is therefore no deeper in approach to the thing-in-itself. I would argue, however, that one of the basic tasks for Marxist epistemological praxis is to give an account of the world which reveals the concrete, material basis of experience. I believe this may be better achieved through Husserl than through Kant despite recent claims.(61) Husserl is close to Kant in the sense that the teleological thrust of the critical spirit is expressed by both philosophers. But to postulate the role of reason in founding a new moral order is not enough to bring it about. What is needed are those theoretical concepts in Marx which clarify social relations, their inherent contradictions and exploitations, and institute praxis to change society. Yet Marx lacks a theoretical structure adequate to explain consciousness and to overcome the stumbling blocks which Kant raised in the antinomies and which are a major barrier to understanding.

Kant is seminal for both Marx and Husserl since in attempting to solve Kantian problems they develop their epistemological standpoints. Kant's denial of validity to 'speculative' metaphysics is compatible with Marx and Husserl, as is his opposition to current philosophical dogmatisms. Yet Kant sets limits on understanding in order to elevate moral freedom and to make the religious ethic central: 'I have therefore found it necessary to deny knowledge in order to make room for faith.'(62) It is important to note that the <u>Critique</u> is aimed at the Schools of philosophy only. Thus science may remain dogmatic, while any future metaphysics must submit to a critique rigorous enough for it to become a science in its own right. Kant's critique is echoed by Husserl's early demands for philosophy to attain scientific rigour. For Kant the monopoly of the Schools over speculative knowledge needed to be broken. But Husserl, being opposed to any form of metaphysics, is, in his view of science, compatible with Marxist theory, whereas Kant is not. To regard Kant as offering to Marxism anything other than an impasse is to misconstrue the situation. By going back to Kant, as an answer to the crisis in Marxism, we will find a conceptual structure possibly

The Possibility of a Synthesis

adequate to deal with questions of ideology and experience.(63) However, such an approach will be limited in its grasp of subjectivity which, despite the critical character of Kant's philosophy, remains within the natural attitude. Husserl takes us back to Kant's 'thing-in-itself' only as the starting point for his investigations of what is given primordially, to discover what he considers is the truly transcendental subjective basis of experience.

Duality and Dialectic

This chapter has outlined the twofold task of examining the synthesis as a theoretical construct and of evaluating phenomenological Marxism as a synthesis in comparison with other forms of Marxist thought. I first conclude that a synthesis is distinct from a theory and should be regarded as a mode of theorising in which there is an interplay of constructs. This mode of philosophical development has been particularly characteristic of twentieth century Marxist theory. Attempts to integrate Marxism with other perspectives has had varying degrees of success which I propose to evaluate.

To recapitulate, then, a synthesis may be thought of as a duologue in which characteristic types of enquiry inform and illuminate each other. Certain criteria have been proposed in order to assess the compatibility of the elements in the synthesis. If, in any area of enquiry, one framework of ideas has been distorted in order to integrate it, then the synthesis must be rejected. The possibility of a phenomenological Marxism has required us to examine the basic traditions from which Marx and Husserl developed. My argument is that both theorists, in their mature works, display considerable movement away from their early positions. Husserl moved from subjective idealism as he developed his theory of the life-world as the central element of an intersubjective phenomenology. In his later work this was given the concrete determinations which make a synthesis with Marx more feasible. Marx rejected a naive abstract materialism. In his critique of Hegel's metaphysics he developed the dialectic of the abstract and the concrete which underpins the analysis in _Capital_ of the structure of social relations.

Taking Kant to be a common antecedent we are able to clarify points of possible compatibility. Both Husserl and Marx stood opposed to Kant's sub-

The Possibility of a Synthesis

jective idealism from very different positions initially. Marx encountered Kant through Hegel's development of a dialectic of history. He rejected an epistemological framework which could not grasp the materiality of the world and the processes through which its truth is obscured by ideology. Husserl's opposition to Kant's empiricism enabled him to develop ideas of the transcendental; the methodology of the epochē; and, more saliently for a liaison with Marx, a theory of the material a priori. Kant's rigorous mode of enquiry into the foundations of science and philosophy gave a stimulus to philosophy to re-examine basic assumptions. However, in Husserl's terms, Kant's analysis did not go far enough, remaining within the natural attitude and failing to enquire into presuppositions. Both Marx and Husserl adopt a more radical attitude to the crisis of philosophy and society.

In conclusion, it should be noted that certain dualisms which Husserl disputes are not bracketed, in the sense that judgement on them is suspended. Indeed, Husserl's goal of reaching an absolute certitude in cognition is pursued in the context of these dichotomies and their analysis. The problem of subjective and objective modes of cognition is resolved; there can be no question that subjectivity becomes the basic tenet of phenomenology.(64) Another duality, the hidden and the revealed, is the basis of Husserl's concept of occlusion and is integral to the methodology. It is retained as a dialectical mode of enquiry in Paci's submission.(65) From the perspective of phenomenological Marxism, the crucial metatheoretical dichotomy of materialism and idealism is the basic antagonism which the synthesis of Marx and Husserl must resolve, and out of which the critique of other Marxist perspectives must develop.

Notes and References

1. The process is defined in the <u>Oxford English Dictionary</u> as 'The putting together of parts or elements so as to make up a complex whole'.
2. This is an orthodox continuist, or gradualist, view of the history of thought. The debate as to whether this is indeed the mode by which thought, and particularly scientific thought, develops is given a thorough airing in Lakatos, I. and Musgrave, A., <u>Criticism and the Growth of Knowledge</u>, Cambridge University Press, 1978.

The Possibility of a Synthesis

    3. Barnes, J., *The Presocratic Philosophers*, Vol I, Routledge and Kegan Paul, London, 1979, pp.236-37.
    4. Kant, I., *The Critique of Pure Reason*, trans. Smith, N.K., Macmillan, London, 1950, pp.99-101. (Second part of the transcendental logic to be termed transcendental dialectic, a critique against sophistical dialectical illusion.)
    5. Fichte, J.G., *The Science of Knowledge*, 1794. See Rockmore, T., *Fichte, Marx and the German Philosophical Tradition*, Southern Illinois University Press, 1980.
    6. Hegel, G.F., *The Science of Logic*, trans. Johnston, W.H. and Struthers, L.G., Allen and Unwin, London, 1966, pp.66-68.
    7. Aristotle, *Topica* in *Collected Works*, Vol I, edited by Ross, W.D., Oxford University Press, 1963.
    8. Ibid., Book I, Ch. 2, p.101b, line 3.
    9. Zaner is one expositor who prefers to view phenomenology as a methodology and thus 'the central discipline of philosophy', cf. Pivčević, op.cit., p.125.
    10. My Introduction, p.1 above.
    11. The term 'levels of analysis' as used here is synonymous with 'types of enquiry' in philosophical parlance. No connotation of order or structure is intended.
    12. Flew, A. (ed.) *A Dictionary of Philosophy*, Pan Books, London, 1979, passim.
    13. Easton, L.D. and Guddat, K.H. (eds.), *Writings of Young Marx*, Anchor, New York, 1967, p.257.
    14. The path of exploration towards this goal appears to veer alarmingly close to irrationalism at one stage. See Roche, M., 'Phenomenology, Sociology and Theories of Deviance', (unpublished article, 1971). Roche traces a parobolic movement in Husserl's thought from subjective idealism through transcendentalism to an intersubjective idealist position.
    15. Husserl, E., *Philosophy of Arithmetic*, first published 1891.
    16. Brentano, F., *The True and the Evident*, ed. Chisholm, R.M., London, 1966, Appendix 1, p.136, 'Letter to E. Husserl'.
    17. Mill, J.S., *A System of Logic*, Longmans, London, 1961.
    18. Husserl, E., *Logical Investigations*, Vol II, trans. Findlay, J.N., Routledge and Kegan Paul, London, 1970, pp.256-58.
    19. Husserl, E., *Ideas: General Introduction to Pure Phenomenology*, trans. Boyce Gibson, W.R.,

Collier Macmillan, London, 1972. Referred to throughout as *Ideas*.

20. Husserl, E., **Cartesian Meditations**, trans. Cairns, D., Martinus Nijhoff, The Hague, 1969.

21. Descartes, R., **A Discourse on Method**, Dent, London, 1957, particularly Part IV, pp.26-32.

22. Husserl, E., **Cartesian Meditations**, pp.123-34. The use of the term 'psychophysical' is problematic since it tends to reproduce the Cartesian error, as Spiegelberg has observed. However, Paci uses it in his definition of the lived body or **Leib** as the point of insertion of the individual into lived space and thus into psychophysical causality (op.cit. (1972), p.464). Husserl, in **Crisis** (p.294), emphasises the unity of this causality and the objectivist imbalance which has resulted from the psychophysical conception of it.

23. Marx, K., **A Contribution to the Critique of Political Economy**, Dobb, M. (ed.) Lawrence and Wishart, London, 1971. (Future references are made to the **Preface** of 1859 and the **Introduction** of 1857 as contained in the **Contribution**.)

24. Husserl, **Cartesian Meditations**, p.34.

25. Husserl, **Ideas**, pp.110-11.

26. Husserl, **Cartesian Meditations**, p.86.

27. Carver, T. (ed. and trans.) **Karl Marx: Texts on Method**, Blackwell, Oxford, 1975, p.163.

28. Paci, E., **The Function of the Sciences and the Meaning of Man**, trans. Piccone, P., and Hansen, J., Northwestern University Press, Evanston, 1972. Referred to throughout as **Function of the Sciences**.

29. Marcuse, H., 'Contributions to a Phenomenology of Historical Materialism', **Telos**, No 4, Fall 1969.

30. Tran Duc Thao, 'Marxisme et Phenomenologie', **Revue Internationale**, No 2, Paris 1946.

31. Vogt, K., **Physiological Epistles**, 1847, quoted in Passmore, J., **A Hundred Years of Philosophy**, Penguin, London, 1975, p.36.

32. Feuerbach, L., op.cit., p.46, quoted in Passmore, J.

33. Marx, K., **Capital**, Vol I, Preface to 2nd German edition ed. and trans. Torr, D., Allen and Unwin, London, 1946, p.xxxi.

34. Marx, **Capital**, 1867 edition, quoted in Passmore, op.cit., p.47.

35. Paci, op.cit., p.161.

36. Marx, **Contribution**, passim.

37. Spiegelberg, H., **The Phenomenological Movement**, Vol II, Martinus Nijhoff, The Hague, 1965, p.666.

The Possibility of a Synthesis

38. Ibid., pp.666-68. Spiegelberg's view has value though it appears self-evident and untheorised in the terms in which he states it. This demonstrates the perennial difficulty for philosophy in operating with well-worn concepts where no meta-language is available.
39. Piccone, P., Introduction to Paci, op.cit., p.xxii.
40. Husserl, E., *The Crisis of European Sciences and Transcendental Phenomenology: An Introduction to Phenomenological Philosophy*, trans. Carr, D. Northwestern University Press, Evanston, 1970, p.60. Future reference is to *Crisis*.
41. Ibid., p.24.
42. Ibid., pp.30-31.
43. Piccone, P., 'Structural Marxism?', *Radical America*, Vol 3, No 5, 1969, p.28.
44. Spiegelberg, op.cit., Vol I, p.103. See also p.82.
45. Ibid., p.107.
46. Husserl, as quoted by Carr, D., *Phenomenology and the Problem of History*, Northwestern University Press, Evanston, 1974. Not identified by Carr except as belonging to the period of *Logical Investigations*.
47. Significant in this respect is Marx's early work, chiefly *Economic and Philosophic Manuscripts of 1844*, Progress Publishers, Moscow, 1974.
48. Kockelmans, J.J., 'Husserl and Kant on the Pure Ego', in Elliston, F.A. and McCormick, P. (eds.) *Husserl: Expositions and Appraisals*, University of Notre Dame Press, London, 1977, pp.269-85.
49. Ibid., p.270ff. Kockelmans gives a comprehensive account of Husserl's 'great affinity' with Kant while making severe criticism of many unexamined dogmatisms. For Husserl, Kant belonged to another tradition.
50. Colletti, L., *Marxism and Hegel*, New Left Books, London, 1973, pp.113-22.
51. Marx, W., *Hegel's Phenomenology of Spirit*, Harper and Row, London, 1975.
52. Marx, K. and Engels, F., *The German Ideology*, Part I, ed. Arthur, C.J., Lawrence and Wishart, London, 1977, and Marx, K., *Grundrisse*, trans. Nicolaus, M., Allen Lane, London, 1973.
53. Husserl, *Crisis*, p.99.
54. Ibid., p.97.
55. Ibid., p.98.
56. Kockelmans, in Elliston and McCormick, op. cit., pp.282-83. Kockelmans' view is that Husserl is superseded by Heidegger's shifting of the subject/

object question out of the epistemological/logical on to the level of ontology.
    57. Husserl, *Crisis*, p.103ff.
    58. Ibid., p.127.
    59. Ibid., p.115.
    60. Ibid., p.116. Husserl makes a case here for 'intentional analysis', an examination of cognitive substrata, as against a psychological analysis, 'a realistic (*reale*) analysis of a naturalistically conceived soul alien to the essence of the mental'. See Ch. 5 below, note 56.
    61. Barker, M., 'Kant as a Problem for Marxism', *Radical Philosophy*, No 19, Spring 1978, pp.24-29.
    62. Kant, I., *Critique of Pure Reason*, trans. Smith, N.K., Macmillan, London, 1952, Preface to the 2nd edition, p.22.
    63. Kockelmans in Elliston and McCormick, op. cit., p.276.
    64. cf. p.22 above.
    65. Paci, op.cit., p.28.

Chapter Two

HEGEL, MARX AND HUSSERL

Together with the demise of positivism as the paramount basis for the social sciences we have seen, in recent years, the toleration of theoretical pluralism in academic philosophy. The acceptability of a turn to speculative metaphysics as a basis for social theory is indicative of these tendencies. A renewed interest in Hegel and Heidegger and a questioning of the meaning of rationalism indicates what could be termed a neo-idealist trend. This climate of thought makes it essential to review the status of Hegelian Marxism as an acceptable direction for Marxist theory. In this chapter I question whether a return to Hegelian philosophy in order to revitalise Marxism can be said to produce an acceptable synthesis. We need to enquire into the nature of this synthesis, looking at the ways in which Hegelian Marxists seek a rapprochement despite the fact that Marx's innovations were conceived in reaction to Hegel. The following questions will be raised:

a) Does Hegel's phenomenology bear any resemblance to that of Husserl? What points of contact can be discerned to adumbrate a possible synthesis with Marx?
b) What does Marx absorb from Hegel's phenomenology as an explanation of the structure of consciousness and as a socio-historical analysis?
c) What status does Hegelian Marxism have as a synthesis? How does it accord with proposals for a synthesis based on Husserl's phenomenology?

Hegel, Marx and Husserl

The Idealist Tradition

Many of the problems in relating Marx and Hegel result from the traditional dichotomies which Hegel, in response to Kant, sought to overcome. From a phenomenological viewpoint these difficulties appear as pseudo-problems, regarded by Husserl as the stumbling blocks of academic philosophy. More problematical is the traditional opposition of idealism to realism and materialism. These broad classifications are freely used in Marxist writings when they are needed to demarcate opposed positions. While they are regarded as essential for critical discussion, they are very often untheorised. Husserl's stricture against naive theoretical positions was an attack on the positivism of his day. This criticism is no less relevant today and has a broader application. However, we can hardly dismiss Hegelian thought and the current 'turn' to Hegel as a naive idealism. There is a revival of interest in Hegel which seems to indicate a desire to return to grand theory in philosophy and the social sciences, an almost inevitable trend after a period of fragmentation and disillusionment with the journeyman status of research in these fields. The impact of European ideas on British philosophy has been slow to develop. Over the last few decades this influence has reached us indirectly, filtering back through the impressive American contribution to philosophy. Hegel's work is perhaps the exception here, having remained a touchstone for branches of philosophy other than Marxism. However, the recent increase of interest in metaphysics is significant, and could be interpreted as a return to speculative philosophy at a period of crisis.

Walter Cerf's Introduction to Hegel's 1802 <u>Essay on Faith and Knowledge</u>(1) exemplifies this turn to metaphysics. Cerf claims a respectability for speculation by redefining it as synonymous with intuition. Hegel's visionary truth is, of course, the system, the wholeness of which is the test of its truth. In Cerf's view, Hegel's achievement was to integrate all aspects of Schelling's Philosophy of Identity and to develop a speculative philosophy 'envisioning the inner unity of God, nature and self-consciousness'.(2) Cerf sees that none of this can appeal to the analytical intellect. In particular, the philosophy of nature had brought speculative theory into disrepute, and it is precisely in this area that Cerf detects a change in attitude: 'The small but noisy army of today's anti-science and anti-technology prophets may joyfully return to the

Hegel, Marx and Husserl

speculative Philosophy of Nature and claim it as an ally.'(3) How are we to account for this reactionary tendency? The consolation of self-revelatory truth probably appeals to many disillusioned positivists. There may also be the desire for the certainty of a system within the anti-science lobby. Yet Cerf seems to suggest that within the logic and corpus of scientific knowledge may arise problems which are explicable only in terms of a philosophy of nature and a speculative idealism. Thus speculative philosophy could reinstate itself by its service to science.

We have seen that Husserl rejects speculative idealism, both for its misreading of the crisis of science and for the solution it proposes. However, phenomenology shares with Hegelian thought a common aspiration - to resolve the dichotomous tensions of reflective (Kantian) philosophy. Hegel and Husserl approach the problem from very different directions. Whereas in reflective philosophy the awareness of such dichotomies leads to scepticism, Hegel's theory attempts to resolve them within the historical logic of its own teleology and thus become the successor to analytic philosophy. Phenomenology stands against such a claim to historical succession. Husserl hopes to establish phenomenology as a first philosophy, breaking new ground and thus overriding the traditional problems expressed by the antimonies. For Husserl, the authentic path to the authentic philosophy is Cartesian in inspiration but goes beyond the dilemmas of metaphysics. The crisis of philosophy in the twentieth century cannot be resolved, in his view, without radical revision.

In the previous chapter we saw that Marx, through Hegel, had examined the Kantian questions of epistemology and the status of scientific knowledge. In Hegel's system of speculative metaphysics Marx did at least find a determination to enquire into fundamentals, for Hegel rejected the mystification and complacency of Kant's schema.(4) He asserted that in no way could scientific knowledge be limited to the phenomena. Everything was accessible to science as the Idea progressed through history, and knowledge unfolded. Though Marx was to overturn Hegel's theory, he was impelled by it towards a more radical enquiry. Marx sought a more profound analysis of the bases of social organisation and consciousness. By turning to economic theory and the analysis of capitalism, Marx exposed the mystique of the social relations of production. He attacked the idealist economic categories of Mill, Say and

Hegel, Marx and Husserl

Ricardo. Though he rejected the crude empiricist reflection theory of knowledge, Marx's view of consciousness is imperfectly realised. The possibility that a synthesis with aspects of Husserl's phenomenology can repair this defect is considered in this chapter.

We first need to compare the two phenomenologies and ask what grounds for a synthesis with Marx exist by virtue of compatible concepts to be found in either phenomenology. This is important because it enables us to review the sources of certain basic concepts in Marx which would be central to any synthesis. Since Marx developed concepts to supersede those of Hegel within a materialist framework, what case can the Hegelian Marxists make for a liaison with Marx? We find that they draw on the early works of Marx where the influence of Hegel is still strongly in evidence. Hegel's Phenomenology of Mind had a profound influence on Marx at this stage. From his position within the idealist tradition Hegel developed a very different notion of phenomenology from that of Husserl. It can be said that Hegel, in reaction to Kant, moved to a more extreme position within the idealist framework. His phenomenology does not challenge the tradition, whereas Husserl's radical attitude allowed him to question the basis of the idealist tradition.

Phenomenology in Hegel and Husserl

Surprisingly for a leading German philosopher and innovator, Husserl makes only scant reference to Hegel.(5) This is not an oversight on Husserl's part and we must therefore take it to mean that he regarded Hegel's work as an irrelevance. Since Husserl does not make a single reference to Marx either, this would appear to be confirmation that he saw himself in a wholly different stream of thought. By preoccupation and intention the early Husserl appears rooted in the German idealist tradition but striving within it for very different answers to the dilemmas of philosophical empiricism from those of Hegel, which appear to offer him nothing.

With so little direct link between them, how should we then proceed to compare the two phenomenologies?(6) In all comparative attempts there is the risk of connotative error. After all, the terminology used by one theorist forms a web of explication; concepts do not have an isolated significance. Therefore, comparison of terminology and usages is of limited value. There is, for instance, a loss of clarity if figurative language is employed. Mure, in discussing Hegel's concept of the Absolute Spirit says that its primary premises are often precariously metaphorised.(7) Not only may metaphors confuse, but terms may be used ambiguously. Kaufmann finds three conceptions of phenomenology in Hegel's work and concludes that '... phenomenology, about which he had thought so long, was incorporated into his system in an ill-considered and arbitrary fashion'.(8) Therefore, it is initially more fruitful to make comparisons of aspects of the philosophical traditions, or standpoints, of Husserl and Hegel. This task is attempted by Lauer who discerns the differences in terms of their approaches to history, philosophy, reason, experience, science and phenomenology.

What dominated Hegel's thinking was the drive to systematise the whole of human knowledge and experience - to elaborate the grand design, which traces the evolution of rational thought and the apotheosis of the Spirit. His phenomenology is not the development and refinement of a critique as it is for Husserl. What Hegel produces, and his stylistic consistency bears this out, is a biography of human consciousness. The Spirit evolves, manifesting itself to itself in dialectical progression. The Mind engages in self-activity and passes through various stages of consciousness towards the Absolute, the attainment of knowledge and truth.(9) Thus we have an historical consciousness, its historical and social being traced phase by phase, so that Hegel's account of human knowledge and the progress of reason comes to create the world: 'the "reason" in history is the product of, but is not reducible to, the reason of individuals in history'. It is a mode of supra-human reason, 'akin to a divine providence'.(10)

The metaphysics of Hegel were entirely rejected by Husserl.(11) He could not accept that consciousness should be transmogrified into a system of concepts and a process of conceptualising alone. According to Husserl, Hegel lacked a method by which to examine concepts, the products of the constituting human consciousness, in any scientific way, to reveal fully the working of consciousness:(12)

> How is it that they remained bound to their style of mythical concept-construction and of world-interpretations based on obscure metaphysical anticipations and were not able to

> penetrate to a scientifically rigorous type of
> concept and method and that every successor in
> the Kantian series conceived one more
> philosophy in the same style? (13)

There is, therefore, very little common ground between Hegel and Husserl, neither epistemologically nor methodologically. Lauer suggests that Hegel and Husserl may be viewed as complementary and that each will benefit from a change of emphasis.(14) Hegel's lack of rigorous method and Husserl's restrictive teleology could both be overcome by adopting aspects of the other's standpoint. I hope in the later chapters to demonstrate that Husserl did, in fact, develop a teleology and extend his theory to embrace history as the concomitant of intersubjectivity. But bearing in mind Husserl's antipathy to Hegel expressed in the later phase of his work, I cannot agree with Lauer's suggestion.

Both Hegel and Husserl are concerned to discover the genesis of consciousness but their epistemological assumptions are very distinct. Hegel's analysis remains at the level of the concept whereas Husserl looks to the level of prepredicative experience for the beginnings of consciousness. We can find 'pre-givenness' in both, but what is given to Hegel's consciousness has already been formulated into objects of thought possessing properties (universal attributes). The sensuous manifold is brought under determinations which identify it, thus ordering it by a conceptual structure. Therefore, consciousness has '... really and rationally determined for itself the object thus sensuously apprehended ...' in observations and experience.(15) Hegel's dialectical method of reflection on ideas is thus both the description of the activity of consciousness and the prescription for the advance of human knowledge. Ultimately by this process the separation of truth and knowing is overcome: 'Being is entirely mediated; it is a substantial content... (it) has the character of self, is notion.'(16) However, Hegel's method is not concerned, as Husserl's is, to examine essences as the core of consciousness. Hegel equates essences with appearances, moreover, and theorises their emerging forms as historical phenomena in the development of Mind.(17) There is no equivalent in Hegel's methodology to Husserl's epochē. In his discussion of Hegel, Spiegelberg states:

> There is no particular interest in insight into
> the essential structures over and above what is

implied in the use of the general dialectic method. Besides, it is exactly this dialectic method with its dubious claim to logical self-evidence that is phenomenologically questioned. (18)

In one area we can discern a purpose common to Hegel and Husserl - the critique of the naive consciousness which operates in the transactions of daily living and mundane thought. This serves to conceal the truth and to mystify what is concrete. But here similarity ends, since the task of phenomenology is different in each theorist. Hegel's purpose is to lead the natural consciousness towards the scientific, whereas Husserl finds in science yet another manifestation of the naive consciousness. If scientific understanding is to be the goal then its basis must be in phenomenology. Hegel describes his task as 'this attempt to vindicate and claim science for conceptual thought'.(19) Bearing in mind the whole philosophical system which he elaborates, it may be claimed that Hegel's view of science is essentially taxonomic and anti-empirical. For Hegel, appearance is not the way an object is given to consciousness (which is Husserl's standpoint) but is, according to Spiegelberg, 'primarily an expression of a developing entity in reality, namely "science"'.(20) By contrast, on the basis of his emphasis on experience, Husserl can be viewed as an empiricist. He is sceptical in the Humean tradition (though critical of Hume) and strongly anti-positivist. While Hegel's view remains bounded by the natural science of his time,(21) Husserl attempts to broaden the concept of science considerably. In fact, Husserl aims to make science philosophical whereas Hegel makes philosophy scientific.

There is an obvious risk of over-simplification if we attempt to draw too precise a contrast between Hegel and Husserl by stating one to be the obverse of the other. It is important to recall the historical circumstances and prevailing traditions against which each strived for an original standpoint. It seems to me essential to recognise, with Spiegelberg,(22) that the central question for Hegel is ontological, whereas Husserl's concern is fundamentally epistemological. This distinction can provide a guideline for a comparative analysis of Hegelian and phenomenological Marxism. The relevance of a discussion of Hegelian Marxism is that it gives us an opportunity to examine the process of

Hegel, Marx and Husserl

synthesis within a particular tradition - idealism. My contention is that such a synthesis would be difficult to establish given the rejection of idealism by Marx. It would require considerable reformulation of both theories. The degree of reformulation should be evaluated in relation to the central ideas of each framework. If it can be established that this restructuring would distort either framework then the synthesis is invalid.

The Concept of Totality

The concept which is central to Hegel, and important for the Hegelian and existentialist Marxist positions, is that of the totality. In considering its development in Hegel's work I also enquire into its significance for Marx and Husserl. Does it have relevance for a synthesis of phenomenology and Marxism? It is evident that Marx's use of the term undergoes a transformation in the works preceding Capital, namely the Introduction of 1857 and the Preface to A Contribution to the Critique of Political Economy of 1859. How extensive was his reformulation of this Hegelian concept? Though Marx jettisoned Hegel's idealism to establish dialectical materialism as a scientific enterprise, was his work impeded by retaining within his new framework vestiges of Hegelian terminology?

The notion of totality in Hegel is indissoluble from the concept of dialectic by the movement of which it is perpetually structured. In Hegel the social and ideational realities, History and Thought, are the external expression of the self-development of the Idea (variously referred to as the Absolute, the Mind or Spirit). Hegel's totality is thus both pre-given and expressive. What is expressed is the essence of the single central contradiction between the Idea and reality. Hegel's system of philosophy is based on the principle underlying this central contradiction, the dialectic of essence and phenomena, the synthesis of which comprises the Hegelian totality. In its ideational form, reality is a continually restructured totality, though knowledge remains incomplete; in its historical form there exists the perpetual struggle of state against state, master against slave. Only at the end of history is the social totality achieved.

Hegel saw the task of philosophy as being to record the process and progress of the Absolute as it has expressed itself in the history of philosophical theories. Since his notion of the Absolute is the totality of all reality, his system is of great complexity. Its circularity and all-embracing character is evident in Hegel's assertion of the crowning stage in the evolution of Mind: 'The final outcome and expression of Absolute Mind is the truth of the Absolute revealed in and through philosophy.'(23) The elaboration of the principles by which the Absolute lives and moves in an intelligible and coherent system constitutes the science of logic for Hegel. In The Phenomenology of Mind, written to precede the Logic,(24) Hegel deals with the nature of experience and the structure of consciousness. Ontologically, man exists as a Becoming; this is made evident in the dialectic of master and slave. At the ideational level the notion (form) and the idea (content) are the elements from which thought is dialectically structured. But all knowledge is partial; the totality is to be revealed only at the end of history.

Having thus outlined Hegel's principal themes we are now in a position to consider how Marx transformed and restructured them. The necessity of grasping Marx's criticism of Hegel's dialectic in order to understand Capital is emphasised by Marxist theoreticians. Into this understanding must enter a consideration of the usage of 'totality' in the works preceding Capital. The seminal epistemological notions which Marx drew from Hegel were progressively modified. By 1857 Marx was still attempting to clarify the problems involved in rejecting Hegelian idealism. It is apparent that in the third section of the Introduction he was still 'coquetting'(25) with Hegelian forms of expression, though he had embraced a materialist position long before. The Preface of 1859, the basic work out of which historical materialism emerged, also makes use of certain Hegelian categories. Though Marx's critique of bourgeois philosophy remained a continuing concern, his growing political involvement shifted the focus of his attention during this period. He undertook a reappraisal and re-presentation of works, his own and others', on the critique of political economy. The 1857 Introduction was written to preface the collection of manuscripts known as the Grundrisse. This text is claimed by certain Marxists as a link between the early and mature thought of Marx.(26) On this basis they argue, in opposition to the scientific Marxists, that there is no foundation for claiming to find an epistemological break in his work. In both the Introduction and Preface the concept of totality occurs and it seems evident that its appearance in Marx's thought at this stage is an idealist residue. By the time _Capital_ was written Marx had adopted an epistemological framework which excluded its use.(27)

In the 1873 Preface to the second edition of _Capital_, Marx stated that he had 'coquetted' with the modes of expression peculiar to Hegel in order to rebut current detractions of Hegel. His object was a connection which would lay open 'the rational kernel within the mystical shell'.(28) By emphasising his indebtedness to the Hegelian dialectic, Marx gave further proof of the deterministic nature of his analysis. The structures of society arise not as the expression of the Absolute but as the social relations engendered by the determining economic base of society. It is in the 1857 _Introduction_ that Marx clearly indicates his rejection of Hegelian idealism. He discusses the philosophical issues arising from the use of the dialectic in some detail, with the aim of finding a correct method of analysis. When Marx writes 'The concrete is concrete because it is the synthesis of many determinations, thus representing a unity of diverse aspects', he is almost quoting Hegel's _Logic_.(29) Yet the epistemological basis of his thought is totally changed. The essence of his critique of idealism lies in the rejection of Hegel's metaphysical subject as the demi-urgos which produces the reality of the world. Marx rejects the notion of the abstract producing the concrete. It is plausible to suggest here that Marx did not jettison the concept of totality completely at this stage since he wished to subject it to a close philosophical scrutiny and then to build his own analysis upon it.(30) Marx had already foreseen the dangers of a simplistic materialist position, and had come to reject Feuerbach's anthropologically-based inversion of Hegel. An examination of the concept of totality enables Marx to explore the subject/object disjunction more thoroughly and thus examine the basis of both the materialist and idealist dilemmas.

Marx criticises Hegel for falling into the illusion of understanding the real as the result of thought and appropriating the concrete as a mental construct present only in the philosophical consciousness - thus Hegel deduces the world. Marx insists that the interiority of this process is false. Conceptualisation, as the production of concepts from within the theoretical process, is unable to achieve perception of the concrete total-

Hegel, Marx and Husserl

ity or the concrete subject. It is able only to perceive the concrete-in-thought, as opposed to the real concrete. The real subject remains locked outside. However, once the correct method is assumed by a correct series of syntheses, the conception arrived at would represent the reproduction of the concrete by means of thinking.

Marx illustrates the theoretical procedure by which the errors of idealist thought can be revealed by examining the methodology of political economy.(31) By an analysis which passes from the concept of society as a whole to its representation in any of its parts, the error becomes apparent. Since the seventeenth century such abstractions as population, production and consumption have been traditionally employed by bourgeois economists. While these categories appear to be dealing with the real and concrete, Marx maintains that they do not lead to a concrete analysis of the economy, but to simpler abstractions such as value, price and labour. Marx insists that the totality be constructed by the opposite method. By taking simple abstract notions such as wage labour, and building more complex determinations, the scientifically constructed whole is achieved. Constructs such as the state, international exchange and the world market may be correctly realised as concrete totalities - the sum of many determinations and therefore a unity in diversity. Thus, the concrete is both the origin and summation of perception and conceptualisation.

As Marx's analysis continued, he no longer referred to the synthesis of the abstract and the concrete in the formation of the totality. He came to adopt a terminology more suited to the discussion of the forces and relations of production. The dialectic became that of the general and the particular. Carver identifies the origin of this change, with certain important qualifications as to its salience. He points out that commodity/money/capital are more nearly the same thing than value/money/capital since value cannot be a tangible thing in quite the same way as money or capital.(32)

The philosophical problems continued, as we see in the early part of *Capital* concerning the theory of value and the commodity, but the major aspects of Marx's analysis became concentrated on the nature of the commodity, money and capital. So far we may conclude that the retention of Hegelian terms such as 'totality' enabled Marx to analyse his methodology prior to *Capital*. Carver points out that Marx's commitment to the method elaborated in the

Hegel, Marx and Husserl

Introduction is confirmed by a reference made in the second volume of Capital.(33) But what of the philosophical implications in his reformulation? It should be stressed that Marx was not merely defending Hegel in the Preface and Introduction, but was practising a synthesis in his own thought. However, it must be remembered that the dialectic is not merely synthetic but cumulative. In Hegel's philosophy the owl of Minerva flies only at dusk. Marx seems to have subscribed to this view. He recognised that Hegel's categories were the result of bourgeois philosophy which had to be transformed and then completed within the framework of dialectical materialism. Thus the totality becomes the mode of production and the dialectic assumes the forms of the construction in historical society, in social life and in thought. For Marx, the key is praxis:

> In the social production of their existence, men inevitably enter into definite relations, which are independent of their will, namely relations of production appropriate to a given stage in the development of their material forces of production. The totality of these relations of production constitutes the economic structure of society, the real foundation, on which arises a legal and political superstructure and to which correspond definite forms of social consciousness. The mode of production of material life conditions the general process of social, political and intellectual life. It is not the consciousness of men that determines their existence, but their social existence that determines their consciousness. (34)

Marx emphasised thought as a product. The concept of totality as a reified form was rejected. Marx's criticism of Hegel is that he produced an illusion of the 'real' by hypostatising concepts as Being or Spirit, thus giving them ontological status. It is implicit in Marx's use of 'totality' that he similarly rejects the concept, in its static form, as an element of bourgeois thought. He retains it only as an element of the process by which he subjects the Hegelian system to analysis.(35)

Hegelian Marxism in Lukacs
Hegelian and phenomenological Marxists share common concerns which again overlap with the interests of

existentialist Marxists. Certain key issues and concepts need to be examined in order to discover the internal consistency in each of these variants of Marxism if we are looking for evidence of synthesis, and questioning its validity and possibilities. The rest of this chapter examines the work of Lukács as proponent of the Hegelian Marxist position. It also looks at themes in Sartre and Kojève which illuminate Hegel's phenomenology from new perspectives. A significant contribution to the development of phenomenological Marxism has come from these sources. Lukács saw his overall task as the establishing of a dynamic, dialectical Marxism freed from the Soviet orthodoxy which was stultifying its development in Europe in the post-revolutionary period. He opposed its dominant scientism by attacking its metaphysical basis in positivistic dogmatism. To provide the impetus for his attack he turned to the early Marx and to Hegel.

We have seen that Hegel claims to achieve the resolution of the problem of the dichotomous structure of consciousness. He deals with the epistemological status of subject and object in the <u>Phenomenology</u>, and his answer to the Kantian dilemma is to make Mind paramount :

> Mind is the only Reality. It is the inner being of the world, that which essentially is, and is per se; it assumes objective, determinate forms and enters into relations with itself - it is externality (Otherness) and exists for itself; yet, in this determination, and in its otherness, it is still one with itself - it is self-contained and self-complete, in-itself and for-itself at once. (36)

Hegel seeks to achieve unity in diversity throughout his system of philosophy and within the structure of the understanding itself. He strives to demonstrate that reason is a process; the totality of the Absolute is not a purely contemplative state but is the concomitant of historical movements. Yet however Hegel attempts to make his analysis concrete, it remains within the framework of Absolute Idealism.

Lukács, in his <u>Preface</u> (1967),(37) traces his own early attempts to transform Hegelian ideas into the driving force of a revolutionary Marxism. The Hegelian identity of subject and object would exist in the proletariat at the point of revolution where full consciousness was attained.(38) With hindsight Lukács realised the error of his attempt to 'out-

Hegel' Hegel - '... the proletariat seen as the identical subject/object of the real history of mankind is no materialist consummation that overcomes the constructions of <u>idealism</u>'.(39) Lukacs' self-criticism developed into a critique of Hegel's concept of alienation - 'this fundamental and crude error' - which equated alienation, a societal category entailing a teleology, with objectification, an epistemological category. Rejecting the idealism of <u>History and Class Consciousness</u>, Lukacs embraced an orthodox Marxism which he later repudiated. He finally opted for a Marxism which enabled him to examine economics and dialectics.(40) The predominant issues came to be the ontological. Lukács makes a major contribution to the examination of ontology in Hegel and Marx. <u>Toward the Ontology of Social Being</u>(41) is an extensive analysis of the ontological assumptions of contemporary philosophies. This leads to a discussion of Marx's debt to Hegel, out of which Lukács develops categories with which to propose solutions to problems of contemporary society. These require an understanding of the ontology of social existence.

In his early work, Lukács' response to Hegel's profound influence was to make his prime category that of the totality. He thus sought to use the dialectical dynamic to synthesise abstract and concrete, whole and particular, theory and practice. Lukács' later work acknowledges that his Marxism, though in need of drastic revision, remained closely tied in spirit to Hegel. In the 1967 <u>Preface</u> he traces the misconception of his 'most radical attempt to restore the revolutionary nature of Marx's theories by renovating and extending Hegel's dialectics and method'.(42) In retrospect Lukács still valued the Hegelian heritage. His failure was in omitting to subject it to a materialist interpretation which would 'transcend and preserve it'.(43) That the Hegelian influence is strongly retained is illustrated clearly by Lukács' contradictory position on this question of the totality.

We find that for Lukács the centrality of totality was a distortion, but at the same time it remained vitally central - a paradox indeed. In the second part of his discourse on social being, Lukács points to Marx's assertion, early in his work, of totality as a directly given principle which is yet abstract and only rendered concrete by genetic knowledge of economic and social relations. It is to this task that Lukács directs his survey of Marx's ontology of social being.(44) The problems which relate to social being are those of dialectical opposition, difference, and appearance and essence. Lukács uses the concept of the totality of social being to indicate the generalising nature of science and the concrete nature of scientific thought.(45) Lukács' statement makes a claim which accords with Husserl's project of asserting the scientificity of his phenomenological analysis in opposition to positivism and the naive realism of natural science: 'We believe that Marx created in this way (by critically considering the reality and significance of individual phenomena) a new form of general scientificity as well as a new ontology.'(46) When Lukács examines the structures of economic being as found in Capital(47) he interprets them in a restricted form. His concern appears to be to avoid the charge of historical relativism for which his work in 1927 was widely criticised. He limits himself to concepts of 'homo laborans' and 'the ontologically central category of the economy' which must remain under socialism as a 'realm of necessity in social life'.(48)

There are two criticisms to be made here before the main question of Hegelian Marxism's validity as a synthesis is considered. First, in his ontological analysis of the social and economic formation, Lukács sees man as man in nature, asserting himself over nature, creative and dominant: even in his aesthetic life man's achievement is wrought out of labour. Therefore, Lukács' category of homo laborans extends to man even under socialism in the post-revolutionary phase. This ontology which Lukács discovers in the early Marx, and in Capital, is idealised labour, a romantic conception deriving directly from Hegel. It is a concept which allows him to unify theory with practice in such a way that the work of the intellectual in the community is given special importance. This interpretation is one with which I take issue on the grounds that it is elitist. However, the main point I wish to illustrate here by outlining the ontology is that Lukács again displays inconsistency. He first of all claims a limited ontological significance for certain concepts and then asserts that his ontology of man has enduring ontological status.(49) It would seem that there is an inconsistent use of certain ontologies by Lukács which constitutes a relativising of his position. The ontological claim is by definition a statement about the nature of being. It is not a category of knowledge about truth which can be subjected to proofs. It should therefore operate as a consistent theoretical construct. My criticism of this aspect of Lukács is directed against (a) his ontology and (b) his inconsistency in employing the ontology.

The second point on which I take issue with Lukács is his elevation of ontology above epistemological argument. He sees the emphasis on epistemology, together with logic, as dominant concerns which characterise positivism and the methods of science. While it may be said that ontological assertions ultimately underpin all statements about the nature of society it seems to me that epistemological analysis is essential to any form of Marxian theorising. To diminish the role of epistemology in any proposed synthesis with another framework of ideas is to run the risk of weakening the claim to validity and explanatory power. In particular, it is most certainly contrary to a phenomenology approach in the Husserlian tradition. In his search for truth Husserl gives priority to cognition. His work is first and foremost epistemological as we have seen in the first chapter.(50) It can be said that the major claim of phenomenology is to have superseded traditional epistemologies. Therefore, any reconciliation of Marx and Husserl will need to take epistemological compatibility as its prime consideration.

Hegelian Themes in Sartre and Kojève

The concept of totality remained problematic for later Marxist philosophers. We have seen that for Lukács, the use of this concept is central to the framework of his ontology. The problem is that the Hegelian dialectic resists his attempted displacement of it into the sphere of political praxis. If the concrete totality could not be achieved by the use of Hegel's categories, neither could it be achieved by the concrete mediation of a postulated proletarian consciousness, Lukács' concept of the totality is essentially normative.(51) While Sartre also experiences problems at the ontological level, he escapes the fetishism of totality that we find in Lukács. The concept of the inert totality is rejected in favour of the notion of 'totalisation'. This allows Sartre to emphasise the dynamics in the dialectical process of Becoming on which his ontology of human life depends. He attempts to escape the hypostatisation of totality by stressing the principle of recurrence in the historical dialectic.(52) The totality is theorised as a detotalised totality.

Sartre's notion of totalisation appears to me to have the merit of extending Marx's idea from the concrete/conceptual to the level of social process. His solution is to emphasise praxis as perpetually restructuring the synthesis which results from man's impact on materiality and which forms the basis of history. The concept of totality, if given these determinations, could be usefully retained. The reformulated term 'lived totality' would serve to convey Marx's intention by retaining the sense of both concrete and conceptual totalities. This would also open the way to a synthesis with Husserl's notion of the lived world. For Husserl, the Lebenswelt is the supreme totalising category, being the foundation of all experience. Its unity is of 'an open horizon of possible experiences for all; it is the world as the universal horizon, common to all men, of actually existing things'.(53) Where Husserl refers to totality per se it is to indicate the naivety of the natural attitude.(54)

An attempt to reformulate Hegel to a position more compatible with that of Marx can be found in Kojève's reading of the Phenomenology.(55) Though Kojève rejected Marx's materialist categories, his account emphasises those elements which Marx transposed from Hegel into dialectical materialism. Contrary to the view that Hegel was a metaphysician, Kojève stresses the atheism and concreteness in Hegel. The Absolute is thus not metaphysical but denotes a complete and self-contained form of the finite. The human individual is a realised self-conscious mind. The structure of this mind is unified, not as a static 'given' (which would lay Hegel's philosophy open to the charge of theodicy), but as a continuous process by which the mind creates 'experience'. The process, the dialectic, is at once a whole and a multiplicity. The world is a single unified whole, a totality or synthesis which is neither a process only nor a static reality.(56) Reason and reality are the form and content of this totality. Kojève insists that this totality is, moreover, concrete. With these formulations he is, therefore, providing a realist account of Hegel. This may be considered a significant reinterpretation by those commentators who seek to establish the contemporary relevance of Hegel. Kojève's claim, that the Absolute is finite, is not, however, compatible with a Marxist view of the material world.

It is evident that Kojève gives us an

essentially humanistic interpretation of Hegel. His work has been criticised by Tran Duc Thao(57) as presenting the whole of <u>Phenomenology of Mind</u> in terms of the master/slave dialectic, thereby emphasising the history of labour and the struggle for recognition which defines the historical being as human being. From the phenomenological viewpoint Tran Duc Thao offers another reading. This takes the master/slave dialectic in its metaphorical form, the dialectical elements being life and self-consciousness.(58)

The Structure of Consciousness

It is evident that the notion of the totality is given ontological status by Hegelian and existentialist Marxists, but it is also reworked and transmuted into a methodology. The term 'totalisation' is retained to describe the structuring of consciousness. Given the problematical nature of the concept, this allows a certain ambiguity to be tolerated within the theory of the structuring/de-structuring process of the dialectical consciousness.(59) The problem with this is how essential Marxist constructs, such as the mode of production, or the economic substructure, can be given ontological status. Again, we have the problem of how the conceptual totality is to become the concrete totality. We have seen that Marx asserts the dialectical process of consciousness, and thus avoids falling into a naive empiricist position when theorising the relationship of base to superstructure. However, this does not overcome the structural problems of how experience and consciousness are related. Such difficulties stem from traditional epistemological categories acting as constraints on even such an original thinker as Hegel. Since Marx inherited these problems and the Hegelian Marxists appear to work within the same constraints, what can phenomenology offer as a solution?

The epistemological dichotomies of traditional theories of knowledge are considered by Husserl to be irrelevancies. Likewise the ontologies which pose problems for realists and rationalists are unacceptable to Husserl. He rejects the idea of a natural science of the world based on a universal a priori. In place of a physicalistic ontology of nature Husserl offers an ontology of the world as 'a world of knowledge, a world of consciousness'.(60) It is the unifying life-world, the preconceptual basis of all experience, that exhibits itself in what appears to consciousness. Even in developing his concept of the life-world as a central ontology, Husserl is concerned to shift the emphasis back to the epistemological level. Thus the life-world becomes the subjective matrix of all experience. Given this overarching 'subjectivity', the traditional epistemologies which oppose subject to object, appearance to reality, abstract to concrete, are nullified in Husserl's view. They are no longer problematical as areas of speculation. We have already seen this demonstrated in Husserl's treatment of the object in Chapter One.(61)

The impetus to break down the subject/object division and investigate the core of consciousness is maintained in the later work of Husserl. Writing on sense-intuition in <u>Crisis</u>, he refers to the ontic certainty of the thing that is given to consciousness and apprehended in all its richness. What is exhibited in such manifold aspects by the continuous alteration of seeing, and by the modalities of sense-perception, is 'a sometimes continuous, and sometimes discrete synthesis of identification, or better, of unification'.(62) Thus, we have a re-statement of Husserl's methodological universal a priori - correlation, a seeking of relationships within a continuous 'unfolding of horizons'.(63)

To establish common ground with Marxism, phenomenology would have to concede the following points on this crucial question of consciousness:

a) methodology - to view the correlative principle as a process compatible with the dialectical structuring of consciousness (Paci considers this tenable if Husserl's theory is implicitly a dialectic of the hidden and the revealed, and Merleau-Ponty contributes to this with his theories of perception);
b) ontology - to render Husserl's theory of the life-world compatible with Marx's structural analysis; the life-world would need to be concretely theorised and given status as an historical a priori, a substructural constant in relationship to changes in consciousness (this is again proposed by Paci, and considered below in relation to the problem of history);
c) epistemology - to reconcile the pervasive subjectivity of Husserl's theory with the Marxist project of scientific enquiry and

concrete analysis; aspects of Husserl which
are of importance here are his theory of
intentionality and the character of the life-
world.

A fuller analysis of these points is dependent on arguments developed in later chapters. At this stage I am concerned to indicate the importance to a synthesis of reconciling Marx and Husserl on the question of consciousness and to suggest those aspects which require closer attention.

In this chapter I have aimed to demonstrate the flaws in attempts to graft Marxist philosophy on to Hegelianism. Such attempts, which claim to provide theoretically sound bases for a revitalised Marxism, can only result in an inadequate and spurious synthesis. Further to this, the idea that phenomenological Marxism is itself a variant of Hegelian Marxism must be rejected. We have seen that there are major differences in the ontologies and epistemologies of Hegel and Husserl. The basis of Hegelian Marxism appears to rest on a contradiction. Since Hegel's philosophy is deeply rooted in the idealist tradition from which Marx broke away, it is only possible to modify it in liaison with Marxism by distortion of the Marxist perspective. Whereas Lukács, Sartre and Kojève adapt Hegelian notions to fit their conceptions of a Marxist synthesis, they still fail to make a convincing case against orthodoxy. Since Husserl takes a radical standpoint, which moves beyond the idealist position, his work is more compatible with that of Marx.

Notes and References

1. Cerf, W. and Harris, H.S. (eds.) <u>Hegel: Essay on Faith and Knowledge</u>, University of New York Press, Albany, 1977.
2. Ibid., p.xii.
3. Ibid., p.xiii.
4. Hegel, G.W.F., <u>The Science of Logic</u>, Vol I, trans. Johnston, W.H. and Struthers, L.G., Allen and Unwin, London, 1966, p.73. Hegel describes Kantian philosophy as 'a pillow for intellectual sloth, which soothes itself with the idea that everything has been already proved and done with'.
5. We find direct references in <u>Logical Investigations</u>, Vol I, p.158. <u>Cartesian Meditations</u>, p.90, <u>Crisis</u>, pp.204-205, <u>Philosophy as Rigorous</u>

Science, trans. Lauer, Q., 1965, pp.76-77.
   6. Kaufmann, W., 'Hegel's Conception of Phenomenology', in Pivčević, E., Phenomenology and Philosophical Understanding, Cambridge University Press, 1975, p.212. Kaufmann mentions Sartre's innovative role in giving prominence to both.
   7. Mure, G.R.G., 'Hegel: How and How Far, is Philosophy Possible?', in Weiss, F.G., Beyond Epistemology, Martinus Nijhoff, The Hague, 1974, p.14. 'In philosophy a metaphor (or) to speak metaphorically is like an overdraft: indispensable at the time but difficult to repay ... Hegel takes important terms from his predecessors, and when he shapes them to his own use they often seem almost synonymous because of his concern to reinterpret them all as exhibiting the triple rhythm of his dialectic.'
   8. Kaufmann in Pivčević, op.cit., pp.226-27. The three conceptions are of phenomenology as: 1) the science of the experience of consciousness; 2) the poetic reflection on the life of the spirit; 3) the study of self-consciousness and reason.
   9. Baillie, J.B., Preface to Hegel, Phenomenology of Mind, Allen and Unwin, London, 1931, p.16. Reference hereinafter is to Phenomenology.
   10. Norman, R., Hegel's Phenomenology: A Philosophical Introduction, Sussex University Press, London, 1976, pp.112-14. Norman discusses to what extent the 'development of reason' analysis develops into a theology. Kaufmann, op.cit., finds that Hegel's 'anti-pluralistic bias was rooted in Biblical monotheism' (p.230) and that the Phenomenology is 'an utterly unscientific and un-rigorous work' which nevertheless allowed him to develop new ways of thinking.
   11. Husserl, Cartesian Meditations, p.90. Husserl dismisses Hegel along with the futilities of 'dialectical argumentation and self-styled "meta-physical" hypothesis (whose supposed possibility may turn out to be complete absurdity)'.
   12. Lauer, in Weiss, op.cit., pp.194-6.
   13. Husserl, Crisis, p.201. Husserl's answer is that transcendental philosophy adopted a mentalistic approach and thus idealism arose out of reflections on conscious subjectivity. Husserl is referring in this quotation to the transcendental philosophers, Fichte and Hegel.
   14. Lauer, in Weiss, op.cit., p.196.
   15. Hegel, Phenomenology, p.284.
   16. Ibid., Preface to Phenomenology, p.32.
   17. Lowenberg, J., (ed.) Hegel: Selections,

'Doctrine of Essence', Modern Students Library, London, 1929, p.164.
18. Spiegelberg, op.cit., Vol II, p.14.
19. Hegel, Phenomenology, p.66.
20. Spiegelberg, op.cit., p.14f.
21. Soll, I., An Introduction to Hegel's Metaphysics, University of Chicago Press, 1969, p.136. Soll states: 'He holds that the natural sciences, which use the finite categories of the understanding, are adequate to the particular task of knowing ordinary finite objects, while traditional metaphysics has the different task of knowing absolute or infinite objects'.
22. Spiegelberg, op.cit., p.14.
23. Hegel, Phenomenology, Baillie's Introduction to 2nd edition, p.29.
24. Hegel, The Science of Logic, (1812).
25. Marx, Capital, Preface to 2nd edition, p.xxx.
26. Nicolaus, M., 'The Unknown Marx', in Blackburn, R., (ed.) Ideology in Social Science, Fontana, London, 1972.
27. Althusser, L., Lenin and Philosophy, New Left Books, London, 1971, pp.90-95, p.121. Althusser's extensive use of the term 'totality' is surprising. He is concerned to detect 'whiffs' and even 'flagrant and extremely harmful traces of Hegelian influence' in Capital, Vol I which Marx intended to eradicate. I suggest that Althusser regards the concept as value-free, finding it essential to convey the 'process without a subject', cf. his quotation from Marx's note to the French edition of Capital (p.121). I have treated 'concept' and 'term' as synonymous in discussing 'totality'. An interesting approach to the study of a concept is made in Overend, T., 'Alienation: A conceptual analysis', Philosophical and Phenomenological Research, Vol XXXV, No 3, 1975, pp.301-22. Overend follows J.L. Austin's distinction of the locutionary and illocutionary forces of a word to signify what I have termed the denotation (sense) and connotation (reference and normative content).
28. Marx, Capital, p.xxx.
29. Marx, Introduction, p.206.
30. Carver, T., Karl Marx: Texts on Method, Blackwell, Oxford, 1975.
31. Marx, Introduction, pp.206-207.
32. Carver, op.cit., pp.134-35, and Marx, Contribution, p.29.
33. Marx, Capital, Vol II, pp.366-67.
34. Marx, Preface, pp.20-21.

35. '... the concrete totality regarded as a conceptual totality, as a mental fact is indeed a product of thinking, of comprehension; but it is by no means a product of the idea which evolves spontaneously and whose thinking proceeds outside and above perception and imagination; but is the result of the assimilation and transformation of perceptions and images into concepts. The totality as a conceptual entity seen by the intellect is a product of the thinking intellect which assimilates the world in the only way open to it...' Marx, Introduction, pp.206-207.
36. Baillie, Introduction to Phenomenology, p.22.
37. Lukács, G., History and Class Consciousness, trans. Livingstone, R., Merlin, London, 1971.
38. Lichtheim, G., Lukács, Fontana, London, 1970, p.64.
39. Lukács, op.cit. (1971), xxiii.
40. Ibid., p.xxxv.
41. Lukács, G., Toward the Ontology of Social Being, trans. Fernbach, D., Part I, Chs. 3 and 4 deal with Marx and Hegel.
42. Lukács, op.cit. (1971), p.xxi.
43. Ibid., p.xx.
44. Lukács, G., Marx's Basic Ontological Principles, trans. Fernbach, D., Merlin, London, 1978, p.10., pp.160-61.
45. Ibid., p.17.
46. Ibid., p.18.
47. Marx, Capital, p.157.
48. Lukács, op.cit. (1978), p.18, cf. also pp.38-39.
49. Ibid., p.163 where Lukács stresses the changing forms which evolve into 'new ontological stages of being'. My comments are in line with the classic criticism made of the historicist position.
50. See Chapter One, p.15 above. Also Kolakowski, L., Husserl and the Search for Certitude, Yale University Press, New Haven, 1975, p.4. Kolakowski sees Husserl's goal as 'how to reach a perfectly hard ground in cognition'.
51. Meszaros, I., Lukács Concept of Dialectic, Merlin, London, 1972, pp.69-71.
52. Sartre, J.P., Search for a Method, Vintage Books, New York, 1968, in which Sartre develops this idea as part of his critique of positivist sociology.
53. Husserl, Crisis, p.164.
54. Ibid., p.204ff.
55. Kojève, Introduction to the Reading of Hegel, Basic Books, New York, 1967.

56. Ibid., p.30.
57. Tran Duc Thao, 'The Phenomenology of Mind and its Real Content', *Telos*, No 8, 1971, p.91ff.
58. Ibid., Thao is referring to Hegel's *Phenomenology*, pp.231-35. His critique is made from a realist standpoint, cf. Mays, W., in Pivčević, op.cit., 1975.
59. Ambiguity being a principal concept in Merleau-Ponty's work, one with which Paci takes issue, viz., Paci, op.cit., 1972, p.346ff.
60. Husserl, *Crisis*, p.265.
61. See Chapter 1, pp.22-24 above.
62. Husserl, *Crisis*, p.158.
63. Ibid., p.159.

PART II

THE CRISIS OF SCIENCE AND THE ANALYSIS OF CAPITALISM

Chapter Three

STRUCTURE AND SCIENTIFICITY

My intention in this chapter is to examine a further attempt to synthesise Marxism with another theoretical perspective, namely, structuralism. The emergence of structuralist or scientific Marxism has provoked a great deal of interest and controversy. In what sense is it a departure from other branches of Marxist theory, and in what respect can it be said to be scientific? Further indication of the current search for direction in Marxist philosophy is the turn towards scientific realism. In the context of the crisis in science it is relevant to challenge the assumptions made by this theory and to ask if it can substantiate its claims to explanatory power. I shall examine certain perennial epistemological problems which have particular relevance for these perspectives - the science/ideology disjunction, the relations of subject to object, abstract to concrete, and the nature of reality.

The Marxist theorist who has commanded most attention in recent years is the French philosopher, Louis Althusser. His work, coming at a point when Marxists were seeking a radical alternative to Hegelian Marxism, was given prominence in the left-wing political upsurge of the 1960s and 70s with which he is identified.(1) Althusser offered a new interpretation of Marx as scientist. The intention was to examine the status of Marx's later work as a scientific theory and to demonstrate that it signified an epistemological break with the ideology which was discernible in the earlier writings. It is essential to clarify the idea of science in Althusser and his use of the term 'scientificity'. We have already seen that a reformulation of the idea of a scientific theory is a hinge-pin in Husserl's work. How does this contrast with Althusser's ideas? He makes several references to

Structure and Scientificity

Husserl as epitomising the idealist stance in the philosophy of science.(2) I shall consider this assessment in the context of the relation of science to philosophy. In Althusser's own work the treatment of this relationship undergoes a change and marks a shift in perspective.

I finally ask what phenomenological Marxism can contribute to the critique of science and capitalism if other syntheses prove inadequate. How do we identify aspects of phenomenology which are compatible with Marx's structural analysis? What are the implications of this approach for substantive analysis of the present crises in science and society?

The Structuralist Synthesis

Althusser's work is an amalgam of orthodox scientistic Marxist theory and structuralist theory of the French school, though he has rejected both these theories as deviations, and attempts to go beyond them (as indeed he must if the foundational character of his work is to be maintained). 'A new science',(3) like Vico's, must assert its distinctive aspect. But in spite of the rigorous making and remaking of his philosophical position, Althusser ultimately fails to achieve an adequate synthesis. Though he attempts to correct the inconsistencies in his work, his self-criticisms are made from within his own problematic.(4) As we shall see, Althusser's self-critique fails because the correction of a theory requires a degree of metatheoretical analysis more radical than that which he applies to his own work. Althusser does not adopt the Cartesian method of enquiring into the foundations of the ideas which he attempts to synthesise. He appropriates concepts from Hegelian Marxism and structuralism, theories which he vigorously rejects. I hope to demonstrate that these constructs are inadequately theorised.

I point first to the importance of structuralism for Althusser by citing his denial of it. In the 1970 'Interview on Philosophy', Althusser states that the role of Marxist-Leninist philosophy is to conduct political struggle, in the theoretical realm, against a bourgeois world outlook of which the current philosophical form is: 'neo-positivism and its "spiritual complement", existentialist-phenomenological subjectivism. The variant peculiar to the Human Sciences: the ideology called "structuralist".'(5) An earlier essay on Freud and

Structure and Scientificity

Lacan contains a mention of the work of Saussure as a source of the 'idealist ideologies' of Sartre and Merleau-Ponty.(6) Saussure is also acknowledged as the basis of Lacan's exposition of Freud (a pioneer scientist in the discovery of the de-centred subject 'constituted by a structure').(7) Althusser's own scientific approach relies heavily on the displacement of the human subject. He does not change this approach despite other shifts in his theory. The anti-subjectivist plea for scientificity evident in his early work also draws on structuralist theory.

The idea of a structure is central to any system of thought and to any proposal to synthesise two frameworks. Therefore it cannot be dealt with on the logical level of concept-, or hypothesis-formation. It is the paramount metatheoretical term signifying a logically and epistemologically coherent whole, an episteme or body of knowledge exhibiting a principle of coherence. Phenomenology and those branches of the human sciences which relate their approach to phenomenology are often criticised for their failure to match the theoretical critique of social formations offered by structuralist theories. The proposals for synthesising phenomenology with Marxism can be viewed as an attempt to rebut such criticism. It will be useful in this chapter to examine how Marx's notion of structure can be allied with Husserl's and to assess its application in the critique of science and the social formation. In contrast, the work of scientific Marxists will be examined to see how their concepts of structure, scientificity and ideology are theorised. Husserl is, as Cutler puts it 'the philosopher who most rigorously reflected the role philosophy has traditionally assumed vis-a-vis the sciences'.(8) As we have seen, his critique of the sciences demands that they must be brought back to philosophy, having lost their meaning and purpose. The occlusion, in human knowledge and practice, of their origins in the pre-conceptual life-world has led to a crisis at the height of their 'success'. Husserl proposes establishing phenomenology as a 'first philosophy' which can restore to the sciences their telos.

Such notions of the crisis of science are rejected by the scientific Marxists. Drawing on structuralist postulates to provide the theoretical framework, Althusser seeks to establish Marxism as a science free from ideological contamination. A basic tenet of Althusser's position is that knowledge, scientific knowledge, is the result of a production process.(9) This process is not anthropologically

conceived as deriving from the practice of human
subjects but as engendered by the mechanisms of the
structure itself. Thus, science is the possibility
for the emergence of knowledge as well as the knowledge itself. Althusser's theory is, therefore, anti-
teleological, anti-subjectivist and anti-idealist.
For Althusser, the social formation arises from the
articulation of the practices of the superstructure.
The point at which the true science of history,
Marxist science, emerges is marked by a break with
the epistemology of former theories in the domain of
theoretical practice. Althusser also makes a break
with philosophy, which he sees as bourgeois and
impregnated with ideology. Marxism becomes a new
science producing knowledge of its objects in a
discrete area, thus enabling distinctions to be made
between science and ideology, and science and
philosophy. According to this schema, however, there
are not clear cut epistemological breaks which could
correspond to synchronically identifiable points of
emergence for new knowledges.(10) The elements of
the structure are in dynamic relation to each other
and there is an unevenness in the development of the
concepts in any science.(11) It is on this ground
that Althusserian theory rejects the notion of a
crisis in science. Moreover, the apprehension of
crisis presupposes a constituting subject construct-
ing a history of knowledge and a history of science
as it emerges from that knowledge. A crisis in
science occurs as a departure from an origin but, as
Cutler puts it, 'The privilege of the origin is the
privilege of the knowing subject', and thus
reproduces the 'vulgar empiricist notion of time',
that is: a continuist history of ideas.(12)

  The problem with this complex and ingenious
theory, with its overt and implied critiques of
Husserl, is that its structuralist basis is at fault.
By appropriating the notion of structure which
characterises the structuralism of the French
theorists, Althusser's system displays a mechanistic
logic in the relations of the parts to the whole.
This logic is the a priori which fixes the moments
of the system in causal interrelationship. The
basic presupposition of this theory is that the
interior logic is inexorable and pervades the whole
episteme. Yet surely to render this logic tenable it
must be argued for and demonstrated in the
propositions of the theory? This objection to
Althusser can be illustrated by reference to Hegel.
It can be claimed that Hegel's system and its logic
inheres in the demonstration which he makes through-

Structure and Scientificity

out its exposition. The fault with Hegel's system is that its central tenet, the Idea, is self-generating; thought reflects itself, the logic lives itself and so forth. This is not merely a stylistic device in Hegel. It is, I submit, crucial to his intention of breathing life into the dialectical logic, of providing the dynamic necessary to a reflexive theory. Now while Hegel can be faulted on this ontological basis, we cannot dispute that the logic is fully theorised and demonstrated in the text. This is not achieved by the structuralists. Structuralism fabricates an elaborate schema on the basis of a metaphor which is limited in character; cognition and knowledge are the products of a geological 'science'. Within the limitations of this extended metaphor we are presented with images of surfaces and underlying deep structures, shifts in levels and strata, of breaks and slippage, of overlapping elements of ruptures and <u>embrayage</u>.(13) Since structuralism gives a depersonalised account of processes in a structure, the imagery, employed here as the epistemological framework, is that of impersonal, inexorable forces of nature, inevitably deterministic in their effects. The image accommodates, therefore, those approaches to language, history and society in which the system has its own dynamic. It is appropriate that Foucault termed his analysis of knowledge and the emergence of scientific discourses an archaeology of knowledge.(14)

Though he rejects structuralism as bourgeois philosophy,(15) Althusser takes the structural model and attempts to synthesise it with Marx's base/superstructure model. The social totality is transformed into the structure in dominance. This articulates with other components in a system of structure/superstructure with which he replaces Marx's construction. It is the process and the mode of articulation which determines the character of historical society. Thus, the mode of production is conceptualised as a decentred totality. Althusser elaborates his model by ascribing relative autonomy to the superstructural ideologies, while the base remains determinant 'in the last instance'. These concepts explain changes within the superstructure which are unaccountable by direct relation to changes in the base. But there are considerable problems in the explanation of the autonomy of the superstructure in terms of ideological production and reproduction. By theorising the totality as the formulation of a process without a subject Althusser is open to criticism. The producing subject is ostensibly removed but, in fact, remains implicit in relation to the posited object or product of the process. Althusser's epistemology retains an analysis of subject and object while denying the human subject. Logically, therefore, the subject must be some other entity. We have seen that Hegel's producing subject is the Idea, the Absolute, the source of his idealism. The entity which operates as subject for Althusser is the concept. When Althusser reintroduces the thinking subject to account for changes in science and knowledge he is merely providing an actor to flesh out the part which the structure assigns to him.(16)

Science and Ideology in Althusser and Foucault

A key distinction for Althusser's epistemology is that between science and ideology.(17) The way in which these are related lies at the heart of the antagonisms between Marxist theories. The opposition of science to ideology is a disjunction over which phenomenology challenges the scientific Marxists. Althusser's intention is to establish the structural invariance of scientific Marxism in order to render it totally distinct from ideologically tainted variants of Marxism. From Husserl's position the reverse is true; science has its foundation in the sphere of human praxis and its originative lifeworld. It is, therefore, permeated by human interests which are evinced in the forms that knowledge assumes.(18) In other words, science is interpenetrated by ideology. The phenomenological Marxists assert that the ideologies of sectional interests operate within the natural and human sciences. They are evident in the institutionalisation of the sciences, in their research policies and funding, in the endorsement of new knowledge, and in the selection and training of scientists, their validation and professionalisation. As Gramsci writes:

> To pose science as the basis of life, to make of science the conception of the world par excellence - which clears the eyes of every ideological illusion, which places man in front of reality as it is - amounts to falling back on the idea that the philosophy of praxis needs philosophical supports outside of itself. But in reality even science is a superstructure, and ideology. (19)

Structure and Scientificity

Gramsci considers the sciences as ideological in their scientism and mechanism. This criticism can be extended to Althusser's version of Marxist science which has not proved impregnable against idealism. The phenomenological Marxists maintain that 'Science must be grounded in a philosophy which is not an ideology'.(20) Ideologies are false, non-universal, fallible and partial. They must be eradicated by the two-edged critique of Marxism and phenomenology.

It would be instructive at this point to contrast Althusser's treatment of the science/ideology disjunction with that of his compatriot, Foucault. Not only should this further clarify the structuralist approach but also, by examining the changes in his position, usefully illustrate the problems which beset Althusser. Foucault also makes a critique of phenomenology which makes his work doubly interesting at this stage of the discussion.

Foucault claimed that The Archaeology of Knowledge marked a radical departure from structuralism and the traditional histories of thought.(21) Rejecting the anthropological theme of the history of ideas, he confines archaeology to the discovery of the discourse of historical 'events'. The discourse is defined as a practice governed by rules for making descriptive statements in a given domain such as psychopathology or political economy. The discursive practices occupy a different territory from the sciences, being neither pseudo-sciences nor sciences in their prehistory. Foucault's archaeology does not aim to describe a coherent conceptual framework but rather the set of rules for arranging statements in series and distributing recurrent elements in ordered succession. Though these rules operate at 'a kind of pre-conceptual level', Foucault is at pains to assert that this refers only to the level of discourse and 'neither to a horizon of ideality nor to an empirical genesis of abstractions'.(22) This is obviously in criticism of phenomenology which he sees as a humanist ideology. His own position is anti-historicist, anti-teleological and anti-realist, yet he denies that he is practising either history or philosophy.(23) So the archaeology appears as a methodology rather than a theory. Foucault sees his task, like Husserl's, as repairing the crisis in philosophy engendered by the Kantian legacy, but includes phenomenology in his attack which is intended 'to free history from the grip of phenomenology'.(24) This is an impossible position to maintain since no methodology can exist in theoretical isolation or, as Foucault consistently

67

maintains, in an untheorised state. In denying structuralism and attempting to go beyond it, Foucault arrives at an impasse. He lacks a theory with which to account for the production of knowledge.(25)

In his account of the archaeological method of identifying discursive practices, Foucault has systematically attacked both the constituting subject of the historicist problematic and the structuralist notion of signification. With so much written off, what does Foucault offer us as the archaeological enterprise proper? He claims that the rules governing any discourse can be taken as the historical a priori of the various verbal performances by which the archive, though only fragmentarily, can be described. Since the archaeological enterprise is not concerned to establish conceptual coherence, it can accommodate contradictions both between and within a discourse, either as subsystems or parallel discourses, such as magic and science. So accommodating is the archaeology of knowledge that it soon provokes the question of how adequate Foucault's approach is in providing a theory of change. His rejoinder here is that he has no theory of change, but only the methodology for its description. Foucault maintains that the archaeology is more adequate and willing than the history of ideas to deal with 'discontinuities, ruptures, gaps, entirely new forms of positivity and of sudden redistributions'.(26) It is evident that there is no concept in Foucault corresponding to the Bachelardian epistemological break. Even if we agree with Brewster and Cutler that the break, in the sense of a total rupture, is absent from Bachelard, there is still no common ground with Foucault. This is simply because Foucault places his archaeological enterprise beyond the epistemological histories which Bachelard and Canguilhem present. Foucault uses terms which occur in Bachelard - rupture, break and shift - in describing 'events' in a discourse.(27) Since these ruptures and shifts are found at various levels in a discourse, a clear-cut break cannot be identified either within or between the various discourses.

To illustrate his notion of a 'fragmented shift' Foucault refers us to his analysis of Ricardo and Marx in The Order of Things.(28) He finds that certain concepts in Marx, for instance, surplus value and the falling rate of profit, can be described on the basis of the system already operative in Ricardo. But these concepts as they

Structure and Scientificity

appear in Marx belong to a 'quite different' discursive practice. This is not a transformation of Ricardo, nor a new political economy, but is part of a separate discourse occurring 'around the derivation of certain economic concepts'. Thus what has been traditionally taken for Marx's critique of Ricardo (providing Althusser with a clear instance of an epistemological break(29)) is no more than a discourse running parallel to Ricardo's, having evolved from a common point of transformation in the analysis of wealth.(30) Hussain is particularly critical of Foucault's claim to be epistemologically neutral by not recognising the pertinence of the distinction between the scientific and the non-scientific.(31) He states that Foucault is therefore without the theoretical apparatus with which to register the moment when theoretical practice 'establishes a science by detaching it from the ideology of its past and by revealing this past as ideological'.(32) Hussain's criticism is that by partitioning the discourses of Ricardo and Marx on the basis of strategic choices, Foucault has totally ignored the crucial distinction made in *Capital* between labour and labour-power. Yet there is value in Foucault's rejection of a mechanistic notion of an epistemological break. Hussain and Lecourt both acknowledge this. It lends support to the argument, put forward by Brewster and Cutler, that there is no break in the sense of a total rupture in Bachelard. Also, Althusser, in his extensive use of the concept of the epistemological break, does not argue that ideology disappears immediately from the domain inhabited by a new science.

Foucault's distinction of non-discursive/discursive practice is seen by Lecourt as an attempt to rethink the science/ideology disjunction.(33) Discursive practice occupies a different territory from that of science though it may express scientific hypotheses and give rise to scientific developments.(34) Science, once constituted, appears against the background of a discourse but does not dissipate it.(35) Thus, a science does not necessarily modify the discursive formation from which it disengages. It remains in relationship to it, a relationship which is the locus where ideology may be detected. This leads Foucault to make the following propositions:

    a) Ideology is not exclusive of scientificity; political economy exemplifies this.
    b) The ideological functioning of a science may

69

> be structurally detected at the level of rules, positivities or scientifically.
> c) Neither by correcting errors nor by rigorous formulation does discourse diminish its ideological content.
> d) To reveal and modify the ideological functioning of a science it must be treated as a practice like any other, not to uncover its pre-supposition, foundations or contradictions, but to tackle its system of formulation, of objects, concepts and theoretical choices.

Despite the antagonism to phenomenology, particularly implicit in the last of the above points, and despite the differences in approach and methodology, Foucault's treatment of the science/ideology distinction appears closer to a phenomenological Marxist standpoint than to Althusser's position.

The centrality of the epistemological break to Althusser's synthesis of structuralism and Marxism indicates his desire to give an impregnable status to Marxist science. Yet we have seen that the structuralist position on the methodology of identifying science and ideology is problematical. Althusser found his own early position vis-a-vis Marxist philosophy difficult to sustain because it demanded too rigid a disjunction between science and philosophy. Marxist philosophy, as 'the theory of the history of the production of knowledge' and as 'a theory of science and a history of science' indispensable to historical materialism, was exposed to the invasions of ideology. Althusser's reformulation of dialectical materialism presented it as a theory of science, a Theory of theoretical practice.(36) Historical materialism was the science of social formations. The insistence on science and the scientificity of his revised epistemology exposed him to the criticisms of elitism and theoreticism.(37) The detachment of science and politics had to be repaired. Althusser moved to his later position where the working-class struggle, philosophy and science become linked in opposition to bourgeois ideology. He finds his justification in what he interprets as Marx's epistemological break:

> The story of Marx's Early Works and his rupture with his "erstwhile philosophical consciousness" prove this: in order to fulfil the conditions that govern the science of history, Marx had to abandon his bourgeois and then petty-bourgeois class positions and adopt the class positions of

the proletariat. (38)

Citing Lenin's interpretation of the Eleventh Thesis on Feuerbach, Althusser states that Marxism is not a philosophy of praxis but a new practice of philosophy which can assist in transforming the world. It seems that Althusser became aware of the elitist assumptions of his position in his <u>Reading Capital</u>. The role of the intellectual had been fixed within theoretical practice, mediating Marxist science to the masses via new forms of ideology. The resultant disunity of theoreticians and class practice was, in effect, a theory of manipulation.(39) But is Althusser's attempt to redress his position any more 'correct'? Geras finds his later formulations of the relations between theory and class 'more adequate', since Althusser ascribes to the proletariat the ability to comprehend its objective class position through education. Thus Althusser moves philosophy to what appears to be a supportive role - 'Philosophy represents the people's class struggle in theory. In return it helps the people to distinguish in <u>theory</u> and in all <u>ideas</u> (political, ethical, aesthetic, etc.) between true ideas and false ideas.'(40) In effect, he has now given the philosopher a metatheoretical task with regard to the discourse of Marxist philosophy, which puts him once more into a privileged position in the fight against ideology. The idealist and elitist tendencies in Althusser have not been eradicated since they are endemic to the structuralist Marxist synthesis.

<u>Structure, System and Totality</u>

In order to enquire whether the Althusserian synthesis can fulfil the task of founding a definitive version of a Marxist science I have so far examined: (a) its ineradicable links with structuralism; (b) the problems of theorising a disjunction of science and ideology; and (c) the question of the subject. At this point I return to the consideration of holism in Althusser. We have seen that this transformation of the Marxist structure confirms his structuralist position, though he claims to go beyond this to establish a new Marxist science. Not only are the idealist structuralist postulates which he has attempted to transform inadequate to a Marxist theory of history; in the process of his own philosophical volte-face he has had also to jettison aspects of the earlier texts. The adoption of a schematic structuralist framework has imposed such a constraint on Althusser's Marxism that much of his theory is assertion and is not fully theorised. We see this in relation also to the Hegelian elements in his analysis; Althusser is unable, as a result of their retention, to adopt a true materialist position.

Althusser's early work employs a number of Hegelian notions and this influence is still strongly felt in the later work, as his examination of Lenin's reading of Hegel makes clear.(41) It may be argued that this essay is of particular importance to substantiate Althusser's newly assumed interventionist role for philosophy. 'Lenin before Hegel' contains a résumé of the new position. Althusser discovers the 'partisanship' of philosophy through the works of Lenin before his reading of Hegel. Turning to the post-Hegel Lenin, Althusser finds confirmation of the scientific validity of the concept of history as a process without a subject. This has great importance for the scientificity of Althusser's schema by giving his system its apriorism. Lenin read Hegel as a materialist and found represented in the Absolute Idea:

> ... simply the absolute method, the method which, as it is nothing but the very movement of the process, is merely the idea of the process as the only Absolute. (42)

This thesis of Hegel provides Lenin (and Althusser) with

> ... a confirmation of the fact that it is absolutely essential (as he had learnt simply from a thorough-going reading of Capital) to suppress every origin and every subject, and to say what is absolute in the process without a subject both in reality and in scientific knowledge. (43)

The positing here of the reality of the method or concept as the absolute does not seem so far removed from Hegel's idealism as Althusser would argue. He shows an awareness of the vulnerability of his own position in using such concepts when he notes that Lenin dismisses Marx's coquetry with forms of idealist language, in the early chapters of Capital, as mere idiosyncrasy.(44) Althusser fails to see that, in the context of the whole work, and in the light of Marx's own intervention in politics, this terminology served a purpose.(45)

Althusser states that Lenin's understanding of

Structure and Scientificity

Marx depended on his study of Hegel's Logic. The significant point for Althusser is that Lenin took the Hegelian ontology as his justification for asserting history to be the process without subject. Althusser claims this as confirmation for the elimination of the subject from his structuralist system.(46) We find therefore that the idealist ontology of the Hegelian dialectic (which in Hegel's schema is history itself) has been transformed and embellished by Althusser into both a logic and a method. Thus while Hegel hypostatised method as an ontology, Althusser converts ontology into epistemology. This confusion over levels of analysis calls into question the Althusserian synthesis. Furthermore, Althusser is not merely attributing to Lenin a materialist reading of Hegel; he is implying that a structuralist viewpoint underpins Lenin's interpretation of Marx.(47)

A similar theoretical transposition occurs with the Hegelian notion of totality. In Althusser's view, the Hegelian and Marxist totalities are completely divergent conceptions. Yet it can be shown in his own considerable use of the concept that Althusser retains aspects of the Hegelian formulation. The social totality is transformed by his system into the structure in dominance. The mode of its articulation with other components in the system determines the character of historical society at any juncture. Althusser's presentation of the mode of production as a decentred totality is certainly distinct from Hegel's conception - an opposed view, in fact. Yet when we compare other aspects of their formulations what emerges has the appearance of a mirror image. Hegel's totality is monistic, historicist, idealist and pre-given; Althusser's totality is decentred, ahistorical, materialist but also, as a structure, pre-given. Thus Althusser's formulation appears as an inversion of Hegel's.

Though Althusser believes he has made an adequate reformulation of the concept of totality, it is an element of Hegelian thought which Marx succeeds in demystifying but which remains a mystification in Althusser. He did not appear to consider that his retention of the term is inconsistent within a scientific Marxist framework. One may well ask why, in attempting to establish a new problematic, Althusser clings to Hegelian terminology. The categories of Absolute Idealism operate at the philosophical level as Althusser acknowledges by stating that the Hegelian philosophy was never in itself a praxis. Yet the concept of totality has ramifications in the sphere of political praxis which Althusser fails to acknowledge or chooses to ignore. As Piccone has pointed out,(48) Hegel's totality, in its interpretation as the expression of the Idea in historical society, has provided the ideological basis for reactionary politics. It has led directly to the hypostatising of the concept of national unity. Surely this cannot be ignored. While one may agree with Althusser's statement that 'the Hegelian totality never provided the basis for a policy, that there is not and cannot be a Hegelian politics',(49) it is important to point out that the concept carries strong ideological connotations. Even in its reworked form within Althusser's problematic these connotations are inescapable.

Marx retained the concept of totality while it was methodologically useful. Having perfected his method he took up his major task of analysing the capitalist mode of production, employing a methodology and terminology which are not mystifying but essentially rational. While Marx emphasised in the works preceding Capital the usefulness of preserving elements of Hegelian thought, it is evident that this concept, which Althusser finds it necessary to retain, was among those idealist constructs Marx came to reject.(50)

Scientific Realism and Phenomenology

One recent attempt in British philosophy to fuse Marxist theory with another perspective has been seen in the development of a realist theory of science which embraces Marxist materialism. Its project is to establish an invincible foundation for a Marxist science, but though strongly influenced in this by Althusserian theory, it does attempt to develop an original approach. This amalgam of ideas is also presented as a possible base for a new Marxist sociology as (a) a critique of positivism, (b) a critique of interpretative social theory and (c) a theory of science which can yield substantive knowledge in the human sciences. In particular, the propositions of Bhaskar, Keat and Urry, and Benton will require comment here.

The phenomenological approach to the analysis of society is considered to be within the interpretative branch of sociology. As a sociology of knowledge it is regarded as foundational for certain areas of microtheory. Its empiricism opposes it to scientific realism.(51) From a phenomenological

Marxist viewpoint, my critique is that the realist theory results, when allied to Marxism, in a metaphysical materialism. At base this is idealist and incompatible with the Marxian project of attaining a scientific analysis of history and society. The basis of my critique is Husserl's sustained rejection of metaphysics in both his early work and in Crisis. According to Findlay, the influence of Brentano's realism is evident in Husserl's early work.

> No-one, we may say, can understand Husserl's phenomenology who has not grasped its transcendental realistic roots in the intentionalism of Brentano, roots which Husserl may have ingeniously "bracketted" in various higher-order conceptions, but which in a sense remained intact and unharmed within such brackets. (52)

The proviso, 'in a sense', detracts from Findlay's point here. Moreover as Roche indicates, it was the existentialist realists who became interested in what was bracketed. This was marginal and uninteresting to Husserl.(53) His analysis of the contents of consciousness brackets out the natural attitude so that questions about reality cease to be relevant.(54)

Findlay further contends that when Husserl in Ideas begins to develop an ontology of transcendental entities he is taking a step towards metaphysics.(55) But the inclusion of an ontology, as we shall see in Chapter Five, enables Husserl to broaden the scope of his analysis to establish the nature of the life-world. I believe that this is in no sense a concession to metaphysics; the concrete, material world is given to consciousness and grasped in subjectivity where all entities have their constituted origin. To postulate the reality of the material world is naive and to argue the reality of processes and logical entities is to assume a Platonic idealism.

Bhaskar makes a closely argued and ingenious case for scientific realism.(56) He proposes a non-positivist critical naturalism which adopts the same principle as natural science but different predicates and procedures. There is no separation in the sciences; they are unified in method but differ in respect to their objects. A later proposal in The Possibility of Naturalism(57) would appear to contradict this formulation since Bhaskar states that different procedures characterise the sciences.(58) If there are differences in the methodologies of the human and natural sciences this will be the result of different notions of scientificity. It is therefore difficult to assert natural science as the paradigm for the study of social objects while at the same time taking up an anti-positivist position. Transcendental realism states that what is apodictically demonstrable is also scientifically comprehensible. Thus the synthetic a priori can be known a posteriori. On this basis it claims the reality of the patterns of causality, revealed in observables, and the reality of conceptual structures in which the concept is logically adequate to the object. Against the charge of metaphysics, Bhaskar asserts that the transcendental elements in his theory of knowledge are those structures and patterns which are detected via their effects. Thus the transcendental realist

> ... regards objects of knowledge as the structures and mechanisms that generate phenomena; and the knowledge as produced in the social activity of science. These objects are neither phenomena (empiricism) nor human constructs imposed upon the phenomena (idealism) but real structures which endure and operate independently of our knowledge,... (59)

These objects are not the events which the empiricist observes, but are manifest structures:

> The "real entities" the transcendental realist is concerned with are the objects of scientific discovery and investigation, such as causal laws. (60)

This claim lifts the analysis out of theory into metatheory, since two domains are established beyond the empirical - the Real and the Actual. Bhaskar elaborates the ontological distinctions between these domains(61) for it is his intention 'to furnish the new philosophy of science with an ontology'.(62) This ontology is grounded in an apodictically derived 'reality' of a domain which theorises the product as it is socially produced by scientists working, presumably, according to nomological-deductive principles. Under laboratory conditions, which Bhaskar terms conditions of closure, the generative structural mechanisms become apparent as the potentialities of things are investigated. These mechanisms operate in the world outside the experimental situation as Bhaskar emphasises: 'If science is to be possible the world must be one of enduring and transfactually active

mechanisms; and society must be a structure (or
ensemble of powers) irreducible to but present only
in the intentional action of men.'(63) The assertion
that such mechanisms obtain in the open systems of
the human world reveals Bhaskar's approach as similar
to Althusser's in its elaboration of causally deterministic structures. The above quotation makes clear
the contrast with Husserl for whom intentionality is
itself basic to the structure of human consciousness
a priori.

The impetus for Bhaskar's scientific realism is
to establish a materialist theory (of the production
of knowledge) compatible with Marxist historical
materialism. With regard to the human sciences, the
theory states that these adopt forms of explanation
analogous to the natural sciences. They operate
with data which are not the brute data of a
simplistic materialism or the sense data of a naive
empiricism but are the acts, intentions and powers
imputed to subjects a posteriori. The significance of
the ontological assumptions is now clear. Bhaskar
states that:

> The central argument of this study, establishing
> an ontological distinction between causal law
> and patterns of events (the independence of the
> domains of the real and the actual, the
> irreducibility of structures to events) has
> turned on the possibility of experimental
> activity. (64)

Since experiment is virtually impossible in the
social sciences the ontological assumptions must
allow the object of knowledge to have an ontological
status parallel to objects of natural science. The
basic material is, therefore, human activity rendered
as atomic facts which are socially produced. Human
beings become the bearers of the structure.(65)

Bhaskar's critical naturalism(66) seems as
inadequate to account for human praxis and consciousness as positivism is. The theory combines with
historical materialism a theory of human self-
emancipation by agents who, in their intentional
practice, are causally determining the process which,
in turn, determines them.(67) We see here that the
Marx of the *Critique* is invoked. But, to use the
dramaturgical metaphor, what we are presented with on
the stage of history are actors ad-libbing their own
lines on the basis of a script. To express this more
directly, action/praxis is rule-governed behaviour,
the rules being a kind of historical accretion.(68)
Bhaskar agrees in part that his theory of

emancipation on the basis of an ontology of progressively emergent powers has links with a utilitarian ethics. But what he and the other realist philosophers are principally concerned with is to establish the scientificity of their approach. They seek an authenticity for the human sciences parallel to that which they see as prevailing in the natural sciences. Bhaskar puts forward the possibility of an emancipatory politics (or therapy) grounded on a realist science. This would gain its epistēmē and explanatory power from a theory of the operation of emergent laws concerning the processes of oppression, and possibilities for transforming those processes. The laws are generative, at the cognitive level, of epistemological objects and beliefs concerning them and, at the conative level, of social practice.

My general criticism of this approach is that it attempts to synthesise a realist theory of human action with a historical materialist which displays a Viconian or Aristotelian orthodoxy. The thoroughness with which the various versions of this neo-realist orthodoxy are explicated is impressive.(69) Its emphasis on logical analysis makes a persuasive appeal on behalf of rationality, but the rigour is deceptive since the premiss is false. It wrongly asserts that its model of human action can be extended into an objective theory of science integrated with a Marxist theory of history. On this basis a Marxist sociology would be untenable.

The refutation of the realist theory of science is that it makes too limited a claim on scientificity by taking the positivistic natural sciences as its point of departure. Benton's thesis is that it is vital to restore to the sciences a conceptual autonomy which would, for example, take the politics out of physics.(70) The result of a disjunction of science and ideology would be a 'purer' conception of scientific work. This purity inheres in the internal coherence of the science within its own problematic - '... the source of the objectivity of scientific knowledge is in the referential character of the theoretical concepts of a science'.(71) Operating thus within its own procedures for identifying entities and establishing validity, the processes and structures will be logically harmonious. The realist theory therefore adopts a coherence theory of knowledge(72) which is hardly radical in its claim to integrate with a Marxist 'natural science of history'.(73)

By asserting that its version of a science of society can be independent of ideology, and by claiming that its processes and structures are real, the realist theory is open to criticism. We are presented with a mechanistic set of propositions which claim to explain scientific development and the production of knowledge. This idealist position is incompatible with Marxist materialism, and its presuppositions are challenged by the view of science advanced by phenomenology.

Structure, Consciousness and Causality

The structuralist and scientific realist positions so far reviewed fail as adequate bases for synthesis with Marxism because of their inherent idealist content which is, in my view, incompatible with Marx's project. The proposal that Marx's materialist theory of history and society could be made inconvertible by grafting it onto a mechanistic theory of scientific knowledge and practice must be rejected. The concept of scientificity which these perspectives advance is intended to counter the positivistic tendencies of orthodox Marxism and to refute humanistic and subjectivistic deviations. It is not, however, a concept of science radical enough to match Marx's conceptions.

What can phenomenology offer as an alternative, bearing in mind the force of argument on grounds of the structural unassailability which is claimed for scientific Marxist theories? This chapter concludes with a review of certain critical areas where compatibility between phenomenology and Marxism might be established on the basis of proposals that:

   a) Husserl's concept of scientificity allows for a broader critique of positivism;
   b) the structural aspects of phenomenology are compatible with Marxist theory;
   c) the basis of phenomenological theory is implicit in the Marxist critique and its epistemological claims are more adequate in relation to Marx's account of cognitive processes and concrete social conditions than other explanations;
   d) the teleological aspect of a phenomenological Marxism is compatible with a notion of scientificity and has greater explanatory power in relation to the dialectical view of consciousness than the mechanistic causality which underpins scientific realism and structural Marxism.

Structure and Scientificity

We have already seen that the scientific realist theory takes the natural sciences as its point of departure and paradigm of scientificity. The phenomenological attitude to science which Husserl expresses is an attack on this claim to scientificity and a call for a new science. The science which is disclosed in <u>Crisis</u> is a phenomenology which can reveal the transformation of the natural sciences into technizations with consequent loss of meaning. The life-world is the occluded foundation of natural science and the means for its restoration. As Husserl states:

> The sciences build upon the life-world as taken for granted in that they make use of whatever in it happens to be necessary for their particular end. But to use the life-world in this way is not to know it scientifically in its own manner of being. (74)

For instance, in his use of Michelson's methods and findings:

> ... Einstein could make no use whatever of a theoretical psychologic-psychophysical construction of the objective being of Mr. Michelson: rather, he made use of the human being who was accessible to him, as to everyone else in the prescientific world, as an object of straightforward experience, the human being whose existence, with this vitality, in these activities and creations within the common life-world, is always the presupposition for all of Einstein's objective-scientific lines of enquiry, projects and accomplishments pertaining to Michelson's experiments. (75)

The object is no reified entity but the human content of an experience. Similarly, the objective 'is precisely never experienceable as itself; and scientists themselves ... consider it in this way whenever they interpret it as something metaphysically transcendent, in contrast to their confusing empiricist talk'.(76) Later, Husserl refers to 'The objective sciences as subjective constructs - those of a particular praxis, namely, the theoretical-logical, which itself belongs to the full concreteness of the life-world.'(77) Thus the sciences are continually related back to pre-constructural concrete experiences, but we should note that the life-world concept is now broadened to include a higher order of constructive praxis, the theoretico-logical.(78) Clearly Husserl intends here

to rescue his concept of the life-world from the
danger of being construed as a naive flux or stream-
of-consciousness. For his theory to have any credence
with scientists it must be recognised that their
particular life-world will include scientific
experience. He is concerned with the difficulties in
establishing phenomenology as a critique of the
natural sciences: '... in order first to free our-
selves from the constant misconstructions which mis-
lead us all because of the scholastic dominance of
objective-scientific ways of thinking'.(79)

As already noted, the phenomenological method of
reconstruction in the natural sciences is exemplified
by the work in the field of optics of Vasco
Ronchi.(80) I am also convinced that the descriptions
by Hanson(81) and Feyerabend(82) of non-conventional
routes to scientific discovery can be claimed as
demonstrating that scientists adopt the approach of
phenomenology, though not its epistemology and
methodology per se. It can be said that the questions
they put to nature are truly radical since they
investigate presuppositional experience.

Phenomenology attacks both the naive realism of
the natural attitude and the naivety of the natural
sciences. Citing Einstein as the great exemplar of
the subjective method, Weyl(83) claims that the
phenomenological mode of enquiry characterises both
empiricism and realism. However, Weyl, who is closely
concerned with demonstrating the subjective character
of scientific experience and discovery, arrives
eventually at a theodicy.(84) His arguments, drawn
mainly from *Ideas*, remain within the realist/idealist
framework and demonstrate the impossibility of hold-
ing a realist position without its idealist concomitant.(85) Where his analysis is salient is in its
assertion that the experience of the life-world is a
praxis of struggle towards a telos.(86)

The key to understanding Husserl's view of
science and his claims to scientificity is to be
found in his final work, though the theme is consistently reiterated throughout his work. It is
through the crisis that the scientist is forced back
to philosophy to review the presuppositions of his
discipline. Husserl had begun his critique of the
positive sciences in the early works. In *Philosophy
as Rigorous Science* (1910) there is criticism of the
formalism and technization which results in 'the
superstition of the fact', the hallmark of the
natural sciences.(87) Phenomenology moves counter to
natural science towards an original knowledge. Yet,
as Kockelmans points out, positive science and

phenomenology are 'profoundly intertwined in their scientific intentionality through the course of the history of reason'.(88) Phenomenology as 'last science' is to bring the positive sciences to the full insight of their role as human praxis. It has not appeared necessary for the successful practitioner in science to possess this rationality; a scientific 'instinct', coupled with a methodology, will suffice to create new knowledge. Yet the outcome is a crisis because 'the progress of science has obscured its origins with a technical superstructure which no longer answers to the self-evident'.(89) Husserl's work is consistent in its teleological import and it is this aspect which governs his insistence on the rationality of phenomenology as 'last science'. With <u>Crisis</u> the task of bringing the positive sciences back to their true function becomes more urgent. Though Husserl's work exhibits a change in method there is no change in direction when it comes to defining the task. It is this task of restoring the telos which phenomenological Marxists insist is compatible with that of transforming society.

Phenomenology is able to supply a theory of consciousness and perception which are in Marx unsatisfactorily theorised in the context of ideology engendered by division of class interest. The contribution of Husserl's analysis of the structure of consciousness is considerable in offering a revised perspective on the following:
(a) The problem of false consciousness - according to Parkinson, most Marxists endorse this concept.(90) We also find that Althusser examines the false consciousness of the oppressed which is thought to overlie a dormant unconscious perception of the truth of their situation.(91) This notion is elitist since it gives a dominant role to the intellectual in disclosing this imputed revolutionary consciousness. The phenomenological Marxist position holds that consciousness is shaped by lived experience grounded in materiality. Consciousness cannot be false since it is not consciousness itself which is occluded but its content. Moreover, Husserl rejects any theory of the unconscious. Phenomenological Marxism makes the critical examination of the contents of consciousness central to its praxis. The methodology of reduction and the critique of capitalism reveal the nature of oppression and the truth of the social relations which shape consciousness. The only sense in which the 'unconscious' can be applicable to Husserl's analysis is in the sense of what is not yet identified in the surrounding world.(92)

(b) The question of the basis of consciousness is crucial. The positive social scientists fail to provide an adequate analysis of consciousness and society. Their theories must be rejected on the grounds of scientism, psychologism and sociologism. Marxist science, conceived in positivist terms, can provide only a naive account of the production of thought. Husserl asserts that consciousness is historically grounded, as he reveals in Crisis. Human experience is concretely based in the life-world. In the conceptualisation of experience, as limited by material circumstance against which humanity strives, we find the possibility of relating Husserl's theory of the life-world to Marx's dialectic of history. Marx's theory of consciousness and perception is locked into the appearance/reality disjunction (though by no means naively because of the Hegelian influence). Husserl's theory of the intentionality of consciousness supplies a more profound analysis. It is this factor of intentionality which, though it was first developed as a key element in Husserl's theory of cognition, is indicative that all aspects of consciousness are projected towards a content. There is, therefore, an intrinsic teleology in consciousness - to reach out and grasp experience in understanding. Marx's work does not extend to a detailed analysis of the structure of consciousness, but the theories of alienation show the development of an ontology and further develop those teleological aspects of his social theory which appear compatible with Husserl's later position.

The project of making a synthesis of Marxism and phenomenology must demonstrate two essential criteria - first, that there are no contradictions in the structural aspects of the synthesis, and secondly, that the question of causality in such a structural theory involves no theoretical inconsistencies. These points will receive fuller consideration in the final chapter. The salient question here is whether Marx's structural analysis, in its causal aspects, can coalesce with parallel elements in Husserl's theories.

In Crisis Husserl centres his analysis on the life-world and, mindful of the need to establish his claim to scientificity (phenomenology being the science of the life-world), he pays close attention to the concept of causality. Its importance is evident from the assertion that: '... through <u>a universal causal regulation all that is together in the world</u> has a universal immediate or mediate way of <u>belonging together</u>'.(93) What we have here is the concept of a regulative principle, a universal causal regulation which is the undeniable, structural basis of the framework. Husserl first developed the notion of causality in relation to the constitution of 'things'. In <u>Ideas</u> causality is firmly linked to materiality: '... the regulated series of appearances which necessarily hold together within the unity of a single appearing object'.(94) The material or substantial-causal thing results from the unity of the constitutive appearance manifolds. From this basis, intersubjectivity confers a higher order of constitutive unity on 'things'. The process of constitution is the synthesising of these apperceptions. In <u>Phenomenological Psychology</u>, Husserl uses the term 'causal style' to denote that which confers stability on an entity in its multiplicity of changes. Each causal property is an index of causal regularities in the dependence of changes - 'all changes of a thing are restricted to a stable style of change in relation to an environment'.(95) Thus the specific character of the thing emerges, allowing prediction to be made. Such instances confirm that, for Husserl, causality is rooted in the material world, an assertion that gives significant grounds for a liaison of phenomenology with Marxism.

At this point it is important to reiterate that there can be no liaison, and particularly no related theory of causality, unless it is established that Marx moved away from a naive and rigidly deterministic materialism and that Husserl moved from an idealist position.(96) It would be impossible to integrate such divergent perspectives. I have taken as a fundamental proposition that both Marx and Husserl in their mature works moved to positions that can be reconciled. Marx's shift from a naive Feuerbachian epistemology brings him eventually to the position in <u>Capital</u> where materiality, as the causal basis, and material conditions, as the determinants of social existence, are affirmed.(97) Similarly, the shift in Husserl discernible in <u>Crisis</u> makes his position consonant with Marx on this fundamental question of causality. When Husserl comes to explicate the <u>Lebenswelt</u> he links ontology and causality into one structure. As Paci states:

> ... "lived" causality is precategorical ... its foundation is in the way it is experienced and lived in the Lebenswelt. This experiencing is occluded; it is the task of phenomenology as the science of the Lebenswelt to disocclude it. This means that we must discover the precategorical

origin of the category of cause in order to become aware that causality is a way in which nature is given to me as material nature'.(98)

Thus we experience nature as spatio-temporal causality. The notion of the concreteness of the natural world becomes, in Husserl's analysis, as in Marx's, the 'circumstantiated' world. 'Things' are related to circumstances and through circumstances. This is a lived causal connection. Causality is thus not an abstract category but is precategorical and material. The material basis is, for Husserl, the experience of matter - opaque, passive, resistant; it is provoking and conditioning. This is the material world which humanity constantly changes and is changed by.

Beyond this level of material things is the level of sensate living experience, a reciprocal endowment of the intersubjective world. Paci sees this as the region of psychophysical causality wherein reciprocal sensibilities operate, and as the region of self-awareness.(99) We have, therefore, in Husserl's theory of the life-world an analysis of theoretical structure, of causality, materiality, ontology and historicity, which is given in <u>Crisis</u> its most concrete expression.

Notes and References

1. The significant works of this period were first published in the 1960s, <u>Pour Marx</u>, 1965, <u>Lire le Capital</u>, 1965, <u>Lenine et la Philosophie</u>, 1968.
2. Althusser, L., <u>Lenin and Philosophy</u>, trans. Brewster, B., Monthly Review Press, London, 1971, p.41 and p.49.
3. Ibid., p.19.
4. Althusser, L., 'New Definitions of Philosophy', <u>Theoretical Practice</u>, Nos 7 and 8, pp.4-11.
5. Althusser, op.cit. (1971), p.17.
6. Ibid., p.208.
7. Ibid., Appendix, 'Freud and Lacan', pp.218-19
8. Cutler, A., 'The Concept of the Epistemological Break', <u>Theoretical Practice</u>, No 4, p.66.
9. Althusser, L., <u>For Marx</u>, Allen Lane, Penguin, London, 1969, pp.182-93 where Althusser describes 'The Process of Theoretical Practice'.
10. This view is opposed to the continuist view of scientific development, ie. a synchronic/diachronic schema.

11. Cutler, op.cit., p.69.
12. Ibid.
13. This metaphor seems almost endemic to the description of language.
14. Foucault, M., The Archaeology of Knowledge, Tavistock, London, 1972.
15. Althusser, op.cit. (1971), p.17 and op.cit. (1969), pp.111-15, where Althusser describes the structure of his system and the problem of autonomy in the superstructure.
16. This dramaturgical metaphor has been developed into a critique by Glucksmann, A., 'The Althusserian Theatre', New Left Review, No 72. See also Benton, E., Philosophical Foundations of the Three Sociologies, Routledge and Kegan Paul, London, 1977, p.181.
17. The key text for Althusser is his critique of ideology in Marx and Engels' The German Ideology, in which ideology means a system of ideas impregnated with distortion. Ideology may also be taken to mean ideation in general.
18. Husserl, E., 'The Origin of Geometry', Appendix IV of Crisis, pp.353-78.
19. Gramsci, A., Il Materialismo, p.56, quoted in Paci, op.cit. (1972), p.315.
20. Paci, op.cit.
21. Foucault, op.cit. (1972), p.15. A useful exposition of this text is given in Williams, K., 'Unproblematic Archaeology', Economy and Society, Vol 3, No 1, 1973.
22. Ibid., p.60f.
23. Ibid., p.206.
24. Ibid., p.203.
25. Lecourt, D., Marxism and Epistemology, New Left Books, London, 1975.
26. Foucault, M., op.cit. (1972), p.175. His 'archaeology' dis-articulates the synchrony of breaks and destroys the unity of change and event.
27. Bachelard, G., The Formation of the Scientific Mind, Vrin, Paris, 1965. Shortland, M., 'Introduction' and Canguilhem, G., 'What is Scientific Ideology', in Radical Philosophy, No 29, 1981, pp.19-25.
28. Foucault, M., The Order of Things, Tavistock Publications, London, 1970, pp.253-263.
29. Althusser, L., and Balibar, E., Reading Capital, New Left Books, 1970, in particular the section on 'The Epistemological Propositions of Capital (Marx, Engels)', pp.145-57.
30. Foucault, op.cit. (1970), p.262.
31. Hussain, A., 'A Brief Resume of the

Archaeology of Knowledge', Theoretical Practice, Nos 3 and 4, 1971, pp.106-107.

32. Althusser, op.cit. (1965), p.168 refers to Foucault, op.cit. (1972), p.12.
33. Lecourt, op.cit. (1975), p.205.
34. Foucault, op.cit. (1972), pp.184-86.
35. Ibid., p.185.
36. Althusser, L., op.cit. (1969), p.168.
37. Geras, N., 'Aspects of Fetishism in Capital', New Left Review, No 65, 1971, pp.69-86.
38. Althusser, op.cit. (1971), p.8.
39. Geras, op.cit., referring to Reading Capital, p.131.
40. Althusser, L., op.cit. (1971), p.24.
41. Ibid., pp.107-25.
42. Ibid., p.123. Althusser later adds: 'Allow me to recall that this divination of Hegel by Lenin, and then his reading of Hegel, were only possible from a proletarian class viewpoint, and with the new practice of philosophy that follows from it. Perhaps we can learn a lesson from this for the present and the future' (p.124).
43. Ibid.
44. Ibid., p.110. 'Marx's manner of expression'.
45. This point is also made above in Chapter Two, p.43.
46. Hirst, P., 'Althusser and Philosophy', Theoretical Practice, No 2, 1971, p.17. Althusser regards his works as investigations, disclaiming the idea that they constitute a system.
47. Althusser, op.cit. (1971).
48. Piccone, P., 'Reading the Grundrisse: Beyond Orthodox Marxism', Theory and Society, Vol 1, No 2, 1975.
49. Althusser, op.cit. (1969), p.203 in 'On the Materialist Dialectic', and p.102, in 'Contradiction and Over-determination'.
50. See Chapter Two, p.44 above.
51. Collier, A., 'Scientific Realism and the Human World', Radical Philosophy, No 29, Autumn 1981, p.8.
52. Findlay, J.N., 'Phenomenology and the Meaning of Realism', in Pivčević, op.cit. (1975), p.146.
53. Ibid., p.152.
54. Ibid., p.158.
55. Ibid., p.157.
56. Bhaskar, R., A Realist Theory of Science, Harvester Press, Sussex, 1978.
57. Bhaskar, R., The Possibility of Naturalism, Harvester Press, Sussex, 1979.

58. Ibid., p.26 and op.cit. (1978), p.246.
59. Bhaskar, op.cit. (1978), p.25. Quotation continues: '... our experience and the conditions which allow us access to them'.
60. Ibid., p.26.
61. Ibid., p.244.
62. Ibid., p.23.
63. Ibid., p.248.
64. Ibid., p.244.
65. We find the concept of the subject as bearer in Althusser. See For Marx, p.182ff.
66. Bhaskar, R., 'Scientific Explanation and Human Emancipation', Radical Philosophy, No 26, Autumn 1980, pp.16-28.
67. Ibid., p.16.
68. Ibid., p.19ff.
69. See Keat, R.N. and Urry, J., Social Theory as Science, Routledge and Kegan Paul, London, 1975.
70. Benton, op.cit., pp.189-91.
71. Ibid., p.198.
72. The coherence theory of truth holds that knowledge is organised as a single system of thought of which truth is predictable. This theory is associated with Hegel and the rationalist metaphysicians or objective idealists, cf. Flew, A. (ed.) A Dictionary of Philosophy, Pan Books, London, 1979, p.61.
73. Benton, op.cit., p.199.
74. Husserl, Crisis, p.135.
75. Ibid., p.125. Michelson's experiments to determine the effects of the earth's motion on the velocity of light yielded negative results but were foundational for Einstein's relativity theory. See also Lakatos and Musgrave, op.cit., pp.159-65.
76. Husserl, ibid., p.129.
77. Ibid. For this broader concept of the life-world Husserl posits 'science as the totality of prepredicative theory'. See Ch. 5, pp.149-50 on variation in the life-world concept, also Ch.6.
78. Ibid., p.129ff.
79. Ibid.
80. See Ch.4, p.107 below and Note 30.
81. Hanson, N.R., Patterns of Discovery, Cambridge University Press, 1961, p.87. See also his Observation and Explanation, Allen and Unwin, London, 1972.
82. Feyerabend, P.K., Against Method, New Left Books, London, 1975. Feyerabend cites Ronchi's influence on p.125, footnote 17: 'I would like to acknowledge at this place that Professor Ronchi's investigations have greatly influenced my thinking

Structure and Scientificity

on scientific method'. Feyerabend's attack on the scientific status quo uses visual perception as illustration and metaphor for understanding.
    83. Weyl in Kockelmans and Kisiel, op.cit. (1970), p.94ff. See also Weyl, *Philosophy of Mathematics and Natural Science*, Atheneum, New York, 1963.
    84. Ibid., p.116.
    85. Ibid., p.107.
    86. Ibid., p.99.
    87. Husserl, op.cit., p.141.
    88. Kockelmans, T.J., 'Phenomenology as the Science of Sciences', in Kockelmans and Kisiel, op.cit. (1970), p.9.
    89. Ibid., p.10.
    90. Parkinson, G.H.R. (ed.) *Marx and Marxisms*, Cambridge University Press, Cambridge, 1982, p.9.
    91. Althusser, op.cit. (1969), pp.141-42.
    92. Paci, op.cit. (1972), p.172.
    93. Husserl, *Crisis*, p.31.
    94. Op.cit., 52b, pp.143-49.
    95. Op.cit., p.102.
    96. See Chapter Two, pp.37-39 and Chapter One, p.19 above.
    97. Marx, *Capital*, p.22f.
    98. Paci, op.cit. (1972), p.161.
    99. Ibid., p.163-65.

Chapter Four

THE CRISIS OF SCIENCE

The theme of crisis has recurred throughout our discussion so far, but we need to look in more detail at its significance for the philosophies of Marx and Husserl. Reacting to the dominant positivism of his period, Husserl saw philosophy in a state of crisis because of its post-Humean enslavement to science. Likewise, Marx's conception of crisis extended to both science and philosophy which he regarded as branches of bourgeois academicism. Yet, for Marx, the state of both was indicative of a wider crisis embracing the whole social structure. This crisis could be understood and resolved only by a new revolutionary science.

If we are to look for common ground here, what is immediately apparent is the urgency with which Husserl and Marx rejected the dominant systems of their day. The case for relating the two theorists through their mature works seems further strengthened by their progressively urgent elaboration of the theme of crisis. From the beginning, Husserl was concerned to establish phenomenology as a rigorous science. The crisis of the positive sciences was a threat to the future of humanity. The restoration of purpose and meaning to the sciences was to be the task of phenomenology as the science of sciences. However, Husserl did not develop an analysis to match Marx's theory of the social structure. His life-work remained within the field of philosophy. Are these substantial enough grounds, therefore, for relating the two analyses? Are the crisis of the sciences and the crisis of capitalism aspects of the same crisis? Surely the emphasis on socio-economic analysis in <u>Capital</u> puts Marx's work in a different category from Husserl's?

First, we need to know how the concept of a science is being used by both theorists with regard to their background and the development of their ideas. Next, an answer to the difficulties of a synthesis may lie in the understanding of the epistemology of crisis. Theorists from different traditions have used this concept as a central metaphor to examine the growth of scientific knowledge, the contradictions of the social and economic structure and the predicament of Western culture.(1) Since the crisis extended to the human as well as to the natural sciences it is necessary to deal with theories of consciousness and intersubjectivity. In a discussion of the structure of consciousness under capitalism I consider Marx's concept of alienation in relation to Husserl's concept of occlusion. The question is raised as to the degree of liaison possible even if concepts such as these appear compatible. There may be, for example, differences in the notion of scientificity which suggest a fundamental incompatibility at the level of epistemology. The task is to identify the critical constructs where compatibility must be demonstrated if a true synthesis is to be achieved. Relevant here is the tension between teleological and causal explanations in the human and natural sciences. It seems at first sight that the teleological explanations of phenomenology are incompatible with an orthodox Marxist view. Would Marxism therefore vitiate its claim to be scientific by a liaison with phenomenology?

The Concept of Crisis

The concept of crisis is fundamental to the analyses of both Marx and Husserl and is, therefore, a common element. In what sense, if any, can it be claimed as a main point of synthesis? What kind of notion is it that acts as virtually the guiding principle both for Husserl's major work, <u>The Crisis of European Sciences and Transcendental Phenomenology</u>, and for Marx's <u>Capital</u>, subtitled <u>A Critical Analysis of Capitalist Production</u>? The term 'crisis' is used to indicate the point of decision, the turning-point, the moment of danger and suspense in historical events.(2) These connotations are carried over into the more dramatic pathological usage of 'crisis' as the turning point of a disease. I would suggest that both Husserl and Marx had in mind the pathological connotation, though neither develops it as an extended metaphor. The implication is that society, science and philosophy are all in a morbid state.

The Crisis of Science

The historical expression of the risk to humanity is seen in the social and political upheavals of the nineteenth and early twentieth century which the two writers span between them. Marx wrote of specific historical events while developing his general theory. In his Preface to the 2nd edition of <u>Capital</u>, he marks 1825 as the initial crisis of modern industry, 1830 as 'decisive' and, likewise, 1848.(3) Writing after the Franco-Prussian War and the Paris Revolution of 1870-71 he states:

> The contradictions inherent in the movement of capitalist society impress themselves upon the practical bourgeois most strikingly in the changes of the periodic cycle, through which modern industry runs, and whose crowning point is the universal crisis. That crisis is once again approaching, although as yet but in its preliminary stage; ... (4)

So, for Marx, the nineteenth century was the setting for a series of crises, all expressions of the same motive forces; in that sense, the Europe of his day was the arena for one protracted crisis.

Marx's fundamental crisis is that of society under capitalism. For Husserl, too, the condition of humanity is at risk, but the crisis is identifiable in a different historical arena. Carr refers to crisis as a theme which became dominant for Husserl in the pre-war Germany from which he was eventually driven (though a crisis of civilisation was sensed more pervasively by him than the political crisis in the early nineteen-thirties).(5) Husserl's Vienna and Prague lectures mark the beginning of work which culminated in <u>Crisis</u>.(6) This work was a vigorous attack on the inadequacy of philosophy to speak to the needs of the time. He attacked existentialism for its irrationality, and logical positivism for its inability to halt irrationalism.

> Antirationalism and anti-intellectualism were everywhere, and not merely "in the air"; they were explicit elements of Nazi ideology and propaganda. Husserl's blanket indictment gives expression to a clear link in his mind between philosophical antirationalism and political anti-rationalism. Heidegger's actual connection with the Nazis at one time during this period simply underlined in fact what for Husserl was a kinship in essence. (7)

There are, in effect, two aspects of Husserl's general critique, one aimed at the spirit of philosophy in the service of humanity, and the other at philosophy in the service of science. He chronicles the 'unquestionable success of the positive sciences' as a result of their adoption of a universal philosophy, and yet the demise of metaphysics, its inability to provide a universal philosophy and its decline into dangerous naiveties and scepticism. Phenomenology must take up the task of unifying philosophy and science, leading the way in a breakthrough to 'universal reason'.(8)

Given the disparities in their backgrounds and ideas, is it at all possible to relate Marx and Husserl through their attitudes to science and philosophy? Husserl wished to return science to philosophy, claiming phenomenology both as a science of sciences and a first philosophy. Since we have already seen that Husserl was anti-positivist, yet an empiricist and a rationalist, the contradictions evident here would require a revised concept of scientificity. On the evidence of <u>Crisis</u>, it cannot be claimed that Husserl was anti-science. What he castigated was the positive sciences' loss of direction and unity, their scientism. Marx's scientificity proceeds from an orthodox empiricist position - 'We have begun from the presuppositions of political economy. We have accepted its terminology and its laws'(9) - but does so to refute its metaphysics, its abstractions and its mystifications of true economic processes.

Marx and Husserl are very different in their methodologies. Marx deliberately employs the terminology and methods of political economy; he selects data, hypothesises and produces law-like generalisations in the mode of the natural sciences.(10) Husserl discards all formalisation in order to return to the phenomena at the precategorical level. These methodological differences are, however, superficial, since scientificity is an attitude, not a method only. It can be claimed that phenomenology is akin to the basic radical attitude of the natural sciences. The reduction to essences, the inspection of the contents of consciousness, throw light on how enquiries come to be initiated and how the formalising processes of science operate. Similarly, it is claimed that because of the 'return to the subject' and Marx's insistence on the concrete, substantial world of mankind, his analysis is phenomenological and therefore truly scientific.(11) The 'scientificity' of phenomenology is in the rational pursuit of truth. The method of disoccluding the truth via the <u>epoché</u> is comparable to Marx's intention to tear the

The Crisis of Science

veil from substantial life. In the *Economic and Philosophical Manuscripts* there is continual reference to what is concealed by political economy from the worker, the subject. In *Capital*, Marx states that the objectification of labour conceals the truth of the subjective aspects: 'The life process of society which is based on the process of material production, does not strip off its mystical veil until it is treated as production by freely associated men, ...'(12)

This dialectic of the hidden and the revealed in Marx's methodology is central to establishing a link with Husserl. The world where science dominates he describes as a sphere where man's true humanity and purpose is occluded. Man, the subject, is reduced to an object, and all his projects and products take on a fetishized appearance. The scientific attitude must be brought back to rationality. The purpose of transcendental reduction is to bracket off the cognitive categories which obscure the true self. The crisis of society is that it uses the sciences while forgetting the true purpose of a rational society. Paci finds, however, that Husserl stops short of the analysis of capitalism:

> What Husserl did not know is that the crisis of the sciences, as the occluded use of the sciences that negate the subject, is the crisis of the capitalist use of the sciences, and, therefore, the crisis of human existence in capitalist society. On the basis of the knowledge, phenomenology becomes the revelation of the capitalist occlusion of the subject and truth, and the disocclusion of every ideology based on such an occlusion. (13)

Was Husserl so unaware of the power of the capitalist class to distort the truth? This seems unlikely. It is evident that his project, aimed at the scientific and philosophic communities, had a different leading edge from Marx's political and social analysis. Husserl obviously thought that the resolution of the crisis and the coming of a rational society would end the exploitation of one individual by another, one group by another. This is implicit in his emphasis on the freedom, individuality and integrity which should prevail within the rational community. In developing his concept of the lifeworld through historical reference, Husserl suggests that a world of purposeful praxis, accomplishment and rich culture is possible.(14) He attacks the specialisation within science that fragments it and denies its purposes and direction. By this turn towards historical analysis Husserl has begun to address the problem of the social world of the subject and its meaning. He asserts that human beings inhabit a world of experience which mathematics, geometry and the sciences have idealised. This world remains as it was - an open infinity of possible experiences - but is given by science 'a garb of ideas' so that 'we take for true being what is actually a method -'.(15) Where sciences becomes an objectified metaphysics Husserl mistrusts it. Renaissance science was a liberating, unifying and ethical mode of enquiry into the truth. But the mathematisation of nature, begun by the Greeks and advanced by Galileo, led to physics being adopted as the norm for all the sciences. Facticity became the mode in which truths presented themselves.

Neither Marx nor Husserl decry the growth and success of the sciences, the extension of knowledge through scientific method. It is the non-critical acquisition of facts as objects, products and results presented as truths, that they see as a travesty. The radical analysis which Marx and Husserl pursue is in the tradition of Vico.(16) Both saw that the crisis needed a new scientific attitude. Marx was concerned with the crisis of capitalism and chose to attack its root causes theoretically via his critique of the political economy and the prevailing Hegelianism of the period. Husserl's life-long task of introducing phenomenology as a new science was given a new direction and urgency by his attention to the crisis of European science.

Scientificity in Marx and Husserl

The making of a strong case for a synthesis of the epistemologies and teleologies of Marx and Husserl requires the demonstration of a common attitude and framework of concepts concerning science and scientificity. It is evident that science is a dominant aspect in their analyses. From this first and most general point of agreement we need to develop a closer parallel from their account of the sciences.

It is argued by Lichtheim(17) that the early Marx is not scientific but is concerned only with the problems of philosophy in order to refute Hegel and Feuerbach. The programmatic aspects of Marx's developing philosophical attitude are a response to the revolutionary crisis of the 1840s. In reply to

The Crisis of Science

Feuerbach's contemplative idealism, Marx proposed the realisation of theory in practice, a doctrine of unified philosophy and action. Lichtheim comments on the Theses on Feuerbach of 1845, that they:

> ... with their proclamation of the need for thought to become "practical" and "change the world", represent a pragmatic doctrine of revolutionary action which cannot by any strength of language be called "scientific".(18)

and again states that

> Viewed from the original Marxian standpoint, scientism and moralism are two sides of the same coin. The "union of theory and practice" is not science: it is a fusion of philosophy and action mediated by the vision of a unique constellation of circumstances: the approach of a social revolution which will inaugurate the reign of freedom.(19)

In Lichtheim's view, Marx does not adopt the terminology of positivist science until Capital. We may agree here, but we should not conclude from this that there is a division between the early and mature works. We have seen the direction of Marx's development with regard to science. He adopts the standpoint of positivist epistemology for a specific purpose - to give credence to his attack on the political economy and philosophy of the later decades. A section of the Economic and Philosophic Manuscripts on 'Private Property and Communism' supplies us with an insight into his view of science.(20) This passage on the unity of origin and purpose of the sciences has remarkable echoes in Husserl's Crisis and it is important for establishing a common approach to scientificity. Marx's analysis aims at disoccluding the essential aspects of private property as self-estrangement. He asserts that a resolution of the antitheses which fragment philosophy and society, perpetuating the social relations of capitalism, will be possible only by practical action. The call for emancipation and the revelation of humanity's essential nature is close to Husserl's project. This is a 'real problem of life' which philosophy cannot solve because it conceives the problem as theoretical only. In a similar vein to Husserl, Marx speaks of the separation of philosophy and science:

> The natural sciences have developed an enormous activity and have accumulated an ever-growing mass of material. Philosophy, however, has

remained just as alien to them as they remain to philosophy. (21)

Parts of his account seem directly to echo <u>Crisis</u>:

> ... natural science has invaded and transformed human life all the more practically through the medium of industry; and has prepared human emancipation, although its immediate effect had to be the furthering of the dehumanisation of man. Industry is the <u>actual</u>, historical relationship of nature, and therefore of natural science, to man. If, therefore, industry is conceived as the esoteric revelation of man's <u>essential powers</u>, we also gain an understanding of the <u>human</u> essence of nature or the <u>natural</u> essence of man. (22)

Marx is, of course, much influenced at this point by Feuerbach's anthropological philosophy. This is evident from the stress on sensuous consciousness in Marx's analysis of human relations. There is no parallel here with Husserl's more radical epistemology. However, it is interesting that Marx gives prominence in this early text to ideas that Husserl expresses in the <u>Crisis</u>:

> History itself is a real part of <u>natural history</u> - of nature developing into man. Natural science will in time incorporate into itself the science of man; just as the science of man will incorporate into itself natural science: there will be one science. (23)

The teleological implications of Marx's position during this period will be dealt with later in the chapter. The theme here is the unity of the sciences in the service of mankind. By linking this with Husserl's project, phenomenological Marxists suggest that there are programmatic implications in <u>Crisis</u>. They reject, however, the anthropological assumptions which remain as a residue from Feuerbach in these early texts.

We have seen that a crisis forces the scientist back into philosophy to restore his presuppositions. It may also move him to eliminate the distinction between science and philosophy and to seek out 'one science' by which he also intends 'one philosophy', the unity of an overarching theoretical framework. For Marx the unifying theory is historical materialism. Husserl's response to the crisis is phenomenology as 'science of sciences', 'first philosophy' and 'philosophia perennis'. The problem with Husserl's

The Crisis of Science

'ideal science' is that while it provides a far-reaching critical analysis, it is not clear how the analysis may be operationalised to examine the social structure. The synthesis which is here sought with Marxism should supply elements of concrete analysis. However, certain aspects of Husserl's phenomenological analysis have implications for the practice of science and its status, which are next to be considered.

Husserl made a vigorous defence of scientific rationality. What he criticises is the misuse and misdirection of science in the name of objectivity. The positivist sciences in their research and development are no more than technologies. This critique extends to the most 'theoretical' of the sciences; physics, taken as the norm for analysis, is in a state of crisis. Any claim to theoretical integrity and purity is a deception since the mathematician, logician and physicist are no more, if no less, than 'ingenious technicians'.(24) This criticism is not intended by Husserl as a denigration of the brilliance of their achievements, their 'great and forever valid discoveries'.(25) (He also commends the 'concrete humanistic sciences' for their 'enduringly compelling successes'.) The crisis concerns the meaning of the sciences for humanity; the critique is that they have lost the sense of their origin in the life-world. Taking physics as his model, Husserl shows that the starting point for the enquiry into physical nature is the given world. The experimental physicist, 'the discovering scientist of nature',(26) builds, however, on the body of knowledge already at his disposal, that is a whole range of assumptions validated by mathematical physicists who present these assumptions as 'the available logical possibilities for new hypotheses which, of course, must be compatible with the totality of those accepted as valid at the time'.(27) This accretion is given the character of an 'unquestioned tradition' which becomes detached from its origin. Through the mathematisation and formalisation of nature '... original thinking that genuinely gives meaning to this technical process and truth to the correct results is excluded; ...'(28) While achievement in science advances, Husserl sees the crisis developing in the direction of irrationality. This is the dilemma of the modern world:

> The exclusiveness with which the total world-view of modern man, in the second half of the nineteenth century, let itself be determined by

> the positive sciences and be blinded by the "prosperity" they produced, meant an indifferent turning-away from the questions which are decisive for a genuine humanity. Merely fact-minded sciences make merely fact-minded people... In our vital need - so we are told - this science has nothing to say to us. It excludes in principle precisely the questions which man, given over in our unhappy times to the most portentous of upheavals, finds the most burning ... (29)

Husserl also stresses the limitations on original thinking which this 'technisation' of science imposes. The loss of contact with its origins can be stultifying for progress within a branch of science, whereas a return to the prescientific level can be fruitful for advances in knowledge. This is clearly demonstrated by Ronchi's discoveries in optics.(30) Theoretical breakthrough in physics also demonstrates that, at the point of discovery, ontological 'certainties' are waived and assumptions are bracketed.(31) The procedures of empirical enquiry require that objectivities be established, and effects grasped, as occurrences in time and space. Judgement as to 'real' objects is suspended. As an empiricist, Husserl also looks to the world as it is experienced, but extends the analysis as a critique of positivism. The return to the subjective, which phenomenology asserts as the answer to the crisis in its ethical aspects, also offers a solution to the epistemological problems of science.

The overcoming of the traditional subjective/objective dichotomy, via a return to the subjective as the dominant mode, is phenomenology's solution to naive empiricism. The object and objectivity are not dispensed with in this schema; it is the epistemological perspective that is altered. The experience of the subject is once more the basis of knowledge. Thus the spurious claim to objectivity, as a raison d'être, which is the chief justification of scientism, is shown to be naive. Science, even in its most 'theoretical' branch, theoretical physics, cannot claim to be more than a technisation, and therefore it is not an end in itself but a practice, the function of which must be given direction. Phenomenology further maintains that science, in its pursuit of the truths of the universe, is none the less dealing with relative knowledge. As Weyl expresses it:

> There is no difference in our experience to which there does not correspond a difference in

The Crisis of Science

> the underlying objective situation (a difference, moreover, which is invariant under arbitrary coordinate transformations). It comprises as a matter of course the body of the ego as a physical object. The immediate experience is <u>subjective and absolute</u>. However hazy it may be, it is given in its very haziness thus and not otherwise. The objective world, on the other hand, with which we reckon continually in our daily lives and which the natural sciences daily attempt to crystallise by methods representing the consistent development of those criteria by which we experience reality in our natural everyday attitude – this objective world is of necessity <u>relative</u>; it can be represented by definite things (numbers or other symbols) only after a system of coordinates has been arbitrarily carried into the world. It seems to me that this pair of opposites, subjective-absolute and object-relative, contains one of the most fundamental epistemological insights that can be gleaned from science. Whoever desires the absolute must take the subjectivity and egocentricity into the bargain; whoever feels drawn toward the objective faces the problem of relativity. (32)

The phenomenological return to the subject has implications for the direction in which science should proceed. If human subjectivity shapes the world, should it not also control it? Husserl sees the starting point of social and ethical change as the recognition by the sciences of their true function. But a return to rationality needs to convince the scientific community intellectually. Since it is fundamentally an epistemological critique, Husserl's analysis of the crisis is of the greatest importance in this task.

<u>Theorising the Life-world</u>
It is already clear in what sense Husserl views the crisis of the sciences; it stems from the loss of a sense of their origins in the life-world. The concept of the life-world is a central element in Husserl's analysis. How then does he theorise it? What could be compatible in this part of his theory with Marx's analysis of capitalism?

When Husserl refers to the life-world it is to a shared world of lived experience. What he postulates is not a constructed cosmology, an epistēmē or a definitive world-view. It is rather the preconceptual basis of all subjective experience - pre-theoretical, pre-suppositionless, pre-predicative and pre-scientific. For Husserl, this is the foundation of which phenomenology is able to make 'foundational' enquiries, and the crises of science and philosophy stem from its neglect. This world of experience which became mathematised and circumscribed by science is only accessible through the reductive and descriptive methods of phenomenology.(33) The task set for philosophy, to restore to science its origins, is of immense difficulty since the life-world is, at base, the world of discrete, experiencing subjects, each subject being at the centre of the matrix.(34) What is distilled out of this experience is expressed and perceived within a cognitive framework of ideas, concepts, predicates, suppositions and constructs. The pre-conceptual becomes the conceptual, the conceived world is brought into being. The life-world, one of Husserl's most fruitful ideas, seems logically the next phase of his theory of intersubjectivity. In this concept we see the possibility of a further link with Marx. To make this effective, Husserl's life-world would need to be reformulated as a world of lived experience which is occluded by the domination of capitalism. This would ensure that both frameworks have a priori a common basis in primary experience as a totality or totalising construct. However, this raises the further question of the exact nature of such a totality. Does Husserl's view of the life-world lend itself to interpretation as a sphere of materiality? If there could be agreement through a concept of the primary experience, a basic objection to synthesising Husserl and Marx could be overcome. This is what Paci's theory rests upon, involving as it does the characterisation of the life-world as a political and economic structure. In contrast, Carr's view is that the life-world, as an historical construct in Husserl's later work, could only be compatible with Marx's ideas of the superstructure. Carr appears to be adopting an idealist stance in his assessment here, since he interprets the 'historical' character of the life-world to indicate political and social aspects only. He is doubtful that materiality can be ascribed to primary experience without presenting Husserl's theory of the life-world in a false light.(35) Carr rightly states that Husserl's account of the life-world is confused and that we cannot directly read into it those attributes which would enable a synthesis with Marxist ideas to be made. It

The Crisis of Science

is therefore necessary to explore the possibility of a common basis at a more fundamental level. Also, certain elements lacking in Husserl, where he does not proceed far enough with his analysis, may be supplied by Marx without distorting Husserl's original intention.

The conformation of the life-world may have been left unspecified by Husserl to avoid the criticism that he has relativised it by giving it a particular character. He is anxious to establish the scientificity of phenomenology by presenting the life-world as an ultimate source of knowledge, an a priori foundation accessible only by transcendental reduction. Since Husserl's analysis does not extend to theorising the structure of society, how is Paci able to build his synthesis on the notion of a common economic base? We have seen that he takes the crisis of the sciences to be a 'special case' of the crisis of capitalism.(36) Paci characterises the life-world as a world of need, basic material needs for food, shelter, survival and so forth. Mankind labours to fulfil these needs and in doing so constructs his society and culture, and develops his capacity to dominate nature. But this process involves the application of rationality to the problems of scarcity and need; thus, eventually science and capitalism are instituted. The ensuing alienation of man is the result of the reduction of subject to object rationally accomplished by applied science. The crisis is the displacement of man and the forgetting of his origins. The totality is 'ruptured' by rationalisation and obscured in man's acceptance of his commodity status.(37) It is not merely the telos that is occluded but the totality of social relations. In bourgeois society these appear in illusory and distorted form. Alienation is for Paci, as for the early Lukács, objectification. His source is the Economic and Philosophic Manuscripts in which Marx makes the analysis that 'The performance of work appears in the sphere of political economy as a vitiation of the worker, objectification as loss, and as servitude to the object'.(38) The resolution of the crisis must be accomplished by the collective praxis of subjects.

From Paci's standpoint, which displays a Hegelian influence, Marx anticipates Husserl. Paci asserts that Marx 'unveiled the foundation of intersubjective alienation in the subject's claim to possess the other, through irreversibility and need, in order to objectify him'.(39) It is the emphasis on the ethical question which enables Paci to create a reconciliation

The Crisis of Science

between Husserl and Marx. The crisis of the sciences and of capitalism requires a moral, as well as a material, emancipation.

Relating the life-world to Marx's base/superstructure model is one of the central difficulties in achieving a synthesis. In the next chapter, other aspects of the concept of intersubjectivity which may be compatible with Marx are explored. At this point, where we are considering materiality as a common basis, it would be useful to establish the related use of a key term in both literatures – 'the concrete'. Mention has already been made of Marx's analysis of commodity status in identifying the crisis. This is a central epistemological enquiry for the analysis of capitalism. Marx's critique of bourgeois economics aims at discovering what is concealed in the process of production and in the commodity. It is interesting that both Marx and Husserl use the visual metaphor extensively to signify understanding. Marx writes of the commodity that it is

> ... at first sight, a very trivial thing, and easily understood. Its analysis shows that it is, in reality, a very queer thing,...

The significance of the metaphor is made more explicit as Marx examines the problematical relation between commodities:

> ... the light from an object is perceived by us not as the subjective excitation of our optic nerve, but as the objective form of something outside the eye itself. But, in the act of seeing, there is at all events, an actual passage of light from one thing to another, from the external object to the eye. There is a physical relation between physical things. But it is different with commodities. There, the existence of things *qua* commodities,... have absolutely no connection with their physical properties and with the material relations arising therefrom. There is a definite social relation between men, that assumes, in their eyes, the fantastic form of a relation between things. (40)

Thus the phenomenal forms, the abstract categories which arise in capitalist society, are what render concrete social relations opaque. Marx's notion of opacity here is suggestive of Husserl's 'occlusion', but the direction of analysis differs. While analysing the cognitive character of 'the thing' Husserl is unable to extrapolate from its status to the societal relations of which it is the objectivised form. There are, however, points on which Husserl takes up a social analysis and, as we shall see in the next section, comes closer to Marx.

It is clear that the analysis of the commodity is much more than a methodological tool for the critique of economic theory. Marx applies to it a dialectic of the hidden and the revealed which derives from Hegel's epistemology. From Hegel, Marx also develops his idea of the concrete. The objective reality for Hegel is what thought can grasp. Thought identifies the essence of things with the universal.(41) Hegel holds the concrete to be the particular, the individual, while the essence is the universal, the species. But Hegel's objective idealism supplies us only with the concrete-in-thought, an abstraction. Marx reverses this by his grasp of the materiality of the world. It is important to stress here that it is not by opposing a realism to Hegel's idealism that Marx achieves this, but by opposing materialism to idealism. The question of the concrete as 'really' concrete, or as the concrete-in-thought, is waived. The concrete is the material world of particulars, of things, of sensate experience. Even more precisely, it is the character of the human world, created by human labour-power. Marx associates the concrete with praxis in __Capital__ where he refers to the concrete useful forms of labour which are crystallised into commodities.(42) Also, in __Contribution__ he points to 'concrete social relations, eg. in education'.(43) The concrete is given its true materiality only when it is grounded in concrete subjects, their praxis and their relationships. Marx makes a forceful critique of Hegel's conceptual synthesis which renders the concrete totality as a conceptual totality:

> Hegel accordingly conceived the illusory idea that the real world is the result of thinking which causes its own synthesis, its own deepening and its own movement; whereas the method of advance from the abstract to the concrete is simply the way in which thinking assimilates the concrete and reproduces it as a concrete mental category. (44)

Husserl applies the same style of critique in his discussion of the mathematisation of the plena:

> The theoretical attitude and the thematization of pure idealities and construction led to pure geometry; ... and later ... applied geometry ... the practical art of measuring, guided by

> idealities and the constructions ideally carried
> out with them: ie. an objectification of the
> concrete causal world of bodies within
> corresponding limited spheres. (45)

Husserl's analysis distinctly refers to the practical world and the development of the practical arts. So the concrete world is a world of praxis which becomes objectified by the theoretical attitude. The surrounding world is experienced by concrete individuals through intersubjective relations which comprise society and culture - a world of praxis.(46)

Both Marx and Husserl make a foundational analysis of the concrete which has epistemological and ontological significance. Moreover, it is essential to their theories of consciousness. Therefore, there is a concordance in this aspect which allows us to identify a genuine point of synthesis. It may be claimed that the phenomenological view of the concrete intermonadic world is an idealist construction. But this is untenable since the concrete is firmly anchored in the life-world of pre-theoretical experience, and this world is given historical and societal grounding. Perhaps the key to Husserl's position is to be found in his analysis of consciousness, the body and intersubjective life. How does this equate with Marx's view of consciousness and experience under capitalism?

Consciousness is, for Husserl, an intentional field. Awareness is always directed towards objects within the immediately given surrounding world. Beginning as he did with enquiries into logic, Husserl came to reject psychological explanations as generalisations from experience.(47) The idea that mental states, objects and rules of thinking could be the foundation for logic or for other fields of knowledge - ethics, theology, sociology and so on - was attacked as absurd, irrelevant and relativistic. It denies the possibility of apodictic knowledge while asserting its own truth. Husserl argued that logical laws could not depend on the unstable characteristics of individuals. He proposed the investigation of consciousness to account for the processes which engendered the theoretical entities of a pure logic. Thus, phenomenology became an analysis of types of thinking, forms of consciousness, and modes of symbolic and direct representation.(48) Psychology would describe actual cases; phenomenology would study essential structures and relationships, providing an epistemology which could test logical claims.(49) <u>Logical Investigations</u> contains, in its first

The Crisis of Science

Introduction, a misleading reference to phenomenology as a 'descriptive psychology'; this was corrected in the Introduction of 1913.(50) Though Husserl had a strong objection to 'psychologism', he nevertheless retained the term 'phenomenological psychology' to the end. Even the outline by Fink, in *Crisis*, for the continuation of Husserl's work states that it is necessary to clarify the distinction and to assert that psychology is 'on the way' to phenomenology.(51)

The theory of consciousness developed by Husserl was innovatory. In the *Logical Investigations* he asserted the doctrine of subjectivity and radical enquiry into the things themselves. The essential character of consciousness is that it is noetic, being always directed towards a content.(52) Later, in *Ideas* Vol I Husserl makes noesis the concrete essence, the formative synthesis which 'shapes material elements into intentional experiences'.(53) The intentionality of consciousness towards a content does not reassert the subject/object dichotomy. There is one point which Sartre raises as an inconsistency here, namely, that Husserl includes the concept of a passive material element, the 'hyle', into his conceptual framework.(54) But, in Paci's view, there is no problem in grasping that matter, or hyle, is a basic ontological element which exhibits itself to perception in complex ways. Yet to base a materialist synthesis on the dichotomy in Husserl's work of a basic (and, in Sartre's sense, passive) material element, which could then be identified as the source of brute data, is a reductive and fruitless exercise. Certainly, Marx rejects this notion as simplistic in his attack on metaphysical materialism. It inhibits the identification of compatible concepts with which to describe the experience of materiality, a principal task, surely, for Marx, as for Husserl in the analysis of the life-world and the origins of consciousness. If we continue to argue for or against the existence of a basic material element we are sustaining the debate which Husserl rejected. Questions of material reality are the precursors of all the problems of empiricism and dualism. Husserl's solution is to acknowledge that the material a priori is given to consciousness; therefore, the world of nature is the totality of objects of possible experience and experiential knowledge.(55) Again the emphasis is on experiencing and knowing. Husserl warns against the natural-attitude pitfall of taking the material world for granted, and the dualist pitfall of asking whether the world is really real or has only a presumptive reality. Carr's references to the role of ontology are helpful here. He points out that, in reaction to Heidegger's ontological emphasis, Husserl reasserts the investigation of the concrete as a basic task for phenomenology.

A key idea in Husserl's description of the life-world is 'kinesthesis'.(56) Since consciousness is constitutive, the ego does not function as a static receptor, but is actively engaged with an ever-changing perceptual field. Husserl is thus asserting a dynamic principle in his analysis of consciousness. To establish a synthesis of Marx and Husserl it is vital to retain this notion of dynamism in order to identify a motive force as a link for both theories of consciousness. Husserl's notion of kinaesthesis, of an active constituting process, can be linked to Marx's notion of praxis if we recognise that the kinaesthetic process of the constitution of the object is dialectical in its operation. Though Husserl never postulated it as such, his descriptions of its operations, particularly in The Phenomenology of Internal Time-consciousness, show perception as a dialectical progression. Merleau-Ponty's analyses of figure/fond perception give further evidence to reinforce the claim that Husserl's analyses exhibit a dialectical process. If we accept the link to be found in their methods of grasping experience, we can take the enquiry forward to the levels where synthesis can be demonstrated:

- a) ontologically, since humanity exists inter-subjectively, both within, and acting upon, nature, changing its circumstances by praxis; and
- b) epistemologically, since the constitution of the object, and the processes of subjectivity and intersubjectivity, also operate dialectically.

My conclusion is, therefore, that there are grounds for attributing to Husserl a dialectical mode in the theorising of consciousness, and that this establishes an essential point of synthesis with Marx.

Alienation and the Ontological Question
The elements examined so far in this chapter, from which phenomenologists have hoped to build a synthesis with Marxism, include:

- a) a reformulation of 'orthodox' Marxist epistemology in order to relate to Husserl's life-world concept;

The Crisis of Science

    b) the identification of an embryonic dialectic in Husserl;
    and
    c) a related notion of crisis.

In this section I intend to examine a further element in this project - that of establishing an ontology basic to both theories. This again raises the question of the significance of the ontological level of synthesis. How important is ontology with regard to Husserl? In Chapter Two my objection to Lukács was that he gave, in his analyses of Marx and Hegel, a disproportionate emphasis to ontology. I concluded that epistemological analysis, which investigates claims to truth, must take precedence. However, this does not diminish the importance of ontology altogether: I would disagree with Carr who finds Husserl's work non-ontological.(57) Such a denial indicates a metatheoretical confusion. The ontological cannot be discounted since all theories make truth claims dependent on certain ontological assumptions.

    For the phenomenological Marxists the identification of an ontology common to Marx and Husserl is essential in providing a structural basis to the synthesis. It is therefore important to explore Husserl's theory in more detail. It might appear contradictory to isolate ontological elements in a philosophical approach which exalts the preconceptual as the basis of knowledge. However, it should be remembered that the methodological postulates of transcendental <u>epoché</u>, while they point to the preconceptual as the source, cannot forgo the ontological assumptions of the method itself. In <u>Formal and Transcendental Logic</u> Husserl identifies the ontological elements (the formal elements) in pure logic as a theory of objects in their a priori structure. To this he adds a material ontology to deal with specific areas of knowledge.(58) These he terms 'regional ontologies'; they are significant for theory of science 'because each science, within its own province aims at "true being" - that is: at categorialia whose forms (if the science is genuine) must be among the forms that are formally - ontologically possible'.(59) Here Husserl is concerned only with founding what he terms a world-logic or genuine mundane ontology.

    Though these distinctions are maintained in <u>Crisis</u>, the central focus of Husserl's attention has become the life-world and its role in the critique of the sciences. Husserl sees the scientific world both as set apart from and as part of the life-world.(60) Moreover, he wishes to establish a science of the life-world while characterising it as pre-scientific. If this is the case then there are inevitable difficulties in giving the life-world a determinate character, or ontological status. As a science of the life-world we would expect its material ontology to be given a more concrete determination. Husserl gives a better indication in terms of the task of investigating the life-world. This is to go beyond a traditional approach which would have treated it purely as an experiential world and made enquiries of its structure. The <u>epochē</u>, he maintains, is a more versatile and penetrating mode of enquiry.(61) Under the designation of material ontologies Husserl is able to extend his enquiries from logic and mathematics to the cultural world and the sciences. Yet even though the programme for the continuation of Husserl's work includes the study of the descriptive sciences of nature (their a priori as the 'ontology of the life-world'), he is not specific in characterising the life-world. In <u>Crisis</u> it is variously designated as pre-linguistic, the horizon of all possibilities, the basis of the cultural community, the 'historical' heritage of Western knowledge, the institutional basis of the community in aggregate, its language, customs, and so forth. While Husserl is at pains to give the fullest explication, the concept remains problematic. As an analytical instrument for examining the experience of the subject in the face of the crisis of science and capitalism, the life-world is too indeterminate. It is acceptable as an ontological element commensurate with Marxism only if it is given a determinate character in terms of the experience of the subject. The difficulty here is relativism. Where the subject is anthropologically conceived, relativism is inevitable and some of Husserl's accounts do appear to forfeit ontological status.

We find a similar problem in the early texts of Marx where a residue of Feuerbach can be detected. Marx is seeking, particularly in his treatment of alienation, to produce an analysis whereby the human subject can be made concrete. The possibility for an ontology of human being which both Marx and Husserl would endorse can best be considered in relation to teleology. Both philosophers regard humanity as an unfulfilled condition. To Husserl, mankind has lost what it once possessed but, to Marx, man has never attained his true nature - he remains in a state of pre-history, of which 'the bourgeois mode of production is the last antagonistic form of the social process of production'.(62) Husserl defines teleology as the departure from an origin. The possibility of a common basis with Marx is that the occlusion of the telos could be interpreted as alienation, for alienation is separation or estrangement. Such a condition also signifies a point of departure from a former state. How closely, therefore, can Husserl's concept of occluded self-consciousness be equated with Marx's notion of alienation?

Alienation is the subject of contextual controversy among humanist Marxists. There is, however, general agreement that the concept is relational. At various points in the development of his ideas Marx employs the term to signify:

i) man alienated from himself;
ii) man alienated from nature;
iii) man alienated from the product of his labour;
iv) man alienated from his fellow men.

A line of development is evident here in the changing emphasis from the particular to the general, from the individual to the social character of human being. Marx's final position places greater emphasis on the mode of production and the social relations of production. It is feasible that Husserl's concept of man's occlusion from the telos follows a similar line of progression. In the initial phase of phenomenology, Husserl's main preoccupation was with the problem of knowledge. This led to his discovery that, by epochal scrutiny, the self could reveal universal truths or essences. By the inculcation of the natural attitude, all access to the truth was blocked or occluded. The resultant process of the objectification of man could be viewed as correspondent with the notion of alienation in the Hegelian sense - the separation of mind from its essence: 'What the mind really strives for is the realisation of its own notion; but in doing so it hides that goal from its own vision and is proud and well-satisfied in this alienation from its own essences.'(63) This Hegelian notion of man's alienation from himself permeates Marx's thought in the <u>Economic and Philosophic Manuscripts</u> and receives extensive treatment in the writings of Lukács and Sartre.

The second type of alienation, man estranged from nature, was formulated by Marx in opposition to Feuerbach's anthropology. Feuerbach had rejected Hegel's doctrine that nature 'is a self-alienated form of the Absolute Mind'. In his view, religion, as a reification of essence, was the cause of alienation. This conception of man separated from nature is paralleled by Husserl's idea of the mathematisation of nature and the occlusion of the telos. It is implicit in this idea of the pre-categorical foundations from which the subject has been displaced.

The alienation of man from the product of his labour and from his fellow men are the two Marxist concepts for which it is difficult to provide any direct parallel. Husserl's analysis does not deal with the mode of production in society or the social relations it engenders. Nevertheless, he does see a form of alienation from other men occurring in time of war and 'upheavals'. Man's productive ability through the growth of scientific knowledge and praxis is, for Husserl, nothing but success. The questions concerning human existence which Husserl found to be the most urgent are 'questions of the meaning or meaninglessness of the whole of this human existence'. A fuller expression of this predicament is found in Crisis:

> But can the world, and human existence in it, truthfully have a meaning if the sciences recognise as true only what is objectively established ... and if history has nothing more to teach us than that all the shapes of the spiritual world, all the conditions of life, ideals, norms upon which man relies, form and dissolve themselves like fleeting waves, that it always was and ever will be so, that again and again reason must turn into nonsense, and wellbeing into misery? ... Can we live in a world where historical occurrence is nothing but an unending concatenation of illusory progress and bitter disappointment? (64)

Husserl points to the 'success' of the positive sciences at several points in Crisis. But the 'prosperity' achieved by this has blinded humanity to its true purpose. He defines humanity in terms of rationality, the rational civilisation being the political and social expression of a universal philosophy of reason. In Crisis the idea of freedom has become central. Questions of the meaning of human existence must concern man as a free, self-determining being with the capacity for rationally shaping himself and his surrounding world. Husserl regards the sciences as having nothing to say in answer to human failure, misery and scepticism. Husserl's assessment of the political and social consequences of the crisis of science and philosophy is stated in only broad terms. Yet, as Carr points out, there is an emphasis on values, on the practical aspects of life and on human problems which suggests in Husserl the awareness of every aspect of alienation as Marx describes it.

Teleology and Causality

Vital to the understanding of Husserl's work, its claim to scientificity and its possible synthesis with Marxist philosophy, is a consideration of the motive principles of each framework. Therefore, a further examination of the issues of teleology and causality in each theory should now be undertaken.

In traditional philosophy a basic dilemma is the disjunction of teleology and causality. There is an irreconcilable dichotomy between those explanations which emphasise deterministic causal laws governing nature, consciousness and history, and teleological explanations wherein human subjects are animated by striving after goals, or where a purposeful principle lies behind the course of history and the vicissitudes of nature. This is such a fundamental dichotomy that the notions of voluntarism and determinism are used to express irreconcilable divisions found in both bourgeois and Marxist philosophy. Certainly within Marxism this distinction has come to characterise its various factions.(65) Marxist 'tendencies' appear divided into two camps; traditional or 'orthodox' Marxisms are opposed to humanistic and existentialist Marxisms. The fundamental question which divides them would seem to be the status of human subjects and their capacity to alter circumstances. What Husserl may be able to provide is some mode of resolving this dilemma which will not forfeit the scientificity or logical coherence of the theories under consideration.

Husserl gave particular attention to the problem I have outlined. He believed that its solution lay in his concept of the <u>Lebenswelt</u>. In his study of the mathematisation of nature he refers to the potential for systematisation that already lies in the pre-given world with its apriorism and its universal causality 'which precedes and guides all induction of particular causalities'.(66) The praxis of the subject is governed by intentionality at all levels. The basic causal level governing man is his organic and material nature. But as a subjective living creature he is both physical and psychical and, as such, is subject to causality in the precategorical sense. Husserl distinguishes between corporeality and incarnated life. This, I believe, is one of his most significant insights, since it resolves the dichotomy and enables him to establish causality and teleology in interrelationship. Thus '<u>Körper</u>', the body in the geometric or physical sense, 'the physical body', is distinct from '<u>Leib</u>', a personal way of being, 'the lived body'. Man, in the corporeal sense, is in nature as part of nature, and subject to its laws, whereas ontologically he is also alive in an attitude of intentionality directed towards the telos. And since he is a subjective living being he is subject to causal regulation in its reformulated sense; cause now signifies a lived experience before it is categorised. Human beings are no longer individual, experiencing monads since they occupy the terrain of causal spatiogenerality. This is the basis of intersubjectivity.(67) By this theory, Husserl claims to have overcome the disjunction of causality and teleology which is paralleled by the Cartesian body/mind disjunction. We now need to ask how phenomenological Marxists find these assertions commensurate with Marxist philosophy.

From the perspectives of orthodoxy and neo-orthodoxy,(68) Marxism is regarded as deterministic, being a general theory positing universally valid scientific laws. Determinism presupposes an immutable structure of nature and a pattern of organisation which governs human thought and activity. Orthodox Soviet Marxism became an ideology built upon a rigid principle of economic and technological determinism. Thus a sterile and naive doctrine of causality became, under Stalin, the justification for the control and exploitation of the Russian workers. Under this type of rigid orthodoxy the teleological perspective, which posits human intervention in the overthrow of capitalism, is rejected. Subjects appear only as bearers of the determinations of the structure. Materialism, while accepted as a cognitive construct, is presented in the mode of naturalism. In opposition to this standpoint we have seen that Husserl rejects the naturalistic view as naive - 'materialism is all but "obvious"'.(69) As for the universality of the dialectic, this assertion is problematical. The early efforts of Marx's followers to establish the dialectic as a law of nature have been questioned.(70) In its application to the socio-historical sphere, however, the dialectic remains paramount in Marxist doctrine. We have seen that Merleau-Ponty attempts to establish the dialectic as the mode of perception. It is evident also that for

The Crisis of Science

Sartre the question of the dialectic in History is central. While the dialectic is a source of controversy, both in its mode of articulation and its degree of importance, there is general agreement that the problems it presents are largely methodological.

How then does the phenomenological Marxist position attempt to resolve these dilemmas? Piccone discovers the ultimate source of the objectivists' confusion in the Cartesian split. He holds it to be the expression of the internal division of class society into the rulers and the ruled. Within Marxism this has given rise to an ideological distortion, the 'determinist, objectivist, mechanical materialist metaphysics'(71) of the orthodox position. According to Piccone, what finally characterises the true Marxist position is praxis, since it distinguishes the materialist from the idealist dialectic:

> What makes the dialectic "materialist" in Marx's sense is placing human activity and operations over and above intellectual elaborations. The "given" is always abstract in the Hegelian sense. It presents itself as natural, thus hiding the fact that it has not only been historically constituted (as in the case of the social world), but that its very apprehension as such presupposes a long series of conceptual meditations which are automatically forgotten in what Husserl called "the natural attitude" ... The "secret" of the materialist dialectic is that it obtains between the categorical and the precategorical, and to the extent that life is prior to thought it must be <u>lived</u> at the same time as it is conceptually articulated. (72)

Piccone develops this theme in a critique of the extension of capitalist production in the present period of late capitalism, and its pervasive and pernicious effects on culture and the ecology. His representation of 'living labor' is of mankind no longer engaged primarily in production but in consumption artificially induced by demand creation. This seems to have important ontological implications which challenge Paci's ideas. Paci argues that in order to equate Husserl's precategorical world with Marx's socio-economic genetic structure, it would be essential to establish it as a world of basic human need. Man is ontologically represented by Paci as <u>Homo laborans</u>. Furthermore, Paci sees labour as essentially expressing the creativity of human life. Piccone counteracts this hypostatisation by asserting that needs, including the need to work, are created and distorted by bourgeois ideology. His emphasis is rather on scarcity as a fundamental human condition, a position similar to that of Sartre. Piccone is concerned to demonstrate the socio-economic implications for the future which result from the natural attitude reflected in economic and political strategy. He holds the view that the displacement of labour by automation in the capital-intensive phase of oligopoly is leading to the depletion of energy resources, and he points to the widespread international implications of the ecology crisis.(73)

Need can be established as an ontological precept, descriptive of human reaction to conditions of scarcity in economic terms, or of any other form of deprivation. While in agreement with Paci on this point, I support Piccone's view that the difficulties in specifying basic needs relate to their manipulation by ideological control. The claim that labour or work is ontologically descriptive of the human condition has been highly effective in justifying exploitation under the capitalist mode of production. For that reason, we must jettison the idea of an ontology of labour expressed as the need to work. By theorising the concepts of 'activity' and 'praxis' in response to 'need', we avoid the connotations of 'work' and 'labour' that are open to euphemistic misconstruction (ideas of the dignity of labour, for example).

The phenomenological Marxists claim that there is one point of agreement between the two frameworks which is the least contentious, and is consequently of prime importance - the telos. Difficulties in agreement would obviously arise in attempting to specify the nature of the telos since this involves assumptions about future conditions. Marxists avoid a naive utopianism for the reason that its proposition would be open to bourgeois ideological distortion. Similarly, it can be argued that, apart from the most general representation, the conceptualisation of the telos would be exposed to relativism if it were historically constituted. When Paci refers to a common telos, it is in the most general terms such as 'the progressive constitution of social reality according to the limiting idea of an "<u>ideal society</u>"'.(74) The most specific account he gives is as follows:

> ... science and technology become the means of realisation of the human <u>telos</u>. When, in their specific fields, they multiply human possibilities, free man from slavery, and adapt

themselves to the causality of nature in order
to dominate it. (75)

and, echoing Marx:

... in an ideal society I would be a professor
and a worker by remaining a man. (76)

The Marxist telos is given a less specific treatment
by Paci in terms of the 'emancipation of the worker',
'integrity' and 'dignity'. The reason for Paci's
account is clear; he regards the telos as an ongoing,
spontaneous, subjectively constituted goal which,
though it is referred to as the human telos, is
transcendental in origin.

Before examining some of the issues raised in
this chapter in greater detail it would be useful to
summarise the points made so far. The starting point
for our enquiry was the nature of the crisis in both
science and society which Marx and Husserl identified.
Marx took the crisis of capitalism as his main theme;
Husserl directed his attention to the crisis of the
sciences. Though Husserl remained within academic
philosophy and did not develop a socio-economic
analysis or political engagement, there is evidence
to suggest that both theorists identified the same
chronic situation - the malaise of nineteenth and
twentieth century Europe required a radical appraisal
of science and philosophy. Thus, the themes of crisis
and scientificity became dominant in their work.

Marx and Husserl each took up the task of
unifying science and philosophy to provide an
analytical methodology which would enable the natural
and human sciences to re-appraise their responsibi-
lities to the human community. This is not to suggest
that either theorist adopted a liberal humanist
position. The central emphasis for both was on
rationality and this required the avoidance of
relativism which humanism implied. Marx's mature work
moved towards a more concrete analysis of political
economy, and the changes in epistemology are significant for any synthesis with Husserl's ideas.
Phenomenological Marxism identifies the common
radical attitude, the emphasis on the concrete, and
the resolution of the subject/object dichotomy as
important points of contact.

In broad terms, both Marx and Husserl can be
labelled empiricist but their conceptions of the
relationship between consciousness and the surrounding world seem very different. By what means can we
relate Marx's central theory of base/superstructure
to Husserl's view of the world which the subject

117

experiences. Husserl's theory of the life-world does not appear compatible at first sight with Marx's socio-economic analysis. Yet Paci's attempted synthesis is convincing in its simplicity since what he does is to reformulate the life-world as a world of experience and of need which is occluded by capitalism. The life-world is thus given a concreteness which relates it to the substructure. Though Husserl did not identify the crisis of capitalism per se, his analysis of the crisis of the sciences extends the important notion of occlusion into a wider historical context where the effects of occlusion appear similar to the effects of alienation. The meaning of man is occluded just as the truth of the social relations engendered by capitalism is concealed and mystified. The notion of intersubjective alienation makes a bridge between the two frameworks.

The theorising of consciousness has always posed a problem for Marxists in analysing the relationship of the material base to the ideological superstructure. A naive correspondence theory was rejected by Marx. Can a liaison with phenomenology help to explain the genesis and structure of consciousness? In Husserl's terms, the basis of such an explanation is subjectivity; it is the experiencing subject who constitutes the world that is given to consciousness in all its concrete determinations. If the structure and dynamics of thought can be claimed to be dialectical, the case for a valid synthesis would be strengthened. Husserl's concepts of the life-world and disocclusion might be construed as elements in a dialectic of the hidden and the revealed. Another central concept in Husserl is that of intentionality, which can be extended to convey the notion of a project to which consciousness is directed. This accords well with Marx's concept of praxis since consciousness, as Husserl also contends, is more than conceptualisation but includes all forms of language and intersubjective experience.

Though it is essential to establish compatibility at the epistemological level, the question of ontology cannot be neglected. We find in Husserl's later work that the concepts of the life-world and the telos are given a more concrete character. Marx's ontology expresses itself in terms of the social relations which shape human existence. This view of social being can be related to the Husserlian analysis through the concepts of the experiencing subject and the life-world.

The Crisis of Science

Notes and References

1. In the proliferation of crisis literature we find a divergence of views on the relevance of Marx to the present situation. For an influential analysis of crisis-containment see Habermas, J., *Critical Sociology*, Penguin, London, 1976. Against the view that there are no immanent mechanisms in capitalism which will lead to its disintegration, we may argue that the crisis is escalating and that the theoretical output on this theme is a contributory praxis.

2. *The Shorter Oxford English Dictionary*. Kockelmans has referred to crisis as a disease of language presumably to stress the dangers of reductionism. The term 'critical' is related (see Glossary).

3. Marx, *Capital*, 1873 Preface, p.xxiii.

4. Ibid., p.xxxi. The passage continues: '... and by the universality of its theatres and the intensity of its action it will drum dialectics even into the heads of the mushroom-upstarts of the new, holy Prusso-German empire'.

5. Husserl, *Crisis*, Introduction, p.xvi. Carr comments that the crisis was perceived in this way notably by the Nazis themselves.

6. Ibid., p.xvii. The Vienna Lecture 'Philosophy and the Crisis of European Humanity' is included as Appendix I, pp.269-300.

7. Husserl, *Crisis*, Intro., p.xxvii, cf. also p.12 where Husserl uses terminology popularised by Heidegger to define the extent of the crisis: 'Thus the crisis of philosophy implies the crisis of all modern sciences as members of the philosophical university; at first a latent, then a more and more prominent crisis of European humanity itself in respect to the total meaningfulness of its cultural life, its total "Existenz".'

8. Ibid., pp.15-16. Bearing in mind Cartesian tradition and his vigorous adherence to rational principles, we may regard Husserl as a rationalist.

9. Marx, *Economic and Philosophic Manuscripts*, p.61.

10. Marx, *Capital*, p.xix. In order to analyse 'the economic formation of society ... viewed as a process of natural history', Marx takes as the phenomena 'individuals ... only in so far as they are the personification of economic categories, embodiments of particular class-relations and class-interests'.

11. Paci, E., *The Function of the Sciences*, p.388.

12. Marx, Capital, p.51.
13. Paci, op.cit., p.323.
14. Husserl, Crisis, p.xli. The problem is raised by Carr as to whether any such specification of the character of the life-world renders it less valid as an epistemological element of Husserl's theory of consciousness. This difficulty is dealt with in Chapter Five where I discuss the grounds of Carr's objection.
15. Ibid., p.51. Husserl refers to physics and mathematics as a means of improving 'predictions', cf. pp.99-100 below, also Kosik, K., Dialectics of the Concrete, Reidel, Boston, 1976, p.54 and p.88, note 20.
16. Vico, G., The New Science (1744), trans. Fisch, M.H. and Bergin, T.G., Anchor, New York, 1961.
17. Lichtheim, G., Marxism, Routledge and Kegan Paul, London, 1964, p.236.
18. Ibid., pp.235-36.
19. Ibid.
20. Op.cit., p.96ff.
21. Ibid., p.97.
22. Ibid.
23. Ibid., p.98.
24. Kisiel, T.J., 'Phenomenology as the Science of Sciences' in Kockelmans, J. and Kisiel, T.J., Phenomenology and the Natural Sciences, Northwestern University Press, Evanston, 1970, p.10. Kisiel gives this quotation from Husserl, Logical Investigations, p.253. See also Kisiel, pp.9-11 and Crisis, p.46ff.
25. Husserl, Crisis, p.4. Psychology, though slower of development because of the methodological problems is based on the ideal of exactness in the natural sciences. See also the introduction to Ideas. On the 'success' of the sciences, see Crisis, pp.4 and 12.
26. Ibid., p.47.
27. Ibid. Husserl's view of science can be described as conventionalist.
28. Ibid., p.46.
29. Ibid., pp.5-6. The significant questions concern 'the meaning or meaninglessness of this whole human existence'.
30. Trogu, G., 'Vasco Ronchi's Revolution in Optics', Telos, No 8, 1971, pp.3-20. Optical theories before Ronchi had failed to take account of seeing, ie. had failed to give importance to what is ordinarily perceived as the 'immediate given'. Trogu records the impact on optical theory of taking account of the subjective.
31. Weyl, H., 'Subject and Object (The

The Crisis of Science

Scientific Implications of Epistemology)' in Kockelmans and Kisiel, op.cit. (1970), p.101ff. This is demonstrated also in the theories of Heisenberg, Bohr and Einstein.
32. Ibid., pp.106-107.
33. Spiegelberg, I., op.cit., p.162.
34. Ibid., p.160. Spiegelberg notes that Husserl made reference to the 'mothers', 'the keepers of the keys to the ultimate source of being', the source of the metaphors being Goethe's Faust, Pt. II. The matrix is the womb, the mould, the source and the formative structure.
35. Carr, D., 'Problem of the Life-World' in Elliston and McCormick, op.cit. (1977), pp.202-12. See also Carr (1974), Ch. 2, p.190ff.
36. Paci, E., op.cit., Piccone's Introduction, p.xxiv, and p.xxvii.
37. Ibid., p.339.
38. Marx, Economic and Philosophic Manuscripts, p.95. See Fromm, E., Marx's Concept of Man, Ungar, New York, 1972, pp.121-22.
39. Paci, op.cit. (1963), p.401.
40. Marx, Capital, pp.41-43.
41. Soll, I., An Introduction to Hegel's Metaphysics, University of Chicago Press, 1969, p.109.
42. Op.cit., pp.5-7ff.
43. Op.cit., p.215.
44. Ibid., p.206.
45. Husserl, Crisis, p.36.
46. Paci, op.cit., p.453.
47. Husserl aimed his attack at the position taken by Mill in System of Logic, cf. Vol II, 8, 5.
48. Spiegelberg, op.cit., Vol I, p.94.
49. Ibid., pp.102-103.
50. Op.cit., Vol I, p.261 (Introduction to Vol II of the German Edition) cf. also Foreword II, Vol I, p.47.
51. Husserl, Crisis, p.399. cf. also the final part of the main text. Para 72, pp.257-65.
52. Op.cit., p.136 and p.552ff. See also Formal and Transcendental Logic, pp.169-75.
53. Husserl, Ideas, p.422. See also p.235ff.
54. Spiegelberg, op.cit., p.451.
55. Paci, op.cit., p.168. Paci citing Husserl, Ideas, p.46.
56. Husserl, Crisis, pp.106-108.
57. Carr, op.cit., p.100.
58. Op.cit., Introduction, pp.11-12.
59. Ibid., p.291.
60. Husserl, Crisis, pp.127-130.
61. Ibid., p.174.

62. Marx, Preface, p.21.
63. Hegel, The Philosophy of History, quoted in Fromm, E., Marx's Concept of Man, Ungar, New York, 1972, p.47. Husserl's preoccupation with the occluded monadic individual gave place to a concern with cultural communities which have lost purpose and fallen into political and social turmoil.
64. Husserl, Crisis, pp.6-7. Part of this passage paraphrases Goethe, Faust, Pt. I, line 1976. The Faustian legend had a special relevance for Husserl.
65. Lichtheim, G., op.cit. (1964), p.298ff. on the problem of history and causality.
66. Husserl, Crisis, pp.39-44.
67. Ibid., p.164.
68. By the term 'neo-orthodoxy' I mean those branches of Marxism which, in recent years, purport to be innovative but which display orthodox tendencies, eg. structuralist Marxism.
69. Paci, op.cit., p.174.
70. Dallmayr, in Psathsas, op.cit., p.325, notes that Paci speculates upon the notion of a dialectic in nature, taking his cues from Engels. Paci is critical of Lukács' failure to see the dialectic as the prevailing mode in both nature and society.
71. Piccone, P., 'Reading the Grundrisse: Beyond Orthodox Marxism', Theory and Society, Vol II, No 2, 1975, p.237.
72. Ibid., pp.243-44.
73. Ibid., pp.248-51.
74. Paci, op.cit., p.92.
75. Ibid., p.191.
76. Ibid., p.190.

PART III

THE SYNTHESIS OF MARXISM AND PHENOMENOLOGY

Chapter Five

THE QUESTION OF HISTORY

The theme of this chapter is the problem of theorising the historical consciousness within the experience of capitalism. The analysis has so far dealt with certain epistemological and ontological issues in an examination of the relationship of Husserl to Marx. It is now essential to extend this analysis to other areas which are relevant to our project, such as history, language and social relations. There are problems in relating the work of Marx and Husserl which demand a reappraisal of these elements of their theories. Within this context I also look at aspects of the hermeneutic tradition and again consider the existentialist Marxist position. Having developed a critique of these attempts to relate Marxism and phenomenology, I finally ask whether there is a unique contribution to be made to the philosophy of the social sciences by a phenomenological Marxism.

Phenomenological analysis has been characterised as the search for the radical basis of the way in which we know the world. But to effect an articulation of this philosophy with Marxism, we need to establish an analytical link without which synthesis would be impossible. The vital dimension for any articulation with Marx is the dimension of history. Is there a case to be made that in Husserl's work we find the basis for claiming that consciousness is historically situated? To discover this as an a priori, consonant with a socio-historical analysis, would further the liaison with Marx's historical materialism.

That there is a problem of history in phenomenology is undeniable and well documented. The question of whether phenomenology can account for the historical is given prominence by Carr[1] and Ricoeur.[2] If it can be established that the central tenet of Husserl's philosophy was transformed from a phenomenological description of essences to an analysis of historical intersubjectivity, then there is a basis for a synthesis with Marxism. I consider Husserl's historico-genetic analysis as a possible solution to this problem.

This chapter raises the question of historicity in Husserl and Marx. It reviews claims that Husserl did develop a theory of the historical a priori. This is followed by a discussion of historicism in relation to the Marxist theory of history. Is the notion of a historical a priori compatible with an element of historical relativism? There is the further question of whether Marx's dialectic of history can accommodate a measure of partial historicism as suggested by Carr.

The question of history is central to existentialist theory and to the hermeneutic tradition in philosophy. A critique of these theoretical positions, particularly where they lay claim to an integration with Marxist ideas, should throw light on the problem. For this reason, the relationships between history, language, knowledge and ontology are considered with reference to the work of Husserl, Dilthey, Heidegger, Sartre and Merleau-Ponty. Husserl defines language as the horizon of all possibilities.(3) We need to enquire into the predicative determinants of those possibilities. The answer seems to lie in our concept of experience. Since it is in the organising of experience that intentionality precedes both language and logic, we continue to examine the concept of intentionality as a central element in Husserl's theory of the structure of consciousness.

Historicity in Husserl

The understanding of the development of Husserl's philosophy depends to a large extent on his treatment of history. There is much evidence to suggest that Husserl's final theoretical position regarding the historical nature of the life-world marked a significant departure from his early thought. The initial project for phenomenology was to disclose the universal sources of subjectivity, the invariant structures of consciousness. If these could be established Husserl could claim to reveal the pre-scientific foundation for all science. Thus, phenomenology aspired to be a science of sciences, investigating the essence of other sciences' objects.(4) Husserl's growing concern with the problem of 'the other' led him to the concept of intersubjectivity, and so inevitably to the recognition of the historical character of the world. In <u>Philosophy as a Rigorous Science</u>(5) Husserl had attacked the natural attitude of the Enlightenment. The scepticism which this era produced, led eventually to a spurious philosophy, historicism, which tied the production of thought to historically and culturally specific determinations. Phenomenology purported to transcend these objectivist constraints to reveal an underlying immutability or, more specifically, a historical a priori. But did Husserl later modify this project and embrace what Carr refers to as a 'partial historicism'? This question, with its implication that phenomenology would thus be inauthenticated as a rigorous science, will be subsequently examined. First, it is important to reconsider Husserl's concept of intersubjectivity and the process of reduction which reveals the nature of the <u>Lebenswelt</u>.

Husserl begins from the assertion, which I take to be ontological, that man is involved in nature; what sets him apart from other animate organisms is his capacity for self-reflexion, his subjectivity:

> Everyone, as a matter of a priori necessity, lives in the same Nature, and Nature moreover that, with the necessary communalisation of his life and of the lives of others, he has fashioned into a <u>cultural world</u> ... Each man understands first of all, in respect of a core, and as having its unrevealed horizon, <u>his</u> concrete surrounding world or his culture; and he does so precisely as a man, who belongs to the community fashioning it historically. (6)

Husserl refers to cultural communities as 'worlds', which can be barred to outsiders at the mundane level but which yield their primordial content to phenomenological and historical reduction. The life-world thus revealed is the sphere of givenness in which the self and others are constituted in a common mode. By the period of the writing of <u>Crisis</u> Husserl is far more urgently concerned with the historical. The work takes the form of a critique of European science and civilisation. Here he develops the notion that, in addition to the phenomenological epochê, a historical reduction is necessary. Since this is a project very similar to traditional histories of thought, there appears to be a conflation of approaches in the historical reduction. It can be claimed as innovative only within the context of Husserl's work. We are further presented with the idea that philosophy is to

be regarded as a historical fact. This poses a
problem for Carr. His case for discovering relativism
in Husserl's theory is based upon the premiss that if
philosophies are the products of cultural development,
then the use of a philosophical epochē to discover
underlying truths will produce truths which are in
themselves relative.(7) But by introducing the idea
of a 'partial historicism' Carr hopes to effect a
compromise solution to this classic dilemma. Its
success can be judged only after a more detailed
exposition of Husserl's method.

What then is the character of the historical
reduction which the philosopher is required to per-
form? Initially, phenomenological method has
bracketed all socio-historical categories. Husserl
now demands in Crisis that serious attention be paid
to historical time and place; the world as a spatio-
temporal sphere manifested in history becomes a
central issue. Perhaps the clearest example of the
type of enquiry Husserl had in mind as historical
reduction is to be found in the appendix to Crisis
on 'The Origin of Geometry'.(8) Here he further
expounds his critique of modern science and philosophy, fundamental to which is the view that the
split between physicalistic objectivism and transcendental subjectivism arose through the mathematisation of nature. In the growth of science which this
facilitated, the human purpose, the telos, was lost
and the 'problem of the world' was conceived. The
basis of this philosophical problem is examined by
Husserl by means of a historical epochē. The Galilean
world is suspended and its origin in the pre-
scientific world is revealed by a 'historical back-
ward reference'.(9) The structures of geometry which
Galileo systematised pre-existed 'as analogous to an
artefact existing within our cultural space'.(10)
The geometer as artificer first grasped the idealised
creation of spatial forms in a mode of self-evidence
as an original being-itself-there.(11) And after the
geometer came the mathematician. The arithmetisation
of geometry was accomplished in the work of Descartes
and Leibniz. As the forms of scientific knowledge
were evolved, so the problem of knowledge as an
objectivist postulate emerged.

Two questions arise immediately in relation to
the type of analysis which Husserl advocates:

    i) Is the historical reduction a purely passive
       reflection upon the origins of Renaissance
       man?

    ii) Is it anything other than the methodology

The Question of History

> which characterises bourgeois continuist history?

In answer to the first question, I would say that Husserl's account is too vague to suggest the mode by which the consciousness of the earliest geometers became structured. Husserl's reply to this would be that the philosopher cannot gain understanding except by carrying out the historical reduction and supplying through intuition the elements of the subjective relationship between man and nature:(12)

> ... even if we know almost nothing about the historical surrounding world of the first geometers, this much is certain as an invariant essential structure: that it was a world of "things" (including the human beings themselves as subjects of this world); that all things necessarily had to have a bodily character ... pure bodies had spatio-temporal shapes and "material" [<u>stoffliche</u>] qualities (color, warmth, weight, hardness, etc.) related to them. Further, it is clear that in the life of practical needs certain particularisations of shape stood out and that a technical praxis always [aimed at] the production of particular preferred shapes and the improvement of them according to certain directions of gradualness. (13)

While this indicates that historical reduction may reveal the 'truths' of the past and the occluding nature of formalised knowledge in the post-Galilean world, it says nothing explicit concerning intentional life. The project towards which man 'intends' himself is not rendered specific. For Paci, this vital element is supplied by synthesis with Marx; the goal is specified as freedom from alienation and the synthesis hinges, as we have seen, on the concepts of praxis and need.

On the second question above, I would answer this by emphasising that historical reduction is not intended to furnish a history of ideas since it remains subsidiary to the phenomenological project. Husserl's principal concern is to illuminate the praxis of rationality - the success of rationalism and the failure of reason. Phenomenology is to be the philosophical solution to the crisis of the sciences which originated from the systematisation of Nature.

Historicism and Hermeneutics

It is essential to the understanding of phenomenological Marxism that the 'historicist' issue is not neglected.(14) Having established that in Husserl's later work history became significant, the question remains of the compatibility of the two tendencies of his thought - the historicality of phenomenology and its scientificity. The question of historicism is relevant to a synthesis with Marx when we consider how strongly historiographical readings of Marx are condemned by those who regard his work primarily as a science. Both Paci and Luporini take the line that historicality, at least in Marx, does not imply relativism and that the scientific basis remains unimpaired. The question of history is evidently controversial. The structuralist Marxists maintain that Marx's mature work signifies a radical departure into a new science where the historical is the determinate outcome of the structural forces. We have already used an analysis of scientificity to question such theories. The present analysis is closely related.

The prevailing confusion over the terminology employed in historical analysis has led to the explication of historicism as either relativism or historicity. Paci gives a very broad reading of the term. First, he reiterates the doctrine that capitalism contains within itself the means of its own downfall as a 'tendential law'; crisis is generated by the loss of the telos in science. Secondly, he states that the return to the present, 'alienated through the becoming-conscious of a part', ie. the exploited class', is to be accomplished by a recall to 'historicity'.(15) However, Paci then equates this with 'historicism'.

> Therefore, historicism must indicate "the historical propensities of a certain epochē", ie. "the presence of a historical direction". This allows the recognition of the possibility of overcoming capitalism and of the peculiar character of a situation, and, finally, the discovery of the means necessary for such an overcoming ... Historicism itself is not necessarily Marxist; it becomes Marxist if it appropriates the means whereby capital has asserted itself and uses these means in order to abolish capital, and if it does not lose the totalising intentionality. (16)

Paci demonstrates here how the problems of definition exercise Marxist theorists necessarily concerned with the question of history. The confused meanings of 'historicism' can obscure important issues. At this

point, therefore, we should attempt to develop terms which clarify matters. Though there may be other denotations, I shall distinguish three main uses of the term:
  a) 'historicism' implying relativism since this approach judges events within the particular set of presuppositions of a particular stage of culture and distinguishes no patterns which can be universalised - we can refer to this as 'relativistic historicism';
  b) 'historicism' as a method of historical explanation emphasising events as unique particulars which can be empathetically understood - the term 'interpretive historicism' can be used here;
  c) 'historicism' as an approach concerned with identifying the process of history as law-governed and universal - we can refer to this as 'structural historicism'.

To effect a synthesis of Marxism and phenomenology, Paci would need to take the second and third meanings of historicism to be the correct bases of historical explanation. In this way the 'historicity' of events, their truth, could be established.

Paci relies heavily on the concept of the totality to make his synthesis. Paci takes Marx's totality to be the concrete world of the process of production and the social relations arising from it. He finds the equivalent to this in the 'cultural environment' described by Husserl as:

> Original, generative historicity, the unity of spiritual life, ... the life of a total community of human persons generatively connected, who, in their singular communified activities, in which all single persons participate, reshape a surrounding unitary world which is theirs, into a surrounding cultural world ... (17)

Husserl intends this in two senses: the world of cultural objects - artefacts, traditions and languages - and correlatively, the amalgam of the entire personal and total horizons which form the intermonadic spiritual communion. Paci uses the term 'intentional totality' to designate Husserl's concept and to make the crucial point that Husserl's totality must be distinguished from the metaphysical expressive totality of Hegelian thought. In Hegel, the totality expresses the development of Absolute Mind towards its culmination at the end of history.

The Question of History

Husserl, in his rejection of metaphysics, begins, not with the Concept, but with the determinate world already given as the world of nature and human praxis. This world is constituted in subjective human experience and is thus infinite and teleological in character. While the Hegelian totality is also teleological, it is predeterminate in the sense that the final stage of history is already fixed. From the phenomenological Marxist standpoint, a concept of totality which asserts a definitive form is open to criticism as hypostatisation.(18)

Paci finds Lukács' notion of totality important for phenomenology. The static conceptualisation is rejected in favour of the expressive totality of subjects engaged in praxis. Lukács found in Marxist orthodoxy the congealed categories of the Hegelian dialectic. The process of the negation of the negation had been denied and thus the revolutionary historical situation had been rendered indistinguishable from capitalism. Lukács is often criticised on the grounds of historical relativism. He resists the charge by making his own attack on historicism and relativism. He asserts that historical analysis is a praxis, 'a continuous and removed process of becoming conscious'.(19) Since this praxis of reconsideration is continuous, the totality and the telos are not lost sight of. Lukács looks for a resolution of such critical dilemmas at the point where prehistory becomes history.(20)

Paci's treatment of relativism is a refusal to accept the view that a self-critical historical praxis in any way detracts from a final telos.(21) He adheres to the concept of totality as a construct which enables the structural analysis of Marx to be synthesised with Husserl's 'surrounding world'. He holds that the historical reflection resolves the problem of relativism:

> The meaning of the totality is maintained in the part through the reconsideration of subjects and of the group. It can be said that the revision, in the sense of "revisionism", tends to break the continuity and the unity, while the reconsideration tends to maintain it. Usually, it is precisely the inadequacy of the reconsideration which provokes the rupture of unity and revision. The ambiguity must be resolved in the historical reflection. The reconsideration avoids historicism as relativism and the transformation of the act of becoming conscious into a preconstituted system from which praxis is

The Question of History

"deduced". Similarly it avoids the transposition of the Cartesian dualism of soul and body (res cogitans and res extensa) into theory and practice.

We have seen in Chapter Two that the concept of the totality unavoidably carries idealist connotations or is, at the least, problematical for a materialist analysis. Here we see that Paci is striving for a redefinition in terms of an ongoing analysis, a methodology of totalisation. A new substantive is not easily available at this juncture. Similarly, his expression of historicism needs more than a negative definition of what it should avoid. His attempts to synthesise Marx and Husserl within these terms would require the fusion of 'interpretive historicism' with 'structural historicism'. Questions then put to history would examine the subjective meaning of events and the forces of 'tendential laws' which structure those events. The notion of historico-genetic analysis could be used without the connotations of relativism which the term 'historicism' carries. It is, of course, important to ask whether, from the phenomenological perspective, the historical reduction is considered to be 'outside history' (and thus non-relativistic). The answer must be no, since Husserl is concerned in Crisis with the historically-situated consciousness. The critical examination of the past, whether by historian, philosopher, or any subject, is always conducted from a particular point in space and time. But this does not invalidate his findings provided the epochē, which includes the historical reduction, is radical. The truth of events is built on the historical a prioris: the structural invariances of space, time, need and irreversibility.

Husserl's 'turn' to history and his awareness of the problems of historicism and relativism is indicated by his assessment of Dilthey.(23) Husserl was strongly critical of Dilthey's adherence to naturalistic or positivistic philosophy and his attempt to found the social sciences on 'categories analogous to naturalistic categories'.(24) In particular, Dilthey's psychology tended to rest on evidence and not to derive from intentional life. Therefore, Husserl believed it inevitably led to a sceptical relativism, the only true source of evidence being the precategorical life-world. Husserl further repudiated the doctrine of Weltanschauung adhered to by the school of Lebensphilosophie which Dilthey founded.(25) However, at a later point

The Question of History

Husserl appeared less antagonistic towards Dilthey and by 1911 had announced that there was no serious difference between them. By the period of <u>Crisis</u> Husserl was referring to precategorical bodily nature as 'a priori a sphere of relativity',(26) a fundamental principle of the life-world, therefore. While this appears to contradict his former attitude, it is evidently an attempt to convey the point that essential structures can be mediated historically.

The influence of Dilthey on the historicist Marxism of Lukács is clear. For Lukács, Dilthey's theoretical foundation of the category of <u>Verstehen</u> assumed importance. Dilthey's basic problem was that of theorising the relationship between the natural and social sciences. His solution was to evolve categories of descriptive science, <u>Erklarung</u>, and explicative science, <u>Verstehen</u>. The significance of the category of <u>Verstehen</u> to Lukács is that it allowed the historically specific to be conceived of as an interpenetration of subject and object in an identity. Husserl found the methodology of <u>Verstehen</u> inadequate to achieve understanding of the self's experience within history. As a method it remained at the level of 'psychologism' of which Husserl was highly critical.(27) For Husserl, insight could be achieved only by the process of reduction. But if Husserl came to adopt a methodology of historical reduction, it marks a retreat from the transcendental <u>epoché</u>. That Husserl introduced the historical reduction in <u>Crisis</u> is undeniable; he refers to this work as 'a teleological-historical reflection'. In the sense that this was a new departure, Carr is correct in claiming that we find a 'partial historicism' in Husserl. Given the terms in which we have defined historicism, Carr's conclusion would be better expressed as a 'partial interpretative historicism'. This might go some way to establishing that Husserl's approach to history does not concede relativism.

In contrast with Carr, Ricoeur and Wagner treat the historical reduction as marking an untenable ontological shift: 'How can a philosophy of the cogito, of the radical return to the ego as the founder of all being, become capable of a philosophy of history?'(28) Wagner criticises Husserl's 'historicist ventures' as an attempt to transcend history that is incompatible with his early work. In the light of our review of Husserl's theoretical trajectory these criticisms do not carry weight. The historical reduction does not mark an epistemological break as here implied. It does not invalidate

The Question of History

Husserl's later finding that phenomenology could be extended to deal concretely with events in the intersubjective world.
In the next section the development of an historico-genetic analysis is discussed. The question is whether an amalgam of the interpretive and structural historicist approaches should be superseded by a different order of analysis, one which would provide the way out of the epistemological impasse which the term 'historicist' creates.

Historico-genetic Analysis in Marx and Husserl

Husserl investigates the genesis of thought in consciousness by framing the question of how the world is given in any objective sense. We find in the Logical Investigations that Husserl searches more deeply into the foundations of apodictic knowledge until he approaches the nature of experience itself. In this work he presents experience as a synthesis of perceptions with the 'phenomenologically unified stream of consciousness of an empirical ego. This itself is a real whole, in reality made up of manifold parts, each of which may be said to be experienced'.(29) The important outcome of this notion of an active experiencing ego was the idea of intentionality. Thus Husserl developed the notion of Akt-Erlebnis as the lived experience of the self in its intending mode of consciousness. But intentionality alone cannot answer Husserl's question of 'how', without the temporal dimension being added. Thus, in the Cartesian Meditations Husserl states that: '... the ego constitutes himself for, himself in, so to speak, the unity of a history'.(30) It should be noted that at this point in his work, 'history' is used in the special sense of the history of the monadic individual. In the later writings on the intermonadic community, the problem is again 'how' others exist, but there is now the additional question of the mode of interrelationships which makes it possible to talk about a common 'history'. Carr detects changes in the usage of the term 'history' from signifying the individual temporal genesis of every act of consciousness, building into a particular unified life, to the wider 'problem of history' which Husserl addressed in Crisis.(31) It seems that the link between these changed conceptions is the notion of intersubjectivity.
In Paci's analysis, Husserl's approach to history is related to Marx's via an essential

135

The Question of History

structural element – the dialectic. Writing of the praxis of philosophy, Paci concludes that:

> He (the philosopher) must discover a pre-categorical history of the life-world from which the sciences arise through subjective operations. Present society needs the history of the past so that it can rediscover and reactivate its genesis in it. The "diachronic" genesis is connected to the "synchronic" principle from which it is impossible not to depart. It is connected to the original presence, which discovers itself by rediscovering the past and by holding and renewing the tradition by re-engaging it and transforming it in the present for the future in a series of permanences and dialectical transformations. (32)

The presence of a dialectical mode in Husserl is asserted by Paci first in connection with the pre-categorical foundations of logic in the structures of the life-world. In the sense that the world is an open totality, the whole is the infinite horizon of which experience grasps only parts. Thus Paci detects a dialectic of the whole and its parts perceived in socio-historical terms:(33) 'The dialectic is a totalisation in process whereby every part is an index of the logical meaning of the world and history'. From this point Paci sees the possibility of integration with the Marxist dialectic. The basis of his insight in Husserl's view of the world as 'the idea of the totality of all individualities and groups'.(34)

The question of the social totality, as Marx conceives it, is central to the discussion of the historico-genetic nature of Marx's mature work. The social totality is a structure of socio-economic relations. This conception, as we have seen,(35) is an inversion of the Hegelian totality, supplying the basis of a model for the critique of bourgeois economy. But the proposition that Marx is laying its foundation of a method and a structure suggests that the historical, in _Capital_, plays a secondary role. _Capital_ has been read as a historical analysis, where the concrete and determinate socio-economic situations which Marx reveals, are treated as relativistic. This historical treatment is characteristic of the Hegelian Marxist position. The antithetical position is to take the Marxist analysis as a structural thesis, reading _Capital_ as an examination of the mode of production in general, as an abstraction only. Marx, in his search for the

The Question of History

correct methodology for a critique of political economy, suggests the disjunction between these approaches:(36)

> ... either we trace the various phases of the historical process of development, or else declare from the very beginning that we are examining one particular historical period, as for instance modern bourgeois economy.

But is it necessary to cling to this disjunction? Marx replies that:

> All periods of production, however, have certain features in common: they have certain common categories.

Here Marx seems to be suggesting that the universal, abstract mode of analysis must take precedence. The socio-economic structure of society must be dealt with synchronically. The abstract mode of analysis is what renders Marx's work scientific. But in what sense is it therefore historical materialism? The answer will depend on our notion of 'the historical'. In the hope of illuminating the problem, I shall look next at the work of another Italian theorist, Luporini.

Luporini(37) makes a critique of the structuralist readings of *Capital* by Althusser and Rancière, rejecting their view of history as a process without a subject. He argues that the real subject of *Capital* is the commodity conceived as an elementary phenomenal form masking the mechanisms of capital production which transform it. The object of *Capital* is the circulation of commodities; thus, the owners of these commodities are objectified. These formulations allow Luporini to read Marx as both a 'phenomenological analysis and a conceptual construction ... What is conceptually constructed is the commodity as a real subject (not merely an epistemological one). It is the real subject of a real process'.(38) This reading of 'subject' as 'form' is, at first sight, merely an extension of a structuralist position. But Luporini modifies it to indicate 'that the forms of which Marx writes must be constituted with reference to the empirical'.(39) But how is this 'constitution' to be explained? Luporini proposes that *Capital* be regarded as entirely synchronic (but with occasional diachronic elements acknowledged, such as Marx's discussion of the working day). The structuralist dichotomy synchronic/diachronic is replaced by a synchronic/genetic formulation, allowing the historical to emerge in the tracing of the determinate development of the forms in the mode of production. Thus, there are two aspects to the synchronic nature of Capital: the genetico-formal and the genetico-historical, that is the systematic development of forms and the empirical elements. These constructs allow Luporini to treat historical elements as empirical elements within the overall synchronic model of the mode of production. In this schema the genetic begins to take the form of a theoretical history, very much akin to a history of ideas. The linking of the two constructions is formalised as follows:

> The presence of this variable, the historico-genetic component, is what makes possible the systematic construction of the model: the genetico-formal which characterises it depends on the genetico-historical variable ... If this were not the case the construction would fall to bits. (40)

Luporini's critique is also aimed at the Italian historicist tradition of Gramsci and Della Volpe. The problem for Luporini is how to include the historical without impairing the universality of Marxist science. The point at which his analysis becomes relevant to a phenomenological approach is where he considers the nature of Marx's treatment of the commodity, money, and exchange value. The question is whether, in undertaking a historico-genetic analysis of the basic concepts in bourgeois economic theory (the analysis of value, for instance), Marx is conducting a phenomenological operation. Does Marx, in fact, practise in Capital an implicit phenomenology in any Husserlian sense? I would agree that Marx's definition of the commodity as 'the concrete social shape of the labour product' does suggest a phenomenological approach, a disocclusion of the concrete. But should we regard this as a 'phenomenology of exchange value' rather than 'a theory or value'?(41) In trying to clarify his approach, Luporini is well aware of the methodological difference between the Hegelian analysis of phenomenal forms and the Husserlian reduction. He does not succeed in demonstrating that Marx, in his materialist analysis, abandoned the Hegelian influence. Marx's reduction, if we can call it that, proceeds from one form, value, to another, the labour theory of value; similarly, he moves from 'labour' to 'labour-power'. None the less, this mode of analysis is akin to the initial line that Husserl takes in Crisis where he uses a historico-genetic

The Question of History

reduction to expose the genesis of formal categories.
For Husserl, the development of the historico-genetic analysis is the concomitant of the return to the life-world, since an understanding of the evolution of categories reveals the processes by which they become occluded. Husserl's main postulate had become the inspection of the essences of intersubjectivity. Essences are perceived as immutable, yet, at the same time, accessible via a historical examination. In both Marx and Husserl there is emphasis on the regulatory power of historical analysis. Writing on the commodity status of labour power, Marx states that:

> ... nature does not produce on the one side owners of money or commodities, and on the other men possessing nothing but their own labour power. This relation has no natural basis, neither is its social basis one that is common to all historical periods. It is clearly the result of a past historical development, the product of many economical revolutions, of the extinction of a whole series of older forms of social production.
>
> So, too, the economical categories ... bear the stamp of history. Definite historical conditions are necessary that a product may become a commodity'. (42)

Historicity is the vital element in order to get behind the concept to the 'concrete social forms'. In <u>Notes on Adolf Wagner</u>, a text which considerably elucidates <u>Capital</u>, Marx gives attention to what lies behind the concept.(43) This approach seems to bear some relation to Husserl's reduction. In <u>Crisis</u> we find the life-world, as Carr suggests, to be not so much the 'cultural community', but rather, a 'scientifically grounded and coloured intersubjectivity'.(44) If Husserl's life-world can be given a determinate historical character, then are we correct in assuming its direct relation to a concrete world of economic and social praxis? No clear-cut indications are available from Husserl to support this assumption. One answer to this dilemma is supplied by Paci who asserts that the precategorical world in Husserl can be posited as an ontology of basic needs and satisfactions.(45) Having characterised the <u>Lebenswelt</u> in basic socio-economic terms, Paci further asserts that it is a conflation of the cultural and scientific worlds' underlying structure. In this way Paci rejects any assumption that the

139

The Question of History

<u>Lebenswelt</u> is ahistorical and non-ontological.

In contrast with Paci, Carr's position on the characterisation of the life-world appears somewhat confused. He refers, at one point in his analysis, to phenomenology as non-ontological, and yet his main emphasis is on the historical. Surely to assume the life-world to be historical, in any sense, pre-supposes an ontology? Carr wants to maintain compatibility between a historical orientation and the transcendental aspects of phenomenology, by reading into <u>Crisis</u> a partial historicism. He concludes that without this kind of compromise the notion of the transcendental is threatened. The only way left open then would be to read the historical analysis in <u>Crisis</u> as a mere self-critique by Husserl. Carr makes the following claims for the historical reduction:

> ... (it) has a dual function in the undertaking of transcendental phenomenology. First, it acts as a counter to the pretensions of any straight-forward reflections that are carried out in historical naivete, warning that such reflections may be mere expressions of historical prejudice ... Second, in exercising this critical function, it at the same time holds open the possibility the reflection can succeed in arriving at a philosophical description which is not encumbered by such prejudices. (46)

Though Carr makes a plausible enough case for 'partial historicism' as an attempt to overcome the difficulties of apparently opposed positions, I would suggest that these problems are of his own making. It is necessary to take, as Paci has, a materialist position with regard to <u>Crisis</u>. The question of retaining the transcendental aspect is then resolved, in the realisation that as Husserl moved away from his earlier position, the notion of the transcendental was no longer dominant.

It appears, therefore, that in <u>Crisis</u> Husserl intends to add a further dimension to phenomenology. The prejudices of the natural attitude are overcome by the phenomenological reduction. Likewise, the prejudices inherent in the legacy of philosophical thought must succumb to the historical reduction.(47) To lay the foundations of his regenerative programme for philosophy, Husserl addresses himself to the community of philosophers:

> ... we are functionaries of mankind. The quite personal responsibility of our own true being

as philosophers, our inner personal
responsibility, bears within itself at the same
time the responsibility for the true being of
mankind; ... we (should) reflect back in a
thorough historical and critical fashion in
order to provide, before all decisions, for a
radical self-understanding ... (48)

Time, Sedimentation and Language

We can extend the scope of this enquiry by now asking what elements of historical processes engaged Husserl's attention. Do these elements receive similar attention from Marxist philosophers and are they important for phenomenological Marxism? I look first at the concept of time. Temporal processes, such as protention and retention, were of early interest to Husserl. The other important theme dealt with in this section is language, also discussed with reference to Heidegger, Paci and the existentialist phenomenologists. The question of historical processes is taken further with exploration of Vico's influence on Marx and Husserl.

Carr and Spiegelberg mention the significance of Husserl's reading of Heidegger's <u>Being and Time</u> before he embarked on <u>Crisis</u>. Heidegger had developed, as a central theme in all his work, a theory of the reifying function of the sciences: 'The reified world is the physical-natural world. Estrangement is the separation of subject and object. What alienates and dehumanises man is science.'(49) Heidegger holds that science is an emasculation of the spirit in man. Empiricism, with its central concern for the problem of knowledge, is in no way able to provide clues about being, the overriding problem for Heidegger. The central fact about being-in-the world revealed by phenomenological analysis is that <u>Existenz</u> is temporal and historical in the sense of being always projected towards the future. It was this sense of the temporality of existence that Husserl drew from Heidegger, despite his rejection of Heidegger's irrationalism, 'an ontologism which naturalizes man'.(50) For Heidegger, human existence develops 'resoluteness', confidence directed towards the future from a return to the past. He had a vision of his own task as a philosopher in reassessing the past. By returning to the problem of Being he hoped to complete the task initiated by the early Greek philosophers. We see in this the influence of Husserl's overall project in recalling philosophy to its authentic goal. It is evident that Husserl's collaboration with Heidegger, and his subsequent critique of the direction which led away from the mainstream of phenomenology, enabled Husserl to constitute with greater clarity his own approach to history:

> For Husserl, the I in the first person becomes revealed, clear and self-aware through self-temporalisation in multiplicity and history. For Husserl, temporal finitude is reflection. Without reflection and its temporal modalities, the subject remains obscure and closed in its unexpressed unity. On the other hand, for Heidegger, real being is what Husserl considered unexpressed, obscure. According to Heidegger, when being falls into the finite world, it becomes lost and hidden precisely because it becomes finite and part of a multiplicity. For Husserl, this becoming finite makes possible the progressive self-constitution in history <u>according to truth</u>, and this constitution renders human civilisation possible. For Heidegger, being originally becomes false and can no longer aim toward the goal of truth because it falls into history. (51)

Heidegger's strongest objection to Husserl's work was his lack of a sense of history. His own compelling interest did not merely lead to an increased emphasis on phenomenological studies as integral to histories of thought, but also to the assertion of historicity in the temporal nature of individual beings. Temporality is what gives meaning to Being in the sense of 'a frame of reference or "horizon" for the projects of human existence'.(52) Expressed in another way, Being temporalises itself. The notion of Being, in the idealist sense of a universal teleology, is also found in Heidegger as a time structure running parallel to the temporality of human being. Likewise, Husserl had examined the nature of time in his early work. One of his early psychological studies under Brentano was the nature of internal time-consciousness.(53) Here he explored the transcendental origins of consciousness and arrived at a conception of the ultimate source of the givenness of the world as a 'time-constituting flux'.(54) At this stage the concept of time impinged on Husserl as of central importance, but as yet this notion was not fully developed, as it later became in opposition to Heidegger's metaphysics.

Husserl's study of time has a further

significance for our understanding of historicity in
<u>Crisis</u>. As he developed the theory of protention and
retention as temporal processes, he evolved the
notion of sedimentation in the structuring of the
self. This idea was to be central to his discussion
of language as the immanent mode of intersubjectivity
Phenomenology is concerned with time as it appears to
consciousness. Husserl wished to establish a priori
that self-generation and self-maintenance are
elements in a process of self-constitution which
displays a characteristic style. The objects given
to consciousness must be examined against the background of intentionality which itself has a genesis.
As a result of self-constitution there are formed
unique 'substrata of habitualities and goals'.(55)
These substrata of experience, awareness and response
fix the self concretely in time, the formative
process being sedimentation. Thus it is possible to
examine the mundane ego and its historicity.(56)
Husserl appears to move from this theory of personal
genesis to a theory of intersubjectivity. But a
theory of the unity of many individual temporalities
surely cannot be abstracted from a notion of common
experience? Husserl cannot merely assert the
community of monadic individuals to be a unity without theorising the specificity of the mode of intercommunication. It is for this purpose that Husserl
turns his attention to language.

If we accept that Husserl's project is to
examine the nature of what is experienced, then
language inevitably poses a problem. How is the
phenomenologist to transcend the language barrier?
Is there, for instance, a mode of empathetic
communication operational at the preconceptual level,
and can this be construed as a language? Obviously,
whatever his investigations yield to his own understanding, the phenomenologist must convey his findings in symbolic form. The existentialist phenomenologists held that language could not be bracketed off
to examine a prior level, since the intersubjective
world, which is foundational to all consciousness, is
itself structured by language. This whole field of
study, which was marginal to Husserl prior to <u>Crisis</u>,
became a central interest for Merleau-Ponty,(57)
whose work, together with that of Sartre, is
considered later in this chapter.

In his lectures on internal time-consciousness
Husserl developed the notion of memory as sedimentation. A similar phenomenological analysis was made
of geometry as a sign system. Husserl perceived that
geometry is transmitted and received as a given. Its

origins are implicit in its structure but are occluded:

> The problem of the origin of geometry is a general historical-temporal problem ... An operation that was present while it was being performed is still here ... as a complex of signs and techniques in which it has been sedimented in order to be repeated an infinite number of times, even if we have forgotten the original operations. (58)

Similarly, the concept of linguistic sedimentation refers to the myriad shared meanings implicit in language as it evolves. In Crisis Husserl somewhat indirectly links the development of language with the development of technology as the means of achieving mastery over nature. Paci takes up this idea and theorises a parallel between a dialectic of language and a dialectic of technology. He asserts that in both spheres the subject is exploited, but fails to make clear the mode of manipulation by language (as in, for example, propaganda, censorship, control of the media, and so on). Paci refers vaguely to 'misunderstanding' and 'objectified and alienated language'.(59) However, on the question of language as the basis for conceptualisation, and its significance for both Marx and Husserl, Paci is more successful in making his case:

> Language is a sedimented praxis that renders reactivation possible. The renovation of meaning implies not only the problem of the body-proper but also that of material nature, technology, and labor. These in turn imply the problem of the precategorical economic structure of the Lebenswelt, and the problem of the subjective and intersubjective founding economic operations according to fundamental structural modalities that Husserl never investigated.

But Paci is able to make this assertion only by going beyond Husserl to claim that:

> ... the precategorical causal structure is also a precategorical economic structure constituted according to the relation "if I do A now, I will obtain B later". It implies the complex relation between means and ends, the possibility that the means are means for the ends, and the possibility of the alienation or annihilation of the end by the means. Along with science, technology must rediscover its own historical intentionality,

The Question of History

its own function as a means of emancipation ... (60)

We find a significant historiographical connection between Husserl and Marx which undoubtedly contributed to their treatments of history and language. Both had read the work of Vico(61) and reveal the influence of his historico-genetic theory. Marx acknowledges Vico's influence in an important footnote to Volume I of *Capital*:

> Darwin has interested us in the history of Nature's technology, ie. in the formation of the organo ... (which) serve as instruments of production for sustaining life. Does not the history of the productive organs of man, of organo that are the material basis of all social organisation, deserve equal attention? And would not such a history be easier to compile, since, as Vico says, human history differs from natural history in this, that we have made the former, but not the latter? Technology discloses man's mode of dealing with Nature, the process of production by which he sustains his life, and thereby also lays bare the mode of formation of his social relations, and of the mental conceptions that flow from them. Every history of religion, even, that fails to take account of this material basis is uncritical. It is, in reality, much easier to discover by analysis the earthly core of the misty creations of religion than, conversely, it is to develop from the actual relations of life the corresponding celestialised forms of those relations. The latter method is the only materialistic, and therefore the only scientific one. The weak points in the abstract materialism that excludes history and its process, are at once evident from the abstract and ideological conceptions of its spokesmen, whenever they venture beyond the bounds of their own speciality. (62)

The principal tenet of historical materialism - that men make their own history - seems to have derived from Vico. The theory of class struggle was drawn, in large measure, from Vico's cyclical theory of historical change. He assumed the organic growth and dissolution of societies to be a natural law. Vico's determinism was extended to his theory of knowledge as reflexivity. His ideo-genetic law was assumed by Sorel to be an anticipation of Marx's account of ideas as functions of the mode of production.(63)

The Question of History

In Husserl's case, the historical and teleological importance he attaches to the Renaissance owes much to Vico's concept of new science. Vico began as a Cartesian, a position from which he derived a sense of the unity of science. But under the influence of Bacon and Galileo, who saw that 'reason has insight only into that which it produces after a plan of its own', he became an anti-rationalist. Vico's <u>New Science</u> typified the theme of regeneration which imbued the Renaissance. Paci finds a parallel between this idea of new science and Husserl's objective for phenomenology as a rigorous science.(64) Vico's new science was a search for philosophical principles to which a study of philosophy could be reduced:

> Philosophy contemplates reason whence comes knowledge of the true; philology observes that of which human choice is author ... (This axiom) shows the partial failure of both the philosophers who did not test their reasoning by appeal to the authority of the philologians and likewise of the philologians in not taking care to give their authority the sanction of truth by appeal to the reasoning of the philosophers.(65)

Dallmayr sees Vico's attempted synthesis as a model for relating phenomenology and Marxism, and finds it useful in delineating their complementarity.(66)

With regard to historicity and language, we find both Marx and Husserl involved in explicating the genesis of concepts. Husserl's study of <u>The Origin of Geometry</u> can be seen as a paradigm for a wider analysis of language. Marx demonstrates his philological skill in <u>Notes on Adolf Wagner</u> where he corrects the linguistic errors in Wagner's reading of the concept of value before clarifying the radically different assumptions employed in <u>Capital</u>. This is evident in Marx's denial that the correct historical and philosophical method starts at the level of concepts. The argument he uses must begin at the level of linguistic categories:

> In the first place (De prime abord) I do not start from "concepts", hence I do not start out from "the concept of value", and do not have "to divide" these in any way. What I start out from is the simplest social form in which the labour-product is presented in contemporary society, and this is the "commodity". I analyse it, and right from the beginning, in the <u>form in which it appears</u> ... (67)

The Question of History

This type of analysis, which I would term
'philologico-phenomenological', is regarded by both
Marx and Husserl as fundamental to their enquiries.
They share the same basic concern for a radical
analysis and, at this methodological level, Marxism
and phenomenology can be said to be compatible. The
restraints of the linguistic categories bear power-
fully upon philosophy. The historico-genetic approach
in the mature work of both theorists is demonstrable
in their concern that concepts and categories are
fully clarified. But the problem of the limitations
of language, of the boundaries of conceptualisation,
are treated by Husserl as surmountable in the eidetic
reduction, whereas Marx demands that the categories
must yield to the force of logical argument.

Consciousness and History in Existentialist Marxism

It has already been suggested that the question of
the dialectic is problematical for any proposed
synthesis of phenomenology and Marxism. The point at
issue is the possibility of discovering in phenomenology those aspects, however embryonic, which might
be construed as dialectical. It is evident that
Husserl's treatment of subject and object within a
subjectivist framework is alien to an orthodox
positivist Marxist approach. That the humanist or
Hegelian tradition can be reconciled with phenomenology through a common dialectic is believed possible
by Paci. The existentialist Marxists have also
attempted a rapprochement on this aspect. These
approaches relate the problem of the dialectic
closely to the necessity for extending phenomenology
to deal with the historical in human experience.
Having considered aspects of historicity in Husserl,
it would now be useful to review Merleau-Ponty's
approach to the phenomenology of perception, which he
attempted to reconcile with Marxism. This attempt,
which he was later to abandon, also brings into focus
some of the epistemological difficulties concerning
the structure of consciousness.

The work of Merleau-Ponty was influenced not
only by Husserl but also by Hegel, Kant and
Descartes.(68) One might say that Merleau-Ponty
sought to apply the Hegelian dialectic to the 'things
themselves' in such a way that he could claim his
phenomenology to be the logical extension of
Husserl's. To avoid the problem of dichotomy he
pursued a middle way between traditional empirical
and rational thought, between realism and subjectivism

and between determinism and freedom. What he
proposed was an ongoing dialectic to avoid the
constraints of the categories of thought.
 The influence of Gestalt psychology is also
strong in Merleau-Ponty. He maintains that in Gestalt
theory the unity of the whole is the guiding
principle dominating our perceptual experience. His
analysis of perception claims that there are
dialectically related levels within the wholeness of
consciousness: '... the figure/fond dialectic is used
to keep explanations of experience from crystallising
into <u>fixed concepts</u>'.(69) The importance to Merleau-
Ponty of Gestalt psychology is evident from his
insistence on relating empirical psychology to
eidetic analysis, in order to establish a final
homogeneity among the different psychologies. He
refers to Husserl's claim that eidetic reduction is
available to all. 'The intuition of essences does
not involve any more difficulties or mystical
secrets than perception.'(70) It seems that his
interpretation of phenomenology enables Merleau-Ponty
to place perception in a central doctrinal position
as a paradigm of ambiguity with which to deal with
troublesome dichotomies. The criticism most frequently
levelled at Merleau-Ponty is that his phenomenology
stops short at perception and fails to consider the
self as a concrete entity. But, as an existentialist,
he is, like Sartre, primarily concerned with the self
in the ontological sense. The notion of ambiguity
enables Merleau-Ponty to hold that Being is a
perceptual synthesis. Thus, Being is made evident in
perception, and consciousness discovers itself in the
world where 'I am given to myself'.(71) From here
Merleau-Ponty moves towards a Marxist analysis of the
individual as a body-subject in the historical world.
 Merleau-Ponty's position as a Marxist is fraught
with difficulty. As an existentialist he views
existence as committed consciousness. The commitment,
to be in the world is not by choice but by ascription.
But the subject and the world reciprocally constitute
one another; there is freedom to act but this is
socially determined. Does this mean that Merleau-
Ponty is in accord with Marx's tenet that man makes
the world but in circumstances not of his choosing?
Apparently not, since the socio-historical world, as
Merleau-Ponty sees it, is not the socio-economic
world addressed by the Hegelian Marxist subject/
object dialectic (that world in which the
appropriation of his labour-power renders man an
object and makes this available as a self-definition).
For Merleau-Ponty, the subjectivity of the world we

perceive, and the 'presence' in it of the reciprocal subject/object as a body subject, presupposes a rejection of the materiality of man, the concrete human being, living in a causal environment. The task of sustaining the 'inseparability' of man via ambiguity is characteristic of Merleau-Ponty's humanism.(72) Ultimately what he seeks is morality of free political action set against the backdrop of history.

The Marxism of Merleau-Ponty leads him to develop a phenomenological account of the rise of proletarian consciousness. Rejecting the objectivist view, he sees class consciousness arising out of the experience of being-in-the world. Perception of the 'sensible and historical fabric', containing other sympathetic groups, is available to the proletariat through situations of conflict.(73) But there is no causal inevitability in the growth of revolutionary action 'as a fact of maturation or maturity'(74) and, therefore, Merleau-Ponty's concept of revolution is an ongoing critique of power which refuses to reify the proletariat as the negating component of the historical dialectic.

Eventually Merleau-Ponty retreated from the Marxist position which had seemed to him at one time to be the inevitable path for a radical humanist.(75) How then can we assess his contribution to the development of a phenomenological Marxism? In his examination of the prevailing dualisms which confront Marxists, Merleau-Ponty made a valuable contribution. His view of reciprocity within the structures of consciousness adds to Husserl's theory the dimension of history. We can also derive, as Paci does, much insight from his concepts of freedom and the embodied subject. Spiegelberg claims that, without Merleau-Ponty, phenomenology would have lost prestige and would long have remained 'a mere tool of existentialism'.(76) The question of how closely Merleau-Ponty's work relates to Husserl's is of little significance, in Spiegelberg's estimation. However, the relevance of Merleau-Ponty's contribution to the task of synthesising phenomenology and Marxism is in its extension of Husserl's theories towards the concrete. Even so, his analysis of consciousness remains at the level of perception. The life-world is, for Merleau-Ponty, a perceived world which is not attained by <u>epoché</u>, but is asserted as that world of which one must become aware inevitably. Merleau-Ponty saw a possible line of approach to relating Husserl and Marx through discerning in Husserl the rudiments of a historically-situated

The Question of History

consciousness; allied with a humanist Marxist position, this notion of consciousness could resolve many of the difficulties in relating the two frameworks.

Merleau-Ponty may be viewed as attempting a synthesis which is in no way an enforced synthesis.(77) He presents us with a dialectic of perception which is instructive but yet lacks elements which would appear essential to relating Husserl and Marx. The fundamental precondition is surely the grounding of phenomenological Marxism historically. For such a project the dialectic is essential but Merleau-Ponty's analysis of perception and consciousness is not, in my view, adequate to the task of theorising the concrete historical world. In this respect, it contrasts with the work of Sartre(78) for whom history is a concrete dialectical process.

Sartre's work bears clear traces of the influence of Husserl, Heidegger and Hegel, though it initially stems from Kierkegaard in the existentialist tradition. Sartre begins with the problem of defining Being in relation to reality. His major work on the structure of consciousness, <u>Being and Nothingness</u>,(79) makes the ontological rather than the epistemological question its central concern. Consciousness is Being - 'the transphenomenal being of the subject'. Sartre's subject is monadic, a free individual paradoxically oppressed by his freedom. The intensely individualistic ontology of his pre-Marxist period was never lost, but the Marxist project appears to have given Sartre a vision of a more benign world than that which he reveals in <u>Nausea</u>.(80) In Sartre's first phase of phenomenological investigation he drew on Husserl but developed a notion of the inspection of essences which differs from Husserl's. By dichotomising the world of things (en soi) and their awareness (pour soi), Sartre was led to postulate the existence of consciousness as Nothingness, as 'other than itself', in the Hegelian sense of existing as a pure lack.(81) Thus Sartre took up Husserl's idea of intentionality, Heidegger's idea of Not-being and Hegel's dialectical notion of overcoming (<u>Aufgehoben</u>). These he fused into the concept of consciousness as a state of Becoming. It is Sartre's awareness of man as a struggling individual which leads him eventually to Marxism. The class struggle is the collective expression of the ontology of man, free yet constrained by materiality, scarcity and need. These constraints are experienced as a lack which is to be

The Question of History

overcome by praxis.(82)

For Sartre, dialectical materialism must be equated with historical materialism. Man exists in the heroic mould, triumphing over socio-economic conditions which comprise the pratico-inerte, the sphere of all material and ideological constraints. History is therefore the dialectical process of overcoming scarcity and need by labour. The process is one of continual retotalisation. Sartre rejects a notion of totality which is open to reification; he conceptualises it as an ongoing synthesis.(83) Marxism is, for Sartre, heuristic. The Marxist analysis should discover a posteriori those totalising processes which form the subject of history. What he criticises in Marxism is any emphasis on science, an apriorism which rejects the dialectical transformation of the world. Sartre's view is anthropocentric, stressing the singularity of the subject. He criticises orthodox Marxism for neglecting history, and thus separating theory from praxis and erecting knowledge as an empty edifice: '... this expulsion of man, his exclusion from Marxist knowledge which resulted in the renascence of existentialist thought outside the totalisation of knowledge'.(84) Sartre wishes to integrate anthropology and history with Marxism. But how does his phenomenology accord with a compatible Marxist position? In Natanson's view, Sartre, by adhering to the ontological argument, proceeds by assertion and does not retain anything commensurate with Husserl's methodology.(85) But Sartre does use a form of historical reduction in his regressive/progressive formula. Also, his notion of a pro-ject which throws man towards a range of social possibles, out of which he must choose, seems to me very similar to Husserl's concept of intentionality.

In criticism of Sartre, it would appear that there is a confusion in his attempt to relate a form of environmental determinism (man is constrained by scarcity) with a possibilism (man is free to choose). It could be maintained that this is a paradox that Marx presents and it must remain so. But it does tend to destroy the ontological stance that Sartre takes up. In fact, it relativises his whole analysis. Though in several respects Sartre is incompatible with Husserl, his theories have been instructive for Paci, particularly in supplying an ontology which Paci ascribes to both Husserl and Marx. Husserl's critique of science and technology, and Marx's critique of capitalism, are both underpinned by the ontological certainty that humanity lives in a world structured by irreversibility and need. A phenomenological Marxism entails the expression of these a prioris in its fundamental historical and socio-economic analyses. The point at which Paci disagrees with Sartre is in his rejection of Sartre's conception of groups and individuals in a circular struggle against exploitation. Paci contends that 'the inexorable reappearance of needs because of irreversibility and consumption does not entail the reappearance of exploitation'. He argues that:

> The revolutionary group must overcome the circle of exploitation, so that a man does not come to be used as an inert means by another man. Ultimately social inertia can be overcome because it is due to human relations, unlike the serialisation of needs which is inevitable. (86)

Therefore, Paci's 'clarified and corrected' version of Sartre's position concludes that an ontology of irreversibility and need does not seal human existence into a state of perpetual exploitation.

My intention in this chapter has been to demonstrate that the new dimension added to phenomenological enquiry - the historical - makes Husserl's work more compatible with Marx's, particularly on the levels of methodology and ontology. Thus we find further aspects on which a feasible synthesis can be established.

We may conclude that Husserl's historical reduction makes for a concrete analysis, compatible with historical materialism and essential for a synthesis with Marxism. We can therefore begin to identify the way in which substantive issues can be approached. The crisis is given a substantive reference for future analysis through historical understanding. The crisis of capitalism demands a concrete analysis. It requires the historical reduction to be applied in examination of the role of science and technology in shaping the socio-economic basis of the world we experience. Reciprocally, Husserl's understanding of the crisis of the sciences is adumbrated in Marx's understanding of the crisis of capitalism.

Yet despite Husserl's turn to history, which reinforces the concreteness of his approach, we look in vain for specific analysis of historical junctures; this must be supplied by Marxist theory since in Husserl we find no more than a general analysis of the crisis. As Carr points out,(87) Crisis was addressed to the philosophical community

The Question of History

'by way of a teleological-historical reflection upon the origins of our critical scientific and philosophical situation, to establish the unavoidable necessity of a transcendental-phenomenological reorientation of philosophy'. Crisis was intended as a philosophical diagnosis and, at the time of its writing, prudence dictated that Husserl's attacks on anti-rationalism should not take the form of political polemics. Yet the historical considerations indicate that Husserl was vitally concerned with the needs of the time and wished the relevance of his analysis to be recognised in the world of affairs. His concern with values, responsibility, community and direction in history appears to have been given more specificity in the earlier Vienna Lecture of 1935. Here Husserl's closing words presented the alternative 'escapes' from the crisis of Europe: either a downfall into barbarity or a phoenix-like rebirth through 'a heroism of reason'.(88) The understanding of the crisis called for historical enquiry into the goals which philosophers have taken for granted, a teleological consideration of history by self-reflection. The call was addressed to a wider audience through the theoreticians, who must strive for a synthesis with the practical attitude and thus achieve:

> ... a new sort of praxis, that of the universal critique of all life and all life-goals, all cultural products and systems that have already arisen out of the life of man; and thus it also becomes a critique of mankind itself and of the values which guide it explicitly or implicitly. Further, it is a praxis whose aim is to elevate mankind through universal scientific reason, according to norms of truth of all forms, to transform it from the bottom up into a new humanity made capable of an absolute self-responsibility on the basis of absolute theoretical insights. (89)

The question of history, as raised in this chapter, has taken us into a discussion of the meaning of historicity and the problematical nature of historicism. I conclude that Husserl's analysis is not relativised by the assumption that consciousness is historically situated. Further, Husserl is able to establish the historical a priori nature of the lifeworld in which all consciousness is grounded. Against the background of these fundamental propositions I have attempted to assess the contributions of existentialist phenomenologists in developing syntheses with Marxism. I have also looked at other theories which attempt to explain consciousness, language and history, but which must be rejected because of unacceptable ontological claims.

Notes and References

1. Carr, D., *Phenomenology and the Problem of History*, Northwestern University Press, Evanston, 1974.
2. Ricoeur, P., *Husserl: An analysis of his phenomenology*, trans. Ballard, E., and Embree, L.E., Northwestern University Press, Evanston, 1967.
3. *Crisis*, op.cit.
4. Lauer, Q., Introduction to Husserl, E., *Phenomenology and the Crisis of Philosophy*, Harper and Row, New York, 1965.
5. Husserl, op.cit., (1965).
6. *Cartesian Meditations*, p.133.
7. Carr, op.cit., p.63.
8. *Crisis*, pp.353-78. This analysis is regarded as seminal by Husserl's commentators and interpreters. Jacques Derrida's 1962 translation and lengthy introduction was particularly influential in French thought.
9. Ibid., p.370.
10. Carr, op.cit., p.202.
11. Husserl, *Crisis*, p.356. This term used by Husserl relates to the concept developed by Heidegger.
12. Ibid., p.374.
13. Ibid., p.375.
14. Carr, op.cit., pp.253-54. Carr's case for 'partial historicism' in Husserl is one response to this problem.
15. Paci, op.cit., p.409. Paci states that we must return to and grasp the meaning of the present situation in order to overcome it.
16. Ibid.
17. Paci, op.cit., p.229 quoting Husserl, *Crisis* (Biemel edition) 1954, p.502.
18. See Chapter Two, pp.46 and 50 above.
19. Lukács, G., *History and Class Consciousness*, p.189.
20. Lukács, ibid. cont.: 'This process begins when the proletariat becomes conscious of its own class point of view. Hence it is highly misleading to describe historical materialism as relativism. For although they share a common premise: man is the

measure of all things, they each give it a different and even contradictory interpretation.'
21. Paci, op.cit., p.332f.
22. Merleau-Ponty, M., Phenomenology of Perception, trans. Smith, C., Heinemann, London, 1974, p.xiv.
23. Husserl, Crisis, pp.222 and 245.
24. Husserl, 'Philosophy as Rigorous Science', in Phenomenology and the Crisis of Philosophy.
25. Lebensphilosophie was a revolt against the idealist and rationalist beliefs of the Enlightenment that progress resulted from the application of reason to the social order. For Heidegger, the influence of Dilthey led to unreason; for Husserl, it led to a critique of science. The concept related to the sphere of values. This is the direction in which Husserl moved. On Weltanschauung, see Spiegelberg, op.cit., p.121.
26. Husserl, Crisis, pp.139-41. Husserl stresses that the life-world structure to which everything that exists relatively is bound, is not itself relative.
27. Ibid., pp.222-23.
28. Ricouer, op.cit., p.145.
29. Husserl, Logical Investigations, Vol II, p.540.
30. Husserl, Cartesian Meditations, p.75.
31. It may be said that Husserl's conception of history remains in the empiricist/continuist mode. Cf. Carr, op.cit., pp.80-81.
32. Paci, op.cit., p.278.
33. Ibid., p.279.
34. Husserl, Crisis (Biemel edition) 1954, p.497.
35. See Chapter Two, pp.43-45 above.
36. Marx, Introduction, p.189.
37. Luporini, Cesare, 'Reality and Historicity: Economy and Dialectics in Marxism', Economy and Society, Vol 4, Nos 2 and 3, 1975.
38. Ibid., p.71 and 202, Introduction to Luporini by Sassoon, P.
39. Luporini's modification is not made too successfully in my estimation.
40. Ibid., p.285.
41. Ibid.
42. Marx, Capital, p.148.
43. Carver, op.cit., pp.189-99. See also p.146 below.
44. Carr, op.cit., p.198 quoting Husserl's Cartesian Meditations, p.136.
45. Husserl, Crisis, p.131.
46. Carr, op.cit., p.263.

47. Ibid., pp.274-75.
48. Husserl, Crisis, p.17.
49. Heidegger, M., Being and Time, quoted in Colletti, L., Marxism and Hegel, New Left Books, London, 1973, p.173.
50. Paci, op.cit., p.126.
51. Ibid., p.91.
52. Spiegelberg, op.cit., Vol I, p.335.
53. Husserl, E., The Phenomenology of Internal Time Consciousness, ed. Heidegger, M., trans. Churchill, J.S., Martinus Nijhoff, The Hague, 1964.
54. Ibid., p.98ff.
55. Carr, op.cit., p.80.
56. The notion of sedimentation as the process of forming the substrata of consciousness is drawn from the same structural metaphor which displayed its limitations in Chapter Three. In Husserl's conceptualisation, however, it is presented as a perceptual synthesis rather than a static element of structure. The sediment forms the horizon of mental judgements achieved in cognition against which experience of the given is evaluated. See Carr, op. cit., p.108.
57. Merleau-Ponty, M., The Phenomenology of Perception, trans. Smith, C., Heinemann, London, 1974, The Primacy of Perception, Northwestern University Press, Evanston, 1964, Signs, Northwestern University Press, Evanston, 1969, The Prose of the World, Heinemann, London, 1974. These texts are particularly relevant here.
58. Paci, op.cit., p.206.
59. Ibid., p.208. Paci is referring generally to the normative attributes of language as a sedimented praxis and does not specify its uses as a means of social control or in the definition of the situation by ruling groups.
60. Ibid., p.214.
61. In particular The New Science (1744). On Vico's relevance for phenomenological Marxism see Paci, E., 'Vico, Structuralism and the Phenomenological Encyclopaedia of the Sciences', in Tagliocozzo, G. (ed.), Giambattista Vico: An International Symposium, Baltimore, 1969.
62. Capital, Vol I, p.367.
63. Vico, G., The Autobiography (1731), trans. Fisch, M.H. and Bergin, T.G., Cornell University Press, New York, 1944.
64. Paci, op.cit., p.6 and p.56.
65. Vico, op.cit., (1744), p.21.
66. Dallmayr in Psathsas, op.cit., p.344.

67. Carver, op.cit., p.189.
68. Langan, T., *Merleau-Ponty's Critique of Reason*, Yale University Press, New Haven, 1966. Like Sartre, he may be termed an existentialist phenomenologist or an existentialist Marxist. Ricoeur has referred to both theorists as 'situated at the confluence of the phenomenological method derived from Husserl and the existential problem-set received from post-Hegelian philosophy'. Ricoeur, op.cit., p.203. See also Mays, in Pivčević, op.cit., p.232.
69. Ibid., (my emphasis).
70. Husserl, *Logical Investigations*, Vol I, p.289ff.
71. Merleau-Ponty expounds the essence of this self-possession in *The Phenomenology of Perception*, op.cit.
72. Paci, op.cit., p.334.
73. Merleau-Ponty, M., *Adventures of the Dialectic*, 1955, trans. Bien, J., Heinemann, London, 1974, p.200.
74. Ibid., p.91.
75. Ibid., p.231.
76. O'Neill, J., Introduction to Merleau-Ponty, *Phenomenology, Language and Sociology*, Heinemann, London, 1974, p.liii.
77. Piccone, Introduction to Paci, op.cit., p.xxxii.
78. Sartre, J-P., *Critique of Dialectical Reason*, Pt. I, *Search for a Method*, trans. Barnes, H., Vintage Books, New York, 1968.
79. Sartre, J-P., *Being and Nothingness*, Methuen, London, 1966.
80. Sartre, J-P., *Nausea*, Penguin, London, 1965.
81. Sartre, op.cit. (1966), p.86ff.
82. Sartre, op.cit (1968), p.xxvii. Sartre gives this point added emphasis in a note to p.171. 'There is no question of denying the fundamental priority of need; on the contrary, we mention it last to indicate that it sums up in itself all the existential structures. In its full development, need is a transcendence and a negativity (negation of the negation insomuch as it is produced as a lack seeking to be denied), hence a surpassing-toward, (a rudimentary pro-ject)'.
83. Ibid., p.24.
84. Ibid., p.179.
85. Natanson, M., *A Critique of Jean-Paul Sartre's Ontology*, Martinus Nijhoff, The Hague, 1973.
86. Paci, op.cit (1972), pp.369-70.
87. Carr, op.cit., p.xxvii.
88. Husserl, *Crisis*, p.299.

89. Ibid., p.283.

Chapter Six

CONCLUSION: PHENOMENOLOGICAL MARXISM

In this concluding chapter I review the nature of the synthesis of Marxism and phenomenology, and reconsider aspects of the synthesising process in the other versions of Marxism already analysed. I propose criteria for a Husserlian Marxist synthesis, examining the scope of such a synthesis as a critical philosophical practice and indicating the directions in which it should be developed.
    Initially, my intention in writing this book was two-fold: to examine the theoretical synthesis as the construct which has typified the development of Marxist thought in the twentieth century, and to appraise the resultant versions of Marxism, in contrast with phenomenological Marxism. My interest in this field of study was provoked by the confusing nature of the various claims to 'correctness' found within the corpus of Marxist writings. My first conclusion was that the many efforts to present the truth of Marx displayed similar theoretical antagonisms; the debates appeared to range over the same set of theoretical constructs to the point of exhaustion or impasse. I set out to discover what was problematical in the various attempts to synthesise Marx's work with other frameworks of ideas.
    The proposed liaison of phenomenology and Marxism exemplified the difficulties in relating two disparate perspectives. Yet phenomenology offered the stimulus of a radical enquiry in so far as it demanded the examination of all presuppositions. The possibility of linking this branch of philosophy with Marxism was recognised by those existentialists for whom Husserl was the mentor. Sartre and Merleau-Ponty found textual confirmation of its potential in Marx's early texts. The theoretical consolidation of phenomenological Marxism was not achieved, however,

Conclusion: Phenomenological Marxism

until Paci's work developed out of his interpretations of the mature texts of Husserl and Marx. This approach was innovative in two respects: first, it opened up the possibility through the later texts of the rejection of idealist and humanistic interpretations of Marx; secondly, it required the rethinking of the concept of a Marxist science, since phenomenology calls the status of science into question.

Husserl's mature writings culminated in a critique of positivism as scientism and a claim for phenomenology to be recognised as a rigorous analysis - a science of sciences. One measure of the claim that phenomenology is sufficiently radical for theoretical compatibility with Marxism lies in the strength of its claim to scientificity. We find that the concept of a science is greatly broadened in Husserl's phenomenology. It is developed as a radical analysis and mode of understanding opposed to all forms of scientism. Husserl identifies the crisis as the result of faith in a science which has lost its purpose and direction. From a Marxist standpoint, Merleau-Ponty expresses a parallel concern: '... the fetishism of science has always made its appearance where the revolutionary conscience was faltering'.(1)

The Nature of the Synthesis

The foundational question of my enquiry has been: what do we mean by a theoretical synthesis? In the first chapter I concluded that in seeking points of coalescence between two discrete frameworks of thought certain levels of analysis can be used to establish the degree of compatibility. These are identifiable by the kinds of question they allow us to pose. While I have attempted to deal with questions of logic, epistemology, methodology and ontology, it has not always been feasible or appropriate to apply them schematically. The discussion of the question of history has demonstrated the need for these criteria to be applied with flexibility of emphasis. For instance, it may be argued that an assertion of the irreversibility of historical experience is either logically tautologous or solely ontological. Yet Husserl argues that this is an informative statement about the world; he gives a synthetic a priori status to his historical a priori. Similarly, the assertion as to the subjectivity of all experience

Conclusion: Phenomenological Marxism

has required discussion at several levels to demonstrate that the proposition is informative and not merely reductive.

The question has arisen as to the relative importance of the levels of analysis. We have seen that both Marx and Husserl attested to the radical nature of their philosophical enquiries by their insistence on concrete experience as foundational. There is unquestionably a common basis in the historicality of both the subject (man in history) and the subject's experience (man operating within and upon history). While a significant case has been made for an ontology which could be interpreted as compatible with a Marxist ontology, it must be restated that the ontological is not the paramount level of enquiry in Husserl, not even in the final phases of his work where he extends the scope of this enquiry to the life-world. (Had this been the case, we might expect further exposition on the nature of the life-world.) Husserl's enquiries remain anchored in epistemological problems. After *Crisis* he returns to the study of logic and language, resuming in **Experience and Judgement** his search for a presuppositionless philosophy. The overriding concern here is with the structure of cognitive experience. In the case of the proposed synthesis of Marxism and phenomenology, it is evident that epistemological compatibility should be established as the primary task. As to the ontological, logical and methodological aspects, it has been concluded that these can only be rendered compatible by a considerable reinterpretation of each framework.

The synthesis was initially defined as a mode of theorising. This term was intended to convey its dynamic nature as an interplay of constructs, a dialectical process entailing critical self-reflection. The merits of this synthetical mode were set against the stasis and reification which beset orthodox theoretical approaches. This notion of synthesis does not appear to be accepted unequivocally by phenomenological Marxists. Piccone has voiced opposition to the idea that a synthesis can be successfully achieved:

> Efforts to reconcile phenomenology and Marxism often take the form of a synthesis, and this is precisely what is wrong with them. Mechanistically contraposed as self-contained entities, they are from the very start condemned to failure, since what results is

Conclusion: Phenomenological Marxism

> the shotgun marriage of two ideologies unable to accommodate each other. Only by seeing Marxism as the outcome of phenomenology and phenomenology as an inextricable moment of Marxism can one attain any sort of reconciliation which simultaneously produces a more relevant phenomenology and a non-dogmatic Marxism. (2)

Piccone is opting for a relationship of complementarity here. While I agree that a 'mechanistically contraposed' alliance is unacceptable, I do not believe that a dialectical synthesis is impossible where the theoretical elements are contraposed, re-evaluated, demonstrated as compatible and then reintegrated. The suggestion that Paci has offered a dialectical solution to this problem is given greater weight in the rest of Piccone's introduction to <u>Function of the Sciences</u>. However, I am not convinced that to characterise phenomenology as a moment of Marxism, and Marxism as the logical outcome of phenomenology, adequately conveys the nature of Paci's endeavour or offers the correct theoretical basis for a revised Marxism. Though I agree with Piccone that a forced synthesis of 'mechanistically contraposed' elements should be rejected, I do not see his solution to the problem of relating Marx and Husserl as satisfactory.

I have taken the position that a synthesis, as a dialectical mode of theorising, is a valid and discrete theoretical construct. The problems which arise are mainly over how to assess and demonstrate the achievement of an acceptable synthesis. By examining the levels at which a synthesis should be demonstrated, and in attempting to develop criteria by which it can be judged on those levels, I have adduced the degree of its success or failure. If no synthesis of Marxism and phenomenology is achieved, we are indeed left with 'two ideologies' which relate to each other either as an ineffective juxtaposition or as a dogmatic Marxism which appends phenomenology as a methodology and nothing more. We can only achieve a revitalised critique, with the irrefutable certitude and authority of a 'first philosophy', if a correct synthesis can be established.

The criticism of other versions of Marxism under discussion has been made on the basis of their inadequacy as synthesis. My assessment was made using orthodox criteria not merely because these are the standard constructs employed in meta-theoretical

Conclusion: Phenomenological Marxism

analysis but because there is a need for a more rigorous enquiry than that found in most expositions of Marxist theory and accounts of phenomenological Marxism. While standard criteria have been used, these have been themselves subject to assessment as appropriate modes of analysis and evaluation. Questions concerning logic, epistemology, ontology and methodology have been raised in evaluating the degree of compatibility within the four syntheses. These criteria have not been applied in a systematic analysis but have received a discursive treatment in the preceding chapters. It is now appropriate for me to offer a more schematic conclusion through a comparative assessment which follows the lines of the original proposal.

This review of the four levels of analysis begins with logic, which I have taken to refer to the structure, cohesion and rationality of each theoretical liaison. I have tried to gauge whether the various frameworks are resistant to the synthetical process.

I conclude that Hegelian Marxism displays a basic inconsistency. The Absolute Idealism of Hegel is a metaphysics which, though it claims to deal with concrete human experience and to present the logic of human history, remains a coherent idealist system. Given Marx's rejection of metaphysics, the rational principle for reconciling Marx and Hegel is lacking. The Hegelian Marxists attempt to overcome this by making a radical reinterpretation. They abstract elements of Hegel's doctrines which they believe will accord with Marx's materialist basis. Lukács' emphasis on the proletariat as the potential subject/object of history is a case in point. Kojève's concentration on the master/slave dialectic is a further instance of the attempt to interpret Hegelian ideas materialistically. Such conceptions draw upon Hegel's idea of dialectic operating in history, where the subjective/objective aspects of the world become resolved in the process of history towards the attainment of the spiritual. But the problems of concretizing the analysis, which developed out of Hegel's objective idealism towards a dialectical logic of history, are not overcome by the Hegelian Marxists. We are left with an unacceptable metaphysical materialism.

Structuralist Marxism is also founded on logical principles which I find incompatible with Marxism. I have argued that the structuralist perspective, the theoretical basis of this liaison, is fundamentally idealist. The logical strength of

Conclusion: Phenomenological Marxism

the structural Marxism position is claimed to be its coherence as a structure and system. But this insistence on logical cohesiveness identifies it as a system which bears a resemblance, as a mirror image, to the Hegelian schema. The scientific emphasis on the principle of structural causality introduces a deterministic logic into the explanation of history, where human subjects act as bearers of that history. To propose a mechanistic system as a science of sciences is to present a neo-positivist version of Marxism. The paradigm of scientificity applied to Marxism is drawn from the emergence of the natural sciences. Though this aims to elucidate their ideological precursors, there is no logical transition from this analysis to a more fundamental disocclusion. Within the system of structuralist Marxism it is logically inconsistent to eliminate the producing subject and to seek the motor of history within the structure itself.

Though the existentialist Marxists contribute innovative versions of Husserlian ideas to a synthesis with Marxism, there remains a logical inconsistency in their reliance on branches of idealist theory. Their approach is eclectic to an unacceptable extent, in drawing from Hegelian sources notions of the totality and the alienated consciousness which are anthropocentric and relativistic. Eventually, the logic which informs Merleau-Ponty's writing falls into ambiguity and becomes, therefore, a dialectical illogic or, perhaps more accurately, an abandonment of the dialectic altogether. Sartre's logical basis is more consistently adhered to. Sartre draws on Hegelian ideas but theorises them in conjunction with ideas from Heidegger and Husserl. The transition to a materialistically based analysis is accomplished through a logic of praxis. Where there is a logical inconsistency in Sartre it is his insistence that individual existence is in a perpetual state of struggle which appears as an ontology unresolvable in the terms of the dialectic of history.

The logic of the case for phenomenological Marxism is grounded in the dialectical structure of the temporal and historical situation as it is subjectively experienced. By basing the analysis in subjectivity and intersubjectivity, a logical principle is introduced to supersede the dualistic logic of science. As Paci says, 'the science of the life-world is not knowledge of an objectified object-in-itself, but the act of becoming conscious of the temporal and historical situation'.(3) The

Conclusion: Phenomenological Marxism

critique of the sciences which makes Husserl compatible with Marx is opposed to 'dualistic metaphysics'. It offers a new conception of science as '... the logos and meaning of truth in the temporal dialectic and in the constitutive operations that progressively reveal the meaning of the world and of history'.(4) The logical basis for discovering the truth is lived experience for both Marx and Husserl. A logic of experience, perceived as a dialectical struggle for truth, allows empirical and rational analysis to proceed complementarily. A case can thus be made for phenomenological Marxism as a rational science.

Epistemology deals with the nature and scope of conceptualisation and the meaning and truth of propositions. A synthesis of Marxism and any other perspective would require a high degree of epistemological compatibility. An initial problem is to identify the epistemology which is basic to Marx, since his work has received so many interpretations. For this purpose I have been guided by Paci who concentrates on the major tests of Marx and Husserl as those texts representing their mature reflection and the refinement of their epistemological frameworks. Other attempts at synthesis give more prominence to the early writings of Marx, or attach significance to the 'break' between phases of Marx's development. I conclude that it is possible to attain more than an asymptotic relationship of concepts and categories despite the differences of tradition and the innovations of the various perspectives under discussion. In an examination of its epistemology, therefore, the synthesis should demonstrate its character as a duologue.

The Hegelian Marxist position, as exemplified by Lukács, focuses on the early Marx, so producing an idealist, anthropocentric version. Lukács' synthesis emphasises revolutionary praxis but 'romanticizes' the proletariat as the dialectical resolution of an epistemological impasse, the subject/object dichotomy. Importance is given to Hegel's anti-Kantian dictum that knowledge of the real is possible. This is in order to make a concrete analysis compatible with Marx. Therefore, as Lichtheim points out, Lukács' materialism becomes an epistemological realism, the abstractness of which stems from its idealist base.(5) Hegelian Marxism attaches great importance to the construct of the totality which is, a priori, the matrix of the Hegelian system. The problems engendered by this concept make it unacceptable as a basis for synthesis

Conclusion: Phenomenological Marxism

with Marx without considerable revision.
     Structuralist Marxism presents an epistemology which, in many respects, duplicates the problems of the Hegelian schema. The basic tenet of this perspective is the concept of Marxism as the science of sciences. To achieve a Marxist science, Althusser has drawn a sharp distinction between science and ideology, mirroring the objectivism of the natural sciences. The consequent elimination of the subject is, however, difficult to substantiate, based as it is on a structuralist principle which cannot be accepted as a concrete analysis. This position is as an idealist metaphysics, or a metaphysical materialism, by its assertion of reality as the concrete-in-thought.
     The epistemology of the existentialist Marxist synthesis is mainly drawn from an amalgam of Hegelian and Husserlian constructs. The concepts with which Sartre explains the structure of consciousness originate in Hegel. The dialectical resolution of these structures is sought through the concept of becoming, in a phenomenological interpretation developed from Heidegger. Sartre retains the Husserlian notion of intentionality in his conception of the individual self and the project. The praxis of the subject and the group is directed towards the telos, the basis of which remains the emancipation of the individual within history. Merleau-Ponty's emphasis on subjectivity as the basis of all conceptualisation is drawn from Husserl. He contributes to the theory of consciousness as historically-situated, which is significant for phenomenological Marxism also.
     Phenomenological Marxism rejects many traditional dichotomies in its critique of misleading and irrelevant epistemologies. Since the basis of truth and meaning in this perspective is subjectivity, the dualism of subject and object is bracketed by Husserl. Subjectivity does not imply relativism as it does in the natural attitude of the positive sciences, but is transformed into an a priori principle of cognition. Husserl explains knowledge as the achieved synthesis of an actively constituting consciousness. For Marxism, Husserl's transition to intersubjectivity provides a basis for an epistemology reflecting the community of subjects. Science cannot, therefore, be set apart from this community and its interests. Science and ideology are not separate areas, or applications, of human knowledge. Thus the critique of science recognises that, not only in its application but also in its

Conclusion: Phenomenological Marxism

conceptual structure, science is ideologically engaged. The science/ideology disjunction is refuted by phenomenological Marxism as a pseudo-problem. The subject/object distinction is negated by the overall subjectivity in phenomenology. Where a subject has apperception of an object it is because this is 'given' to consciousness and then constituted from particulars available to experience. This process differs from that described by subjective idealism, where the object is constituted in the sense of being created by consciousness.

The syntheses which I have reviewed give varying importance to the ontological aspects of their systems of ideas. Ontological problems concern the description of entities, their modes of being and questions of their 'real' existence and appearance. The study of existence in the sense of metaphysical 'being' is an issue only for the existentialist Marxists and is, perhaps, only incidental to their central material ontology.

The Hegelian Marxists tend to give primacy to ontology, since the central concept of the totality involves definitions of being-in-the-world. Lukacs develops an ontology of social being, which is central to his understanding of Marx. His analysis of social existence and alienation is, however, humanistic and relativistic. His ontological stance in the early Marxian texts was adopted in order to revitalise a moribund orthodoxy. Marx's position in the later texts was a rejection of the early ontology which, though it was anti-Hegelian in intent, had failed to remove certain crucial residues of Hegelian thought. Lukács' ontology of labour is a Hegelian residue, one which surfaces in Paci's work and which I reject since it is a construct that hypostatises the dignity of labour and presents an unacceptable anthropocentrism.

The ontological priority in structuralist Marxism is given to the structure itself. The structuralist basis of this perspective negates the constituting consciousness of the human subject and thus the ontology of human being. It postulates the reality of theoretical entities as the real-in-thought, an idealist construction. The mechanisms of the structure are perceived as real in their effects on historical occurrence. It is evidence that this attempted synthesis draws on Hegelian concepts in its ontology, though the emphasis is on Marx's scientific revision of Hegel. The Hegelian ontology of the origin and its negation (being = nothingness)

Conclusion: Phenomenological Marxism

is interpreted as the subject negated in the dialectic of history, a supposition that is theorised to accord with the structuralist approach.

The existentialist Marxist synthesis draws upon both the Hegelian and Husserlian frameworks for its ontological basis. In Merleau-Ponty and Sartre the human being is characterised dialectically as a becoming. Sartre's early work makes an analysis of the monadic subject striving for a Heideggerian authenticity when faced with the negativity of existents. Merleau-Ponty characterises being as a perceptual synthesis, the individual as a body-subject. In Sartre's later work, ideas of the subject's existence as a member of the group and the community gives a structural strength and relevance to his writings on the Marxist struggle. His ontology of scarcity and need appears to derive from Marx's socio-economic analysis. However, it stems originally from the Hegelian conception of a lack as the fundamental expression of existence. To translate this notion into an economistic conception of scarcity is inappropriate. It can be argued that scarcity is a social effect of capitalist organisation. This is all too evident in recent years where the concomitant of the production of the surplus is scarcity 'management'.

The ontology of the phenomenological Marxist position is centred on Husserl's life-world construct. This is the key to his radical analysis of society, language and history, providing the basis for a synthesis with Marx. The claim is that the life-world is the shared domain of the human community, an equivalent to the base in Marx's structural analysis. It is, a priori, a sphere of preconceptual experience which is universalised. Closely related to this is an ontology of the human subject as a lived body experiencing irreversibility and need. Conceptions of man as embodied labour or scarcity are unacceptable. Paci stresses the ontology of need as more consistent with Husserl's notion of the reasons for crisis and Marx's concept of the unfulfilled condition of human existence. I am in agreement here, though the concept of need is problematical.

The ontology of the life-world is linked with Husserl's subjective ontology through the concrete material basis of both. Husserl posits a notion of the concrete basis of cognition. He presents this as a non-formal material a priori accessible to experience. This is the basis of the life-world, which is a pre-conceptual, pre-predicative sphere of

Conclusion: Phenomenological Marxism

intersubjectivity, apprehended empirically but not as an idealist concrete-in-thought. The question of whether the ontology of the life-world could be synthesised with a reformulated concept of the totality as a 'lived totality' has been raised. Though rejected on grounds of its idealist connotations, there is no reason why it should not be considered to be transformed in this sense as one explication of the life-world concept.

We come finally to the question of methodology in the synthesis under discussion. Each synthesis should demonstrate a measure of compatibility in the procedures and organising principles of its enquiries, despite the disparate traditions brought together. In method and principles Marxist theory is radical and scientific. The nature of this scientificity will determine the appropriateness of the methodology.

The methodology of Hegelian Marxism is critical and reflexive, but its analysis of the socio-economic structure is historicist and consequently relativistic. As I have already argued, the basis of this position is idealist. In Lukács' work we find a reflexive methodology which is unable to supply a concrete analysis, though it claims to be a materialist analysis of history and to offer the unification of theory and practice. Although Lukács claimed that his later revised analysis was materialist in essence, it appears to be a revision of Hegel's method and dialectic.

Structuralist Marxism attempts an anti-historicist, anti-humanistic liaison of structuralist theories and Marxist science. Its methodology is descriptive of a process without a subject, taking the form of an analysis of the structure, and of those aspects which are dominant at a particular historical conjuncture. The emphasis is on the process of the production of scientific ideas and the generative mechanisms of the system. The analysis of historical events is undertaken to discover the effects of the structure.

Existentialist Marxism examines history and consciousness through a reflexive methodology. Consciousness is taken to be historically situated and dialectically structured. Aspects of phenomenological method are used in the disocclusion of the structures of language and perception as the means of grasping the possibilities of concrete existence. A historico-genetic method is applied to the understanding of the individual in society, though in Sartre this methodology bears a

Conclusion: Phenomenological Marxism

resemblance to psychoanalytic enquiry. Merleau-Ponty's emphasis on the processes of phenomenological perception. However, we find no epochē comparable with Husserl's. We need to ask, therefore, if his methodology can provide a radical investigation of the essential structures of consciousness. In Sartre, the transposition of the concept of the totality into a process of totalisation is an attempt to de-reify this problematical concept. Interestingly it appears to reverse the positivist tendency of ontologising a methodology. Sartre's solution can alternatively be viewed as both an ontological construct and a method.

Phenomenological Marxism uses a historico-genetic methodology which was developed as a radical critical analysis in Husserl. This methodology is compatible with Marx's concrete analysis in its power to disocclude, through the epochē, the ideological barriers to understanding. The reduction allows the reflexive examination of the contents of consciousness. By bracketing naturalistic assumptions we can attain an understanding of concept formation and of how the 'objects' of those concepts are given to consciousness and constituted. This provides a methodology by which to discover how language and thought become repositories of truth or ideology. Paci claims that this methodology is used by Marx, particularly demonstrated by the analysis of commodity fetishism and the labour theory of value. It is also arguable that this methodology is the habitual practice of philosophers and scientists. Yet Husserl's phenomenology is not merely a methodology but a critical attitude. It is this radical awareness that Husserl finds lacking in philosophical practice. Phenomenological Marxism extends this attitude to a critique of society in crisis.

After considering the four levels of analysis and their disparities, we have some picture of the inconsistencies which make any synthesis difficult to establish. I find that there are differences in theoretical emphasis attaching to the levels of analysis. Hegelian and existentialist Marxism display a primacy of emphasis on the ontological. For structuralist Marxism the logical and epistemological aspects take priority. Paci's phenomenological Marxism tends to emphasise ontology but, in my view, a synthesis with Husserl requires an epistemological emphasis. I conclude, therefore, that the interplay of constructs in a valid synthesis must display

Conclusion: Phenomenological Marxism

compatibility at the level of epistemology as a prime requirement. I have tried to demonstrate that the other attempts at synthesis fall short of what is necessary for a duological relationship.

In discussing possible frameworks of compatible ideas I have rejected the eclecticism which is to be found in certain theorists, as this tends to weaken the conjunction of two perspectives. Being dialectical in operation, a synthesis can allow two perspectives to inform and illuminate each other, but only, I contend, where there is demonstrably common ground on the basic points I have indicated.

The analysis demonstrates that phenomenology and Marxism in their synthetical relationship are able to supply theoretical constructs which each lacks. Marxism is beset by problematic antimonies which present obstacles for its theoretical validity. It lacks a theory of the structure of consciousness which phenomenology can supply in characterising consciousness in the mode of intentionality. This makes possible a theory of rational choice and decision-making towards the telos. Phenomenology lacks a concrete societal analysis, though an embryonic social analysis can be claimed in Husserl's presentation of the crisis of the sciences and his turn to history. A synthesis of phenomenology and Marxism can be developed into a more effective critique of science and the crisis of capitalism, in reasserting the telos, and in ensuring that theoretical inertia and mystification do not impede praxis.

Phenomenological Marxism - the Contribution of Enzo Paci

Having made a comparative assessment of phenomenological Marxism, I now summarise what I consider to be the main lines of argument in Paci's attempted synthesis and evaluate these in the light of his critics. In this way I hope to indicate the main problems for a phenomenological Marxism and to suggest possible solutions.

We have seen that Paci takes as basic to the task of reconciling phenomenology and Marxism the return to subjectivity, the denunciation of scientism and the recognition of a new scientificity. The crisis in the sciences is that their true character - the open-ended and non-dogmatic enquiry after truth - has been occluded by positivism. Truth has been reduced to facticity, and science no longer

Conclusion: Phenomenological Marxism

functions as a 'philosophical kind of existence',(6) liberating and ethically reconstituting humanity in political and social life. Husserl sees phenomenology as the means of redressing the position and restoring man's subjectivity to him, for it offers a rigorous, rationally-based philosophy of science. This project is grounded in Husserl's view of the historical role of the sciences: to struggle against occlusion, to pursue rationality and to progress according to a telos of permanent and perfectible values. It is to ground the sciences transcendentally and lead them back to their teleological and rational function '... as branches of one science, of philosophy understood as "the new science"'.(7)

Crisis presents a universal task for phenomenology in establishing the direction for the development of the European science and civilisation. Marxism also has a universal task in transforming society. Paci turns to *Capital*, claiming to find in it themes commensurate with phenomenology. He argues that 'the most profound and most authentic aspects of Marx's work' are the concepts of the critique of political economy.(8) Marx's critique has a paradigmatic character in revealing the process of objectification in the sciences and in societal relations. But, as already indicated, it is not theoretically sound for Paci to proceed towards a synthesis by assertion or hermeneutics, merely achieving a reconstructed phenomenology or a critical Marxism. Paci's enterprise must be evaluated by his ability to produce a genuine theoretical rapprochement and to avoid a forced synthesis. The task is to find a basis for the articulation of the two frameworks. I have isolated several lines of connection by which his work proceeds: the methodology of the dialectic, the notion of a common ontology, the relationship of theory to practice and the establishing of a common telos. Certain problems in Paci's work centre upon these concepts.

The generally accepted view of phenomenology is as a search for a horizon of truth, a telos to be achieved by the process of transcendental reduction. What are set aside, or bracketed, are the objectified forms which occlude the truth to consciousness. This process is usually read as non-dialectical, a stripping-away of occlusions to reach a true essence, rather than a progression towards truth via antithetical concepts. If we regard phenomenology as a theory of cognition only, it

Conclusion: Phenomenological Marxism

would appear that Paci gives a misreading of Husserl. The constituting consciousness builds up the meaning of the world not by a dialectical progression but piecemeal. But Paci considers that, by extending phenomenology through concepts of intersubjectivity and the historical reduction, Husserl demonstrates a dialectical mode in consciousness. Paci conceives this dialectic in terms of the interconnections in the processes of cognition and of social life. This is difficult to establish, though Paci strengthens his case by characterising the task of disocclusion as a dialectic of the hidden and the revealed.

The problem of the dialectic is linked with that of relating theory and praxis. Paci insists that the dialectic is concretised in human experience: 'if there are a formal logic and totality, there must be a totality of meaning of the dialectic and a direction of truth of all groups and struggling communities.'(9) Paci appears to derive this proposition from Husserl's assertion that philosophy (theory) is 'a praxis of philosophers in the society of scientists' which unites them 'with practically struggling men and the human socialities <u>in the world</u>'.(10) Schmueli comments that Paci is grounding his argument in social theory rather than philosophy by collapsing theory into praxis. The subject is no longer transcendental, but sociological and political since the dialectic is present in the struggle of groups with the negation of the negation to be performed by the proletariat.(11) Against Schmueli, I have argued that Husserl's work demonstrates a transition away from the transcendental to a historically-situated consciousness. This is essential, as Paci realises, for establishing a synthesis with Marxism.

Paci interprets Husserl's final position as a scientific praxis which is both the theoretical foundation of phenomenological description of the world and the means of transforming the world. But this can only be accomplished in conjunction with the Marxist project. Having conflated theory and praxis, Paci goes on to distinguish mundane praxis (an occluding self-interest) from disoccluded praxis, free of the mundane, of fetishism and open to the telos. But, as Schmueli argues, this is what Husserl claims for the operation of theory, implying that Paci distorts Husserl's use of the terms. He seems to be arguing that theory and practice should be separated. Yet Husserl's distinction of theory from praxis does not exclude the possibility of a synthesis and we should regard this as a valid

Conclusion: Phenomenological Marxism

theoretical practice. The Marxist synthesis must be safeguarded from elitist disjunctions of theorist and practitioner. Husserl defines philosophical theory as 'the science of the totality of what is' which can only be achieved through phenomenology.(12) Praxis is given two distinct aspects: first, scientific, dogmatically-based praxis operating like logic, and second, praxis based on transcendental reflection - 'the motif of enquiring back into the ultimate source of the formations of all knowledge, the motif of the knower's reflecting upon himself and his knowing life...'(13) Husserl's concept of theory has ethical implications for science since, by abandoning the ideal of true theory, the scientist had lost insight into the true nature of the world. For Husserl, the telos of the new praxis is nothing less than the transformation of mankind into 'a new humanity made capable of an absolute self-responsibility on the basis of absolute theoretical insight'. When this occurs it will be 'the highest synthesis of theory and practice'.(14) In this sense Husserl unites theory and practice. Paci extends this idea to a conflation of social theory and praxis on the basis of Husserl's teleological implications for a phenomenological Marxism. Marx's vital contribution is in opening up the possibility of other praxes towards the same goal.

Paci also finds in Husserl's phenomenology its definite implications for Marxism via a common telos and a universal community:

> The unity of spiritual life is the intentional-historical meaning which is maintained in the totality of ... real men who in their dialectic tend toward an open meaningful synthesis, toward the meaning of truth that dialectically develops in the clashes and encounters of men and cultures.(15)

Paci reasserts the discovery of a dialectic in Husserl, which renders his work valid as a continuing critique of objectivist scientific dogma, a scientism that reduces the dialectic of history to a naturalistic struggle for survival.

In his exposition of dialectic as a point of synthesis for Marx and Husserl, Paci stresses the primacy of the teleological. The dialectic of political praxis in Marx is the class struggle. To parallel this, Paci claims the intermonadic relationship to be the sphere of political praxis.

Conclusion: Phenomenological Marxism

The struggle of humanity is towards a common telos, towards the meaning of man and the fulfilment of human needs. For Paci, this rests on an ontological presupposition which he again finds common to Husserl and Marx. Leading out of Paci's discussion of the dialectic, and concomitant with it, is a notion of human nature. Thus an ontology is implied even before it is made explicit with his reading of Capital. What Paci is basically asserting is that if it can be established that phenomenology is ontological then the convergence of the two approaches is inevitable. As Dallmayr puts it:

> Both the Crisis and Marx's analysis of the capitalist economy (Paci argues) are critical efforts designed to rescue human experience from reification and estrangement. Once the life-world is interpreted as incorporating the level of basic needs and of material production, phenomenology and Marxism are destined to converge. (16)

But how far is Paci justified in reading a common ontological basis into Husserl and Marx? To render the ontology underlying Capital consonant with Husserl's, he must find in Husserl's 'world of human operations' a world of materiality and, more specifically, a world where needs can be taken as a precategorical foundation upon which everything depends. If Paci can establish the life-world as a world of needs which are to be satisfied by man's labour this will make the vital connection with Marx's analysis. Paci finds a basis for the assumption by arguing that both Crisis and Capital are efforts to rescue man from reification and estrangement, and to restore him to himself. Before reviewing this aspect of Paci's thought, it would be useful to recapitulate the nature of the ontological and its place in Husserl's development.

Ontology is traditionally the study of being, of proofs of the existence of God, mind and matter. With the rise of rationalism and empiricism, ontology was dispersed into the spheres of logic and epistemology. Central questions became those dealing with knowledge of existence. From Husserl's early work on the basis of logic and its presuppositions, he evolved concepts to describe its fundamental aspects - apophantic logic, a logic of judgement, and formal ontology, an a priori science concerned with objects in general.

Conclusion: Phenomenological Marxism

With its emphasis on origin and meaning, phenomenological enquiry prepared the way for a new ontology as a fundamental tenet. According to Pivčević,(17) phenomenology is an ontology. For Paci, however, the posing question enables him to explore aspects of Husserl vital to his proposed synthesis. The basis of this is to be found in an ontology of the life-world.

Husserl's phenomenology developed into a critique of the sciences with the intention of founding a new science grounded in the life-world. Its scientificity is grounded in the capacity of consciousness to illuminate what is hidden in precategorical life. Thus Husserl postulates an a priori of the Lebenswelt from which the objective a priori of science is in turn derived:

> Husserl considers it a fundamental result of phenomenology that the Lebenswelt must precede and found the a priori of the sciences. The precategorical a priori must in turn be explained by a special 'new science'. Only this science, phenomenology, can really ground the objective sciences on an authentic scientific basis. The same can be said of logic. The science of the Lebenswelt is the foundation of logic on the universal a priori.(18)

The ontology of the life-world is an extension of Husserl's ontological principle that unrelated things are transformed into relations, thus grasping the presence of a universal horizon:

> ...the ontology that reveals the essence of the spatio-temporal onta is the progressive explication of the horizon of truth of the world that is implicit in every reality and finite individuation. In the ultimate analysis, this is phenomenological relationism. So understood, ontology is, tout court, phenomenology. Therefore, in order to be sustained, it does not need a fictitious ontology in either the traditional or the Heideggerian sense, because it has arisen precisely in order to overcome the fetishization of being.(19)

In this way Paci asserts that phenomenology is ontological, scientific, and dialectical in its revelation of truth. He considers this to be a basis of conceptual equivalence from which to build a

Conclusion: Phenomenological Marxism

genuine synthesis with Marxism. These ideas must be articulated with Marx's ontology, which changes character as his work develops.

Central to Marx's early position is the notion of man under capitalism alienated from his true human potential. The basis of this anthropology is specified as an ontology of needs, concrete material needs for food, shelter, survival. Man is dignified by the labour he undertakes to fulfil these needs. In Marx's mature work the focus shifts to an analysis of the capitalist mode of production. Man's needs are here interpreted as the means of subsistence, that which the capitalist must provide as part of variable capital necessary to sustain the labour force and facilitate the reproduction of the means of production. Needs evolve and are articulated at the ideological level in commodity fetishism – a total enslavement, since man is himself given a commodity status. Paci reads into <u>Capital</u> an ontology of need which hypothesizes labour as endemic to humanity as a basic need, a point on which I disagree with his analysis.

A major difficulty confronting Paci is not the problem of ontologizing Marx, but that of establishing need as Husserl's precategorical foundation in such a way that it is compatible with Marx. The difficulty lies in Husserl's lack of explicitness as to the nature of the precategorical world. Though he sees this as a world of human operations: 'Husserl never dealt with the problem of relating the sphere of needs and satisfactions and the conditioning, precategorical sphere, nor did he treat phenomenology of needs experienced and lived in the first person.'(20) Commenting upon this, Piccone states that Paci regards Husserl's analysis as truncated. The task is to extend Husserl so that the crisis is given its correct source in Marx's critique. Husserl gave the root of the crisis as philosophy's failure to retain the telos which had guided western culture up to the Renaissance, but he does not state why at this particular period, the telos was lost:

> Here Husserl would have had to give an intersubjective, ie. social, explanation of the historical event of forgetting, or of the birth of the Enlightenment. At this point a developed phenomenology coheres with Marxism as a dialectical account of how men make themselves and their institutions in the laboring process. This is the same process that the knowledge

Conclusion: Phenomenological Marxism

> examined by phenomenology was supposed to
> mediate. Hence, phenomenology as a whole can
> already be found <u>within</u> Marxism as a necessary
> and essential moment of the whole structure,
> and the crisis of the sciences can be seen as a
> special case of the capitalist crisis.(21)

I agree with Piccone that Paci's major contribution is in identifying the crisis in these terms. But there remains the problem of reconciling the life-world, unspecified by Husserl in concrete terms, with the world of material needs in the critique of political economy in order to claim a common ontology. In his paper on the Frankfurt School, Rovatti considers its rejection of an ontology of need on the grounds of ideological subjectivity – 'each time a "model" of need is solidified it is destined to become the ideological prop for a fetishized praxis'.(22) He finds in Marcuse the constant theme of the need for freedom and fulfilment. In Adorno, the philosophical need for consolidation leads to a naturalistic standpoint. In Marx, Rovatti finds the concept of need to be also naturalistically-based; its ideology lies in the hypostatisation of need as a classical ideological component of political economy. But this criticism would be difficult to sustain against Paci's analysis, since phenomenological Marxism is grounded in the scientificity of Husserl and Marx, a case which I believe is fully demonstrated:

> ...Marxism is, in principle, not an ideology but
> a critique of ideologies... In phenomenological
> language, the sciences must be brought back to
> the subject and to the world of precategorical
> life. Science must be <u>grounded</u> in a philosophy
> which is not an ideology.(23)

Towards Husserlian Marxism

In this concluding section it seems relevant to consider how the term 'phenomenological Marxism' reflects the relationship of the two branches of philosophy. This term has been adopted without fully questioning its adequacy to convey the equivalence of the perspectives in the synthesis. The term 'Marxist phenomenology' reproduces the problem. To reflect the themes of this book it would be appropriate to adopt the term 'Husserlian Marxism'. This would distinguish our discussion from other

Conclusion: Phenomenological Marxism

attempts to establish a phenomenological Marxism, which we have seen to be a spectrum of theoretical opinion. It would also focus attention on the two main theorists in a relationship of greater equivalence, in the same way as Hegelian Marxism centres attention on Hegel's significance. Though there is no direct historical connection to be reflected in the case of Husserl and Marx, it is to their theoretical integration that the term 'Husserlian Marxism' would give prominence.

It is evident that in synthesising Marx and Husserl, teleology assumes great importance. Though Husserl stated the telos in general terms only and did not develop a political analysis, there are indications in <u>Crisis</u> that are of a sufficiently programmatic nature to suggest that praxis towards the telos would involve a) an end to exploitation and oppression, and b) collective decision-making as to the direction for scientific and technological advance.

While not made explicit, we know that Husserl's personal experience of oppression is reflected in <u>Crisis</u>. He expresses profound desolation at the loss of human dignity and high purpose in the European heritage. His aspirations for humanity are in accord with Marx's revolutionary task, to end oppressive systems and the ideologies which distort human potentiality. Paci's phenomenological Marxism emphasises ethical and spiritual reconstruction, reflecting the Hegelian influence in his work. Husserlian Marxism, while drawing on Paci's ideas, would reject his eclecticism in looking to Hegel for an ethical and spiritual 'completion' of Marxism. A problem for Paci's perspective is for it to avoid becoming a theory of ethics. The pursuit of the telos, a goal-oriented liberating praxis, inevitably involves questions of what human life ought to be. But any specific view would be difficult to reconcile with the Marxian idea that a post-revolutionary future cannot be delineated in terms of present conditions.

Paci's solution is to emphasise human need as the guiding teleological principle, but this is not easy to substantiate. Beyond the basic needs for survival, biological and social, how is need to be determined? Do we think in terms of physical, emotional or spiritual fulfilment? Such a broad definition seems of little use in initiating praxis. Yet with more detailed specification there is a problem of relativism to be answered. Needs can be and are stimulated, manipulated and distorted

Conclusions: Phenomenological Marxism

through the dominant ideology in any culture. Even the basic need to survive may be overruled where altruism or despair prevails, and debates over absolute and relative levels of deprivation continue. The capitalist system requires a vast apparatus for demand creation, engendering needs which further stimulate acquisition through technological advances. The servitude which the system enforces on all is the price of its 'success' in Husserl's estimation, as it is in Marx's. In a period of late capitalism we see an increasing exaggeration of these tendencies. The overall contradiction is that the logic of a rational system is revealed as an illogic; rationality has become irrationality.

The theme that only a new order can restore reason is expressed in both Marx and Husserl. But Schmueli, in criticising Paci, finds Husserl's vision incompatible with Marx's:

> Is Husserl's philosophy complementary to Marxism in the sense of adding a new dimension - namely the emphasis upon transcendental subjectivity - for a theory of knowledge and for a comprehensive ontology? It is difficult to acknowledge that such a theory can be related to Marxism, except by a misinterpretation of both systems.(24)

I have tried to demonstrate that this criticism is a characteristic misreading of the complementarity of Marx and Husserl. Furthermore, it exemplifies what we may call a theoreticist critique. It discounts the critical force of the two theories which when combined could be powerful in instituting praxis. The main point is that Husserlian Marxism should avoid the formulation of an ethical system which would become a reified theoretical praxis or dogma, a new orthodoxy.

The search for a regulatory principle involves an ongoing critique of science and philosophy. The control of knowledge is a vital issue in the discussion of a rational telos. The society of the classical age to which Husserl looks for a paradigm was limited in the extent of its knowledge. Rationality prevailed because of man's insight of the telos. But with the growth of science as a technology and the ensuing accumulation of capital, knowledge has become appropriated and given commodity status. On the point that the appropriation and accumulation of knowledge has led to its exploitation, there is no difficulty in reconciling

Conclusion: Phenomenological Marxism

Marx with Husserl. It is ironic that Husserl cites the Renaissance as the modern origin of the occluding natural attitude. The process of the mathematization of nature had been superseded by the technization of nature, the rise of the modern state, and the growth of science in the wake of the Enlightenment. For Husserl, the rebirth of learning culminated in the decline of wisdom.

What evidence is there for a reassertion of the telos? We can observe a piecemeal rejection of the consequences which result from its loss. There is a growing consciousness of the waste of material resources and of human potential, and an awareness of the technization of control and manipulation as a result of the growth of corporate and monopolistic power. Such arguments as those advanced to promote the conservation of world resources are made on the grounds of logic as well as morality. But the enlightened liberalism of such moral and rational arguments is no threat to the capitalist system which is sustained by the ideology of an illusory rational progress. The dominant ideology combats dissent by co-option and containment; the state promotes individualism, privatism and limited participation as mechanisms of control. It is in order to disocclude these mechanisms that Husserl's critique requires the structural force of Marx's analysis of the social formations in capitalist society, and Paci presents us with a powerful argument for the synthesis of Marxism and phenomenology:

> ...capitalism as a closed system leads to the falling rate of profits. The tendency for profit to fall is countered by various antagonistic forces, eg., technological inventions and scientific discoveries, as well as imperialist expansion which removes the law from the closed system for which it was formulated. The contradiction inherent in capitalism is not a function of the law of the falling rate of profits. The contradiction develops in two immediately obvious complementary directions: (1) the fall of the intentionality of the function of the sciences, ie., the crisis of the sciences and technistic alienation (science at the service of capital); and (2) war, and science at the service of war. The result is the alienated use of atomic energy and the possible total alienation of all humanity. The atomic bomb is the last metamorphosis of capital: its extreme _persona_ and subjective incarnation

Conclusion: Phenomenological Marxism

> vis-à-vis the men-objects. It is the final consequence of the reversal of the subject into the object, and if humanity does not want to be alienated and degraded to the level of inorganic nature, it must bring about the reversal, ie., the return to the subject.(25)

Husserl's view of the crisis in the social sciences is that, as in the natural sciences, the telos is obscured. The behaviouristic sciences are problem-oriented, adopting the ontology of medical pathology, whereby human beings are regarded as material rendered inert (or hyletic). The 'lived body' experience is negated in the manipulative techniques engendered by such attitudes. Ideological control is efficiently served through the technization of the social sciences and their increasing deployment in bourgeois institutions. How does a Husserlian Marxist analysis address these substantive issues? Because the tendency in proposing the synthesis has been to concentrate on a theoretical liaison, it should not be forgotten that the basis of the synthesis has been sought in the concreteness of each analysis. The crisis of the sciences and the crisis of capitalism are expressive of the same concrete historical situation. The aspects of its analysis to which Husserl's theories contribute significantly are the structures of consciousness under capitalism. The analysis of intersubjectivity and the return to the life-world direct us to the intentionality of consciousness, and to its origins. But the origin is also the point at which we can rediscover the possibilities for rational action directed towards a telos.

Phenomenology cannot supply Marxism with 'a psychology'. We have seen that Husserl rejects any such reductionism in his critique of positivist social sciences. Psychologism - and, most importantly for a structural analysis, theories of the unconscious - must be identified as ideology. Phenomenology provides the theoretical basis for understanding the mechanisms and effects of ideological controls - the occlusion of the rational telos which persists at all levels of cultural-technical institutionalisation - in science, education and politics.

We have seen that Husserl and Marx undertook their philosophical investigations in response to crises in both philosophy and the concrete historical situation. We are further aware that the first attempts at a liaison of phenomenology and

Conclusion: Phenomenological Marxism

Marxism were in response to a crisis within Marxist theory and practice. At the present juncture the crisis of the human condition is more acutely evident than ever. As for Marxist theory, this is still fragmented and unable to initiate strategy in any consistent way. The contradictions of capitalism are masked in confused polarities of analysis, attitude, action and response, for Marxist and non-Marxist alike. What could we therefore expect in substantive terms from the adoption of Husserlian Marxism? And what directions should further research take? The extension of a Husserlian Marxist programme should be directed towards:

a) a challenge to the philosophy of science to reinstate the human subject as the central concern of science and the rediscovery of the telos as a primary task;
b) a recognition that orthodox science is impregnated with ideology, thus making a more forceful critique of scientific practice;
c) the disocclusion of those bourgeois ideologies which construct the institutional controls, processes of decision-making, control of resources, demand creation, knowledge creation and control at all superstructural levels;
d) the reinforcement of historico-genetic rather than psychological and psychoanalytical explanations of human behaviour which reinforce the above ideologies;
e) the further development of a Husserlian Marxist critique of idealist critical theories, their obscurantism and occlusion of the concrete;
f) an emphasis on the basis of consciousness as intersubjective experience grounded concretely in the life-world. The genesis of rational collective human experience will emanate from the restructuring of the socio-economic base only when conceived in the broader terms of this analysis.

In conclusion, I hope I have demonstrated that a theoretical synthesis of phenomenology and Marxism is possible when grounded in the mature works of Husserl and Marx. Such a synthesis is proof against the criticisms made of other branches of Marxist theory. Husserlian Marxism does not merely 'complete' by reciprocity the gaps in the discrete theories it combines; it holds them in dynamic dialectical

Conclusion: Phenomenological Marxism

relationship. This synthesis demonstrates its scientificity in questioning and extending the concept of science itself. It thus rejects the mystification and irrationality inherent in positive science. The Husserlian Marxist synthesis is able to examine concrete human experience and, by answering the problem of history and consciousness, clarifies the issues involved in the changing of consciousness and society.

Notes and References

1. Merleau-Ponty in O'Neill, op.cit., p.175.
2. Paci, op.cit. (1972), Piccone's Introduction p.xxxiii.
3. Ibid., p.282.
4. Ibid., p.284.
5. Lichtheim, op.cit., p.109.
6. Paci, op.cit. (1972), p.5. See also Husserl Crisis, p.389. 'Philosophy as science ... - the dream is over.'
7. Ibid., p.154.
8. Ibid., p.413.
9. Ibid., p.279.
10. Ibid., p.276. Paci quotes Husserl, Crisis (Biemel edition), 1954, p.494. See also Chapter Five, p.145 above.
11. Schmueli, op.cit., pp.174-75.
12. Ibid., p.176, quoting Husserl, Crisis, p.8.
13. Husserl, Crisis, p.97f.
14. Schmueli, op.cit., p.176. See also Husserl, Crisis, p.111 on theoretical praxis.
15. Paci, op.cit. (1972), p.230.
16. Dallmayr, in Psathsas, op.cit., p.318.
17. Pivčević, E., Husserl and Phenomenology, Hutchinson, London, 1970, p.25.
18. Paci, op.cit., p.59.
19. Ibid., p.60.
20. Ibid., p.289.
21. Piccone's Introduction to Paci, op.cit., p.xxiv.
22. Rovatti, 'Critical Theory and Phenomenology' Telos, No 15, 1973, p.40.
23. Paci, op.cit. (1972), p.315. See Chapter Three, p.71 above.
24. Schmueli, op.cit., p.179.
25. Paci, op.cit. (1972), p.436.

GLOSSARY AND BIBLIOGRAPHY

GLOSSARY

Apodicity
    Self-evidence. The idea of necessary truth applies not only to knowledge but to the objects of knowledge and methods by which they are known.
Apperception
    The mind's perception of itself. Self-consciousness allows analogous perception of others, and reciprocal experience of the material world.
Appresentation
    In perception, the presenting of one property mediated through another. As in deducing another self through the presence of another body, or in patterning the hidden dimensions of a perceived object.
Aufgehoben
    The culminating process in dialectic whereby the opposed elements are drawn into a synthesis which embodies and goes beyond them, surpassing them. Process of sublation which preserves the rational elements of the triad of thesis, antithesis and synthesis.
Cogito
    The experiencing consciousness in all its operations. A transcendental domain where the meaning of what is given to experience is grasped.
Conative
    Concerning the will. Willing desires or projects to be put into action.
Concrete
    The experience of the subject and the surrounding world is always intersubjective and based in the world of the lived body, in materiality.

Glossary

Dynamis/Energia
Inherent capacities become functionalised. Potentiality becomes actuality.

Ego
The Self, the experience of the subject. The ego is maintained in reflecting upon itself. Egological reduction – to set aside immediate experiencing subjectivity.

Eidetic enquiry
Enquiry into universal essences, into a prioris. Enquiring from particulars to universals. The inspection of essences by the epoche.

Embrayage
The interlocking of elements, coupled together by friction of force.

Empathy
The ego experiences by analogy what others feel, thus an affective intersubjectivity is established.

Engagement
The commitment of consciousness to the world, and involvement in praxis.

Epistēmē
A body of knowledge exhibiting related conceptual structures and claims to truth.

Epochē
The suspension of beliefs and knowledge claims. The setting aside or bracketing of belief in factual existence.

Essences
General or universal essences and the relations between them are grasped by insight in the special sense of phenomenological intuiting. Essences are not realities but are a priori the basis of knowledge.

Experience
In phenomenological terms, the 'lived' mode of experience is a state of awareness consciously directed towards objects of experience, affective and cognitive.

Hermeneutics
A science of interpretation, connoting the divination of sacred texts.

Hyle
Matter, elemental substance, passive material of which the universe is constructed. The basic parameter of our experience of the world.

Glossary

Intentionality
: The mode of consciousness itself as being directed towards the intentional object. Also the mode of intersubjectivity - intentionality operates as the intermonadic experience of concrete individuals. As a teleology, it directs us towards a future society of subjects.

Intuition
: Insight into essences (q.v.).

Irreversibility
: A dominant universal principle of transformation in time which is a priori irreversible. In phenomenology, temporal irreversibility allows the genesis of the present to be disoccluded in order to understand the past and prefigure the future.

Kinaesthesis
: The evolution and mutation of the way things appear to consciousness.

Körper/Leib
: The physical or material body in its inert aspect is opposed to the lived body experience, the Leib. Husserl also uses the terms inorganic and organic body.

Lebensphilosophie
: A school of philosophy founded by Dilthey as a revolt against the idealist and rationalist beliefs of the Enlightenment. Influential in the critique of science developed by Husserl.

Life-world/Lebenswelt
: The precategorical sphere which is the basis of all human experience. At the fundamental level, every animate creature is subject to spatiotemporal causality, need and irreversibility. Because of these a priori structures, Husserl claimed the possibility of a science of the life-world.

Metatheoretical
: Of theories concerned with the analysis and description of theory itself.

Monad
: The concrete ego. Individuals share a surrounding world which is intermonadic, intersubjective.

Natural attitude
: An unreflecting attitude to the world as taken-for-granted. Naturalistic acceptance of the world and a naive belief in its existence.

Noema/noetic
: Processes of the intellect. A noetic act (or noesis) is directed towards the intentional

Glossary

object (or noema).

Nomological-deductive method
Deduction of the laws of nature.

Occlusion
The process and effect of the natural attitude. The closing up of the understanding. The hiddenness of the truth of things by the veil, or garb of ideas.

Ontic
Of structures inherent in being.

Owl of Minerva
Significant metaphor for Hegel's system, signifying the incompleteness of knowledge and truth until the final stage of history.

Phenomena/Noumena
Kantian distinction of appearances and the things-in-themselves. For Husserl, phenomena are investigated to yield knowledge of essences.

Phenomenological reduction
The process of disclosing by setting aside the natural attitude. The phenomenological attitude of reflection which suspends naive belief in the existence of the world.

Plena
Basic substance or material substratum. That which is given to consciousness and perceived as sense data.

Praxis
Action, the realisation of theory. In Husserl the field of praxis is the world and its historical becoming. Inert praxis is passivity.

Problematic
A framework of related ideas, provoking the examination of its conceptual structures. See Epistēmē.

Protention/retention
In protention we hypothesize what will happen. In experience the present is transformed and made available by retention. It is accessible to recall. Thus we can reconstruct the historical past by means of this temporal dialectic.

Psychology/psychologism
Husserl was critical of 'psychologism' as a reductionist explanation of perception and cognition. He continued to revise his conception of a phenomenological psychology. Transcendental and 'pure' psychology appear co-terminous with transcendental phenomenology.

Glossary

Regional ontologies
: The life-world comprises spheres of precategorical experience which are conceptualised as spheres of knowledge by the sciences. The regions are material, animal and spiritual.

Sedimentation
: Structures of meaning which are laid down in the memory can be passively recalled to memory and reactivated in language. Husserl points to the *seduction of language*, since there is 'unavoidable sedimentation of mental products in the form of persisting linguistic acquisitions' (*Crisis*, p. 362). What are taken as self-evident propositions must be questioned.

Sense data
: What is immediately given to consciousness in encountering the surrounding world. The sense-qualities of objects, the properties of colour, smell, tactile qualities, warmth and so on that are apprehended by the sense organs. The sensuous manifold.

Transcendental reduction
: Beyond the suspension of belief in the facticity of things, it is possible to examine the mode of subjectivity by which pure phenomena are constituted. The reduction to the life-world which is the foundation of intersubjectivity.

SELECT BIBLIOGRAPHY

Althusser, L., and Balibar, E., Reading Capital (1965), New Left Books, London, 1970.
Althusser, L., For Marx (1965), translated Brewster, B., Allen Lane, The Penguin Press, London, 1969.
Althusser, L., Lenin and Philosophy (1968), translated Brewster, B., Monthly Review Press, London, 1971.
Benton, E., Philosophical Foundations of the Three Sociologies, Routledge and Kegan Paul, London, 1977.
Bhaskar, R., A Realist Theory of Knowledge, Harvester Press, Brighton, 1978.
Bhaskar, R., The Possibility of Naturalism, Harvester Press, Brighton, 1979.
Blackburn, R. (ed.), Ideology in Social Science, Fontana, London, 1972.
Carr, D., Phenomenology and the Problem of History, Northwestern University Press, Evanston, Illinois, 1974.
Carver, T., (trans. and ed.) Karl Marx: Texts on Method, Blackwell, Oxford, 1975.
Cleaver, H., Reading Capital Politically, Harvester Press, Brighton, 1979.
Colletti, L., Marxism and Hegel, New Left Books, London, 1973.
Craib, I., Existentialism and Sociology: A Study of Jean-Paul Sartre, Cambridge University Press, Cambridge, 1976.
Dallmayr, F.R., 'Phenomenology and Marxism: A Salute to Enzo Paci', in Psathsas, G. (ed.) Phenomenological Sociology, Wiley, New York, 1973.
Elliston, F.A. and MacCormick, P. (eds.), Husserl: Expositions and Appraisals, University of Notre Dame Press, Notre Dame, Indiana, 1977.
Feyerabend, P.K., Against Method, New Left Books, London, 1975.

Select Bibliography

Flew, A. (ed.), *A Dictionary of Philosophy*, Pan Books, London, 1979.
Foucault, M., *The Order of Things* (1966), Tavistock, London, 1974.
Giddens, A. (ed.), *Positivism and Sociology*, Heinemann, London, 1974.
Hanson, N.R., *Patterns of Discovery*, Cambridge University Press, Cambridge, 1961.
Hegel, G.W.F., *The Science of Logic* (1812), translated by Johnston, W.H. and Struthers, L.G., Allen and Unwin, London, 1966.
Hegel, G.W.F., *The Phenomenology of Mind* (1807), translated by Baillie, J.B., Allen and Unwin, London, 1931.
Heidegger, M., *Being and Time* (1927), translated by MacQuarrie, J. and Robinson, E., Basil Blackwell, Oxford, 1973.
Huppert, G., 'Divinatio et Eruditio: Thoughts on Foucault', *History and Theory*, Vol. 8, No. 3, 1974.
Husserl, E., *The Phenomenology of Internal Time-Consciousness* (1905), edited by Heidegger, M., translated by Churchill, J.S., Martinus Nijhoff, The Hague, 1964.
Husserl, E., *Ideas: A general introduction to pure phenomenology* (1913), translated by Boyce Gibson, W.R., Collier-Macmillan, London, 1972.
Husserl, E., *Phenomenological Psychology* (1925), Martinus Nijhoff, The Hague, 1962.
Husserl, E., *Phenomenology and the Crisis of Philosophy* 'Phenomenology as a Rigorous Science' (1911); and the Prague Lecture (1935), translated and edited by Lauer, Q., Harper and Row, New York, 1965.
Husserl, E., *The Crisis of European Sciences and Transcendental Phenomenology: An Introduction to Phenomenological Philosophy* (1936), translated by Carr, D., Northwestern University Press, Evanston, Illinois, 1970.
Husserl, E., *Experience and Judgement* (1954), translated by Churchill, J., and Ameriks, K., Illinois, 1973.
Husserl, E., *Logical Investigations* (1900), translated by Findlay, J.N., Routledge and Kegan Paul, London, 1970.
Hyppolyte, J., *Studies on Marx and Hegel*, translated by O'Neill, J., New Left Books, London, 1973.
Keat, R.N. and Urry, J., *Social Theory as Science*, Routledge and Kegan Paul, London, 1975.

Select Bibliography

Kockelmans, J. (ed.), *Phenomenology*, Doubleday Anchor, New York, 1967.
Kockelmans, J., and Kisiel, T.J., *Phenomenology and the Natural Sciences*, Northwestern University Press, Evanston, Illinois, 1970.
Kojève, A., *Introduction to the Reading of Hegel* (1939), Basic Books, New York, 1967.
Kosik, K., *Dialectics of the Concrete* (1961), translated by Kovanda, K., and Schmidt, J., Reidel, Boston, 1976.
Lakatos, I. and Musgrave, A., *Criticism and the Growth of Knowledge*, Cambridge University Press, London, 1970.
Lecourt, D., *Marxism and Epistemology*, New Left Books, London, 1975.
Lefebvre, H., Dialectical Materialism (1940), translated by Sturrock, J., Cape, London, 1968.
Lichtheim, G., *Marxism*, Routledge and Kegan Paul, London, 1964.
Lukács, G., *Marx's Basic Ontological Principles*, translated by Fernbach, D., Merlin Press, London, 1978.
Lukács, G., *Toward the Ontology of Social Being*, translated by Fernbach, D., Merlin Press, London, 1978.
Lukács, G., *History and Class Consciousness* (1967), translated by Livingstone, R., Merlin Press, London, 1971.
Luporini, C., 'Reality and Historicity: Economy and Dialectics in Marxism', *Economy and Society*, Vol. 4, Nos. 2 and 3, 1975.
Marx, K., *Economic and Philosophic Manuscripts of 1844*, translated by Milligan, M., Progress Publishers, Moscow, 1974.
Marx, K., *A Contribution to the Critique of Political Economy* (1859), edited by Dobb, M., Lawrence and Wishart, London, 1971.
Marx, K. and Engels, F., *The German Ideology*, Part I, edited by Arthur, C.J., Lawrence and Wishart, London, 1977.
Marx, K., *Grundrisse*, translated by Nicolaus, M., Allen Lane, London, 1973.
Marx, K., *Capital* (1867), edited and translated by Torr, D., Allen and Unwin, London, 1946.
Marx, W., *Hegel's Phenomenology of Spirit*, Harper and Row, London, 1975.
Mays, W., 'Phenomenology and Marxism', in Pivčević, E., *Phenomenology and Philosophical Understanding*, Cambridge University Press, Cambridge, 1975.

Select Bibliography

Merleau-Ponty, M., Adventures of the Dialectic (1955) translated by Bien, J., Heinemann, London, 1974.
Merleau-Ponty, M., The Primacy of Perception, edited by Edie, J.M., Northwestern University Press, Evanston, Illinois, 1964.
Natanson, M., (ed.), Phenomenology and the Social Sciences, Northwestern University Press, Evanston, Illinois, 1973.
Paci, E., The Function of the Sciences and the Meaning of Man (1963), translated by Piccone, P. and Hansen, J., Northwestern University Press, Evanston, Illinois, 1972.
Parkinson, G.H.R. (ed.) Marx and Marxisms, Cambridge University Press, Cambridge, 1982.
Passmore, J., A Hundred Years of Philosophy, Penguin, London, 1975.
Piccone, P., 'Reading the Grundrisse: Beyond Orthodox Marxism', Theory and Society, Vol. 1, No. 2, 1975.
Piccone, P., 'Phenomenological Marxism', Telos, No. 9, 1971.
Pivčević, E., Husserl and Phenomenology, Hutchinson, London, 1970.
Pivčević, E. (ed.), Phenomenology and Philosophical Understanding, Cambridge University Press, Cambridge, 1975.
Psathsas, G. (ed.), Phenomenological Sociology, Wiley, New York, 1973.
Ricoeur, P., Husserl: An Analysis of his Phenomenology, translated by Ballard, E. and Embree, L.E., Northwestern University Press, Evanston, Illinois, 1967.
Sartre, J-P., Being and Nothingness (1943), translated by Barnes, H.E., Methuen, London, 1966.
Sartre, J-P., Search for a Method (1960), translated by Barnes, H.E., Vintage Books, New York, 1968.
Smart, B., Review of Paci, E., The Function of the Sciences and the Meaning of Man, Theory and Society, Vol. II, No. 3, 1975.
Soll, I., An Introduction to Hegel's Metaphysics, University of Chicago Press, Chicago, 1969.
Spiegelberg, H., The Phenomenological Movement, Martinus Nijhoff, The Hague, 1982.
Vico, G., The New Science (1744), translated from the 3rd edition by Bergin, T.G. and Fisch, M.E., Garden City, New York, 1961.
Zaner, R., The Way of Phenomenology, Pegasus, New York, 1970.

INDEX

Adorno, T.W. 178
alienation 4, 92, 103, 108-13, 118, 129, 181
Althusser, L. 3, 61-66, 70-74, 82, 137; on Hegel 64-66
Aristotle 10, 11

Bachelard, G. 68, 69
Bacon, F. 146
Benton, E. 74, 78
Berkeley, G. 25
Bhaskar, R. 74-78
Bolzano, F. 25
Brentano, F. 15, 24, 75, 142
Brewster, B. 68, 69

Canguilhem, G. 68
capitalism 4, 37, 82, 92, 95, 97, 101, 103, 115, 118, 125, 132, 177, 180-82; see also crisis
Carr, D. 5, 93, 102, 109, 125-28, 134, 139-41, 152
Carver, T. 45
causality 20, 79, 83-85, 113-18
censorship 144
Cerf, W. 36, 37
class struggle 150
commodity 45, 105, 137; status 104, 139, 177;
fetishism 177
concrete 104-06
consciousness 5, 14, 20, 39-41, 53, 79-83, 92, 98, 118, 125-26, 147-54, 173, 183, 184; false 82; Husserl's analysis of 105-07, 120n; structure of 4, 53, 166
corporeality 114
crisis 4, 27, 91-96, 119n; of capitalism 3, 4, 91, 96, 104, 110, 117; of Marxism 1, 28; of philosophy 1, 30, 102; of science 2, 4, 63, 64, Ch. 4 passim; of social sciences 1
culture 92, 106, 115, 127
Cutler, A. 63, 64, 69

Dallmayr, F.R. 122n, 146, 175
Della Volpe, G. 138
Derrida, J. 154n
Descartes, R. 2, 16, 128, 147
dialectic 2, 10, 11, 29, 30, 83, 105, 114, 115, 118, 136, 173-75
dialectical materialism 2, 14, 19-24, 42, 70
Dilthey, W. 2, 5, 126,

197

Index

133, 134, 155n
ecology 115, 116
economics 104
education 182
Einstein, A. 80, 81, 88n, 120
empiricism 81, 100, 107, 175
Engels, F. 122n
Enlightenment 127, 155n, 181
epistemology 2, 12, 37, 50, 53, 73, 84, 92, 117, 163-66
epochē 16, 22, 40, 94, 109, 110, 127, 128, 133, 134, 149, 170
ethics 78, 179
Europe 93, 117, 153
existentialism 149, 157n
existentialist Marxism 47, 147-52, 164, 168, 169

Feuerbach, L. 20, 71, 96-98, 110, 111
Feyerabend, P.K. 81, 88n
Fichte, J.G. 10, 26, 55n
Findlay, J.N. 75
Foucault, M. 3, 65-69
Franco-Prussian War 93
Frankfurt School 178
Freud, S. 62, 63

Galileo 96, 128, 146
Gestalt psychology 148
geometry 23, 128
Geras, N. 71
Germany 93
Glucksmann, A. 86n
Gramsci, A. 66, 138

Hanson, N.R. 81
Hegel, G.F.W. 2, 10, 15, 16, 20, Ch. 2 passim, 66, 105, 131, 147, 167; Lenin on 72-73; Logic 43, 44; phenomenology 39; Phenomenology of Mind 38, 51, 52; revived interest in 3, 36
Hegelian Marxism 3, Ch. 2 passim, 136, 163, 165, 167, 169
Heidegger, M. 5, 35, 93, 126, 141, 142, 150, 155n, 164, 166; Husserl and 11, 141, 142
hermeneutics 5, 129, 172
historical materialism 23, 70, 77, 98, 125
historicism 35, 129-35, 153; definitions of 131
historicity 131, 139, 153
historico-genetic analysis 5, 126, 135-41
history 5, Ch. 5 passim
humanism 117
Hume, D. 25, 41
Hussain, A. 69
Husserl, E. 2, Ch. 1 passim, 66, 82, 83, Chs. 4, 5, 6 passim; Cartesian Meditations 16-18, 135; Crisis of European Sciences and Transcendental Phenomenology 23, 25, 53, 75, 82, 85, 92, 93, 98, 107, 112, 127, 128, 134, 135, 138, 140, 141, 143, 152, 153, 161, 172, 175, 179; development of ideas 14-17; Experience and Judgement 161; First Philosophy 25; Formal and Transcendental Logic 25, 109; Hegel and 3, Ch. 2 passim; Heidegger and 119n;

Index

Ideas 16, 18, 25, 75, 81, 84, 107; Logical Investigations 16, 25, 106, 107, 135; methodology 27, 28; Origin of Geometry 128, 146; Phenomenological Psychology 84; Phenomenology of Internal Time-consciousness 108; Philosophy as a Rigorous Science 81, 127; Philosophy of Arithmetic 25
Husserlian Marxism 3, 6, 178-84

idealism 17, 18, 30, 36-38, 42, 44, 75, 97, 105; Absolute 16, 20, 47, 73; realism and 22, 26; subjective 2, 14, 19-24, 29
ideology 30, 69, 86n, 178, 180, 181; science and 4, 66-71, 78
intentionality 5, 17, 24, 27, 54, 83, 107, 118, 143, 150, 151
intersubjectivity 4, 84, 92, 102, 126, 143, 182
irreversibility 151, 152

Kant, I. 2, 10, 16, 24-29, 147; Hegel on 54n; Husserl and 26-29, 33n; Marx and 25, 26; Marxism and 28, 29
Kaufmann, W. 39, 55n
Keat, R. 74
Kierkegaard, S.A. 150
Kockelmans, J. 27, 33n, 81
Kojève, A. 47, 50-52, 54, 163

labour 45, 105, 112, 115, 116, 138, 151, 167, 168, 177
Lacan, J. 63
language 5, 141-47, 156n
Lauer, Q. 39, 40
Lebensphilosophie 133, 155n
Lebenswelt 51, 84, 113, 139; see also life-world
Lecourt, D. 69
Leibnitz, G.W. 25, 128
Lenin, V.I. 71-73
Lichtheim, G. 96, 97, 165
life-world 4, 27, 53, 75, 80, 81, 83, 85, 99, 101-08, 118, 126, 133, 136, 140, 161, 168, 175, 176, 182
Locke, J. 25
logic 2, 12, 50, 163-65, 175
logical positivism 93
Lotze, H. 24
Lukács, G. 3, 46-50, 54, 103, 109, 111, 122n, 132, 163, 165, 167, 169
Luporini, C. 130, 137, 138

Marcuse, H. 19, 178
Marx, K. 2, Ch. 3 passim, 84, 91-98, 101-05, 106-11, Ch. 5 passim, Ch. 6 passim; Capital 21, 42-46, 49, 74, 84, 92, 97, 105, 136-39, 145, 146, 172, 175; Contribution to the Critique of Political Economy, Introduction and Preface 42-44, 46, 76, 105; development of ideas 14-17; Economic and Philosophic Manuscripts of 1844 95, 97, 111;

Index

Feuerbach and 20; The German Ideology 86n; Grundrisse 43; Hegel and 3, Ch. 2 passim, 105; Husserl and 3; Notes on Adolf Wagner 139, 146
Marxism Chs. 1-6 passim; branches of 11; orthodox 79, 114; phenomenology and 2-6, Ch. 1 passim; Soviet 47, 114; see also existentialist Marxism; Hegelian Marxism; phenomenological Marxism; structuralist Marxism
materialism 30, 36, 74, 84, 105, 107, 114
Merleau-Ponty, M. 5, 24, 53, 63, 108, 114, 126, 143, 147-50, 159, 160, 164, 166, 168, 170
metaphysics 3, 28, 29, 37, 75, 76, 94, 166
methodology 1, 11, 12, 16, 53, 82, 152, 163, 169, 170
Michelson, A.A. 80, 88n
Mill, J.S. 15, 25, 37
mode of production 145, 177
Mure, G.R. 39

Natanson, M. 151
Nazis 93, 119n
need 103, 115, 129, 150-52, 168, 178, 179
Norman, R. 55n

ontology 2, 12, 49, 50, 52, 53, 73, 84, 108-12 passim, 118, 150-52, 167-69, 175, 176; of labour 4, 116; of life-world 75, 110, 176; of need 177

Paci, E. 2-4, 19, 20, 22, 30, 32n, 103, 116, 117, 122n, 129-32, 135, 136, 139-41, 144, 147, 151, 160, 162, 164, 165, 167, 168, 170, 171-81
Paris Revolution 93
Parkinson, G.H.R. 82
perception 82, 149, 150, 170
phenomenological Marxism 1-5, Ch. 1 passim, 115, 116, Ch. 6 passim, 171-78; see also Paci, E.
phenomenology 2-6, Chs. 1 and 2 passim, 67, 74, 75, 79-82, Chs. 4, 5 and 6 passim; as philosophy 14, 94, 153, 172; as science 82, 94, 96, 172
philosophy Chs. 1-6 passim; Hegel on 43; Husserl on 14, 15; lines of enquiry 11; social sciences 1, 6; see also crisis, science
physics 99, 100
Piccone, P. 4, 22, 74, 115, 116, 161, 162, 178
Pivčević, E. 176
Plato 10
political economy 94, 95, 117, 172
politics 72, 78, 182
positivism 35, 49, 50, 74, 77, 79, 91, 100, 160, 171
proletariat 71, 149, 154n, 173
psychologism 15, 83, 107, 134, 182
psychology 15, 120n, 148

Rancière, J. 137
rationalism 15, 27, 129, 175

200

Index

realism 22, 36, 49, 81, 105; scientific 4, 61, 74-80; transcendental 76; see also Bhaskar, R.
relativism 132, 133
Renaissance 96, 146, 177, 181
Ricardo, D. 38, 68, 69
Ricoeur, P. 5, 125, 134
Roche, M. 31n, 75
Ronchi, V. 81, 88n, 100, 120n
Rousseau, J.J. 25
Rovatti, P.A. 178

Sartre, J-P. 5, 47, 50, 54, 63, 107, 111, 116, 125, 143, 148, 150-52, 159, 164, 166, 168-70
Saussure, F. de 63
Say, J.B.L. 37
Schelling, F.W. 26, 36
Schmueli, E. 173, 180
science, 41, Ch. 3 passim, Ch. 4 passim, 181, 183, 184; ideology and 2, 66-71; philosophy and 2, 92, 97, 117, 180; relision and 26
scientific Marxism 3, 61; see also structuralist Marxism
scientific realism 4, 74-80
scientificity 49, 81, 96-101, 160
scientism 83, 94, 100, 174
sedimentation 141, 143, 156n
social sciences 35, 77, 125, 182
socialism 49
sociologism 83
sociology 74, 78
solipsism 16, 17
Sorel, G. 145
Spiegelberg, H. 20, 32n, 33n, 40, 41, 141, 149
Stalin, J.V. 114
structuralism 3, Ch. 3 passim, 79
structuralist Marxism 3, Ch. 3 passim, 130, 137, 163, 164, 167, 169
subjectivity 23, 30, 53, 107, 127, 178
synthesis 1, 5, 9-14, 29, 35, 38, 54, 73, 96, 104, 125, 129, 146, 160-71, 183; criteria for 11, 12, 160, 170, 171

technology 99, 116, 144, 145
teleology 83, 110, 113-18
telos 81, 82, 112, 116, 117, 130, 132, 171, 172, 174, 175, 179, 180, 182
totality 3, 42-46, 50, 52, 71-74 passim, 102, 103, 105, 107, 131, 132, 136, 151, 169; Althusser on 56n, 65; Marx on 57n
Tran Duc Thao 52

Urry, J. 74

value 45, 138
Verstehen 134
Vico, G. 62, 96, 141, 145, 146
Vogt, K. 19

Wagner, A. 134
Weltanschauung 133, 155n
Weyl, H. 81, 100

Zaner, R.M. 31n
Zeno 10

For Product Safety Concerns and Information please contact our EU representative GPSR@taylorandfrancis.com
Taylor & Francis Verlag GmbH, Kaufingerstraße 24, 80331 München, Germany

www.ingramcontent.com/pod-product-compliance
Lightning Source LLC
Chambersburg PA
CBHW052115300426
44116CB00010B/1668